MORTAL REMAINS

Bouncers Lane Cemetery, Cheltenham, Gloucestershire, 1863-5; main promenade to the chapels; buildings designed by W. H. Knight, Gothic pinnacle in memory of the Reverend Andrew Brown, d.1879.

MORTAL REMAINS

The History and Present State of the Victorian and Edwardian Cemetery

Chris Brooks
with
Brent Elliott, Julian Litten, Eric Robinson,
Richard Robinson and Philip Temple

WHEATON

Published in association with
THE VICTORIAN SOCIETY

First published in Great Britain in 1989 by Wheaton Publishers Ltd.

ISBN: 0 08-037098-5

British Library Cataloguing-in-Publication Data

Brooks, Chris
Mortal remains: the history and present state of the Victorian and Edwardian cemetery.
1. England. Cemeteries. History
I. Title II. Victorian Society
942

Typeset by P&M Typesetting Ltd, Exeter
Printed and bound in Great Britain by
BPCC Wheatons Ltd, Exeter

Wheaton Publishers Ltd
Hennock Road, Marsh Barton, Exeter, Devon EX2 8RP
Tel: 0392 74121; Telex: 42794 (WHEATN G)

SALES
Direct sales enquiries to Wheaton Publishers Ltd at the address above, or to The Victorian Society, 1 Priory Gardens, London W4 1TT.

Wheaton Publishers Ltd is a member of Maxwell Pergamon Publishing Corporation plc.

Of the photographs in this book, those of Undercliffe, Philips Park, and Weaste cemeteries were taken by Geoff Baker; of Harton and Oakham, by Geoff Brandwood; of Caister Cemetery in Great Yarmouth, by Damian Eaton: I am grateful for their kindly allowing me to use them here. Acknowledgements for illustrations are also due to: the Royal Commission on Historical Monuments for Newcastle General; English Heritage for the Glenesk mausoleum in St Marylebone; Camden Library Services for the view from Highgate terrace; and Sheffield Library Bibliographical Services for the print of Sheffield General. All the other illustrations are my own. For letting me take photographs in Highgate, and use them here, I would like to thank the Friends of Highgate Cemetery.

Thanks are also due to John Smith for providing large-scale prints of the photographs.

CONTENTS

PREFACE

In 1972, J.S. Curl first drew attention to the importance of Britain's Victorian cemeteries, and to how widespread was their neglect. Soon after, increasingly alarmed by the damage being done, the Victorian Society set up a committee to gather information about the present state of Victorian and Edwardian cemeteries. Despite the post-war revaluation of Victorian art and architecture, the committee found a history of indifference, incomprehension and, not uncommonly, hostility. Far from being cultural and environmental assets, unique products of architecture, sculpture and landscape design, historic cemeteries were persistently regarded as mere financial liabilities. Arguments of economic expediency – used to justify the destruction of buildings, monuments, whole landscapes – also served to mask deeper motives. Our later twentieth-century culture has signally failed to find a coherent response to the fact of death – partly, no doubt and ironically, because two world wars have brought death unprecedented, both in its scale and in its impersonality. Death has been emptied of meaning, or, at least, we have lost the cultural means by which mortality can be invested with individual social significance. As Philippe Ariès has said, 'we ignore the existence of a scandal we have been unable to prevent; we act as if it did not exist'. As a result, the Victorian cemetery has become an embarrassment, its funerary eloquence a constant reminder of our own inarticulacy. The Victorian Society decided that its committee's findings should be incorporated in a wider study of the social and cultural identity of the nineteenth-century cemetery that would review management and conservation strategies from a historical perspective, and that would include a representative gazetteer of historic cemeteries. This book is the result.

My first debt of gratitude is to the Victorian Society's Cemeteries Committee, particularly to Brent Elliott, who chaired it, Julian Litten, Eric Robinson, Richard Robinson and Philip Temple; also to others who contributed to its final report: James Stevens Curl, Mark Hanson, Michael P. Kearney, Colin Plant, and Tom Slack. The committee's report is the basis for Part 2 of the present book, and I am conscious of how far it informs the rest of my text. Many details have come from Victorian Society members who sent in reports on cemeteries in their area. I have read all these with interest and with profit: to everybody who contributed in this way, my thanks; particularly to B. I. Bagnall, A. S. Brooks, Alexander Chablo, David Evans, Peter de Figueredo, Chris Hammond, Ruth Harman, Peter Howell, Christopher Marsden, Julian Orbach, D. A. Smith, and Julian Treuherz. Several people have helped me directly in assembling material, undertaking research, sending me reports and photographs, taking me to visit cemeteries. For their time, their advice and their expertise, I am especially grateful to Geoff Baker, Geoff Brandwood, Martin Cherry, Jo Cox, Damian Eaton, Malcolm Holmes, Lawrence Inman, and Erik Seedorf. Thanks are also due to the staff of many libraries and county record offices. In particular: the city libraries of Birmingham, Liverpool, Manchester, Norwich, and Sheffield, and the Devon and Exeter Institute; in London, Camden Borough Library Services and the Guildhall Library; the county record offices of Bedfordshire, Devon, Leicestershire, Somerset.

In the process of production, I have greatly appreciated the support of Simon Butler, Andy Jones and Peter Whitehead. As always, I am indebted to Jo Cox for all kinds of ideas and for many hours of discussion. Finally, this book would not have been written without the Victorian Society. I owe much to friends and associates among its members and on its committees; in particular, for their commitment, their advice, and the sympathy with which they have listened to my various musings among the tombs, I want to thank Peter Howell, Teresa Sladen and Robert Thorne.

Chris Brooks
University of Exeter
4 August 1989

1

THE HISTORY

The Age of Great Cities

A BOY BORN IN MIDDLESBROUGH in 1830 would have opened his eyes on a small village with a population of some 150 souls. Before he was ten years old he would have witnessed the transformation of the village into a railway town with over 5000 inhabitants. In 1842, by which time he may well have started work, he would have seen the opening of Middlesbrough Docks. In the year he came of age, ironstone was discovered in the Cleveland Hills: with easy access to the Durham coalfields, the town became a centre of the ironmaking industry inside a decade. As his children grew up in the early 1860s, Middlesbrough's population passed 20,000. By the 1870s that figure had doubled, and by the 1890s doubled again.

Having lived out his Biblical seventy years, he would have died in the same year as the century: by then, the village that as a child he could have toddled across in ten minutes had become a close-packed, industrial conurbation that stretched for more than two noisy miles along the Tees, and as far again inland from the riverbank. Its population had already passed 90,000 and would exceed 100,000 before the First World War.

The making of Middlesbrough is a dramatic epitome of those forces of industrialization and urbanization that created Victorian England. It is also the most signal example of the unprecedented growth in population that underlay those forces, feeding them and fed by them. In 1801 the total population of the United Kingdom was nearing 16,000,000; by 1851 it had reached 27,500,000; in 1901 it was 41,500,000. The increase was steepest in England and Wales, where a population of 9,000,000 at the beginning of the nineteenth century had become 32,500,000 at the end. Such figures are astonishing enough; as astonishing is the speed with which that ever expanding population was urbanized. In 1801 less than 20% of the inhabitants of England and Wales were town-dwellers; in 1851, the year of the Great Exhibition of the Works and Industries of All Nations, that figure had become 50%; in 1901, 75% of the population lived and worked in towns and cities. When the nineteenth century opened there was no city in the British Isles, other than London, with more than 100,000 inhabitants: when it closed there were twenty, of which four – Glasgow, Manchester, Liverpool and Birmingham – had populations in excess of half a million. London's population had grown more quickly than any: from 865,000 in 1801, to 2,362,000 in 1851, to 4,536,000 in 1901. By the time Edward VII died in 1911, his empire's capital city and its suburbs covered 700 square miles.

The scale of population increase in the nineteenth

century, mass industrialization, and the concentration of people into towns, generated the period's characteristic social, political, administrative and cultural structures. The century was indeed, to use a favourite Victorian phrase, The Age of Great Cities. But it would be wrong to interpret this in any narrow sense, for the dynamics that formed the cities came to be felt in every part of Britain. If the Condition of England Question, to quote Carlyle's famous formulation, was posed most insistently by Ancoats, Ladywood and Bethnal Green, it could also be heard in cathedral closes facing the reform of privileges and pluralities, in market towns confronting the end of an agrarian Golden Age, and in coastal villages receiving the first day-trippers and works' outings. The city, in this sense, was everywhere, and with it came its crises, so much so that Matthew Arnold at his most lugubrious saw only:

> ... this strange disease of modern life,
> With its sick hurry, its divided aims,
> Its heads o'ertaxed, its palsied hearts ...

If Arnold's complaint was, to an extent, the groaning of an élitist culture under stress, he nevertheless was right to see the problems of his age as psychological as well as physical. Those problems differed from any facing earlier societies not only in degree, but in kind, and integral to them were the mental habits and strategies of individuals, organizations, whole social groups even, who sought – or were obliged to seek – solutions. Indeed, the very idea of the social problem as a phenomenon to be identified, quantified, analysed and solved, is peculiarly nineteenth-century in origin.

Few nineteenth-century social issues were more fundamental than the question of how to dispose of the dead. And few, in the way they were perceived and handled, were more characteristic. The origin of the problem was, of course, demographic: just as there were ever more people who needed to find somewhere to live, to get work, to ensure they had food to eat, so also there were ever more people who died and needed burial. It was a problem that first became critical in the cities, but subsequently affected communities throughout the country. As it did so, its intimate association with a range of other social issues became clearer, particularly with questions of sanitation and public health. It involved the conflict between the socio-economic doctrines of *laissez-faire* and the crying need for legislative intervention. It was one of the issues on which local administration was challenged by centralization; it was an area fought over by conflicting religious groups; and inevitably, it was a problem that, in its formulation and resolution, was defined and, in part at least, determined, by social class. Out of the whole complex of argument and interest emerged one of the great social achievements of the Victorian period: the provision of public cemeteries.

Seventeenth-century Beginnings

At the start of the nineteenth century the only available means of disposing of the dead was by burial, the ancient practice of the Christian church. Every person had a common-law right to be buried in the churchyard of the parish in which he or she died, and relatives could claim that right for those who died outside their own parish. The duty of burying the dead lay with the Church of England. The parish priest could not refuse to bury and to read the Burial Service as prescribed in the Book of Common Prayer, except when the dead person was unbaptized, excommunicate, or had committed suicide. Such provisions originated in the Reformation settlement that envisaged the established church as the only church in England, to which all people would belong. That theoretical position had long been exploded by historical events: in the seventeenth century, by organized dissent that had been powerful enough to execute one king and help depose another, as well as largely disposing of the Church of England for a decade; in the eighteenth century, by the growth of a vigorous nonconformist culture and by the emergence of Methodism independently of the Anglican Church. Despite all such changes, however, burial in the early nineteenth century was still essentially the prerogative of the established church. The understanding whereby any form of Christian baptism, whether or not by an Anglican minister, was recognized as valid for the purposes of burial in consecrated ground, proved an ambiguous concession. Nonconformist ministers were not allowed to conduct burials in the parish churchyard, and the parish priest, even if not so inclined, was obliged by law to read the full Anglican Burial Service over the dissenting dead. In thousands of parishes throughout England and Wales at least, the sole recourse for burial of nonconformist congregations was to the parish churchyard. In such parishes, Baptists, for example, could have parents who were members of that tradition, be baptized into that church, could be married by a Baptist minister, and could bring up their children as Baptists, but could find burial only under the auspices of a church of which they had never been members, and to which they had never conformed. Among nonconformist communities, the pressure to find an alternative to burial in the parish churchyard began as early as the seventeenth century, and the burying-ground of Bunhill Fields in the City of London, in existence by 1665, may be seen as setting a precedent for burial outside the Establishment monopoly. In many provincial towns which had strong dissenting communities, non-Anglican burial grounds were established in the eighteenth century.

However, as early as the second half of the seventeenth century, the inadequacy of churchyards in towns, and particularly in London, was apparent to Anglicans themselves. Nor was the problem only that of the churchyards. Interment beneath the floor of the church itself had been practised from time immemorial. But what originally had been a privilege restricted to clerics, had been gradually extended to important lay nobility and patrons; then, in the later middle ages and, even more so, after the Reformation, to the merchants, lawyers and businessmen who were the arbiters of local power in the towns and cities. Further impetus to the practice was given by the accession of William of Orange in 1688, for intramural burial was a widespread mark of status in the United Provinces; so much so that churches like the Oudekerk in Amsterdam or the Groote Kerk in Breda, their floors a patchwork of ledger stones over the dead below, took on the character – which they still have – of indoor graveyards. In the 1660s John Evelyn described the City of London churchyards as already over-full, and denounced them as an affront to public decency. Wren too, among his proposals for the replanning of London after the Great Fire, argued that burial within churches should be forbidden, for the practice was 'not only unwholesome, but the pavements can never be kept even, nor the pews upright'. Churchyards were also 'inconvenient', for 'the ground being continually raised by the graves, occasions in time a descent by steps into the church, which renders it damp, and the walls green'. Answering his own question, 'where, then, shall be the burials?', Wren proposed 'cemeteries seated in the outskirts of the town' where 'a piece of ground of two acres, in the fields, will be purchased for much less than two roods amongst the buildings'. Neat and rational, he saw each cemetery 'enclosed with a strong brick wall, and having a walk round, and two cross walks, decently planted with yew trees' so that 'the four quarters may serve four parishes'. Wren's proposals, like so much of his brave new scheme for London, were never acted upon.

Outside the capital in the old provincial towns, often hemmed in by their medieval walls and boundaries, the churchyards were similarly overcrowded. In Exeter, which was the third largest town in England by the late seventeenth century, the common graveyard of the city was in the Cathedral Close; astonishingly, as archaeological investigation has revealed, burials had taken place there since the Dark Ages. In 1636, when an outbreak of plague brought hundreds of pestilential corpses to the packed ground, the situation became intolerable. The graveyard was closed and, in the following year, a new burial-ground opened in Bartholomew yard, inside the south-west corner of the city walls. Less than thirty years later more space was needed. Another burial-yard was opened in 1664, this time just outside the walls in Southernhay, south east of the city. In 1689, just twenty-five years after it had been opened, the Southernhay ground was described in an act of the Exeter Corporation as 'overfilled'.

Protests at the state of the urban churchyards continued in the eighteenth century. Vanbrugh argued against burials in the new London churches, urging instead, in a phrase he surely borrowed from Wren, that 'there must . . . be cemeteries provided in the skirts of the Town'. Against the arguments of propriety and convenience, however, was ranged a whole series of commercial interests. While churchyards had a monopoly on interment, burying the dead could turn a tidy profit. Burial fees were an important part of Anglican clerical incomes, additional charges were often levied by vestries and parish clerks, and sextons had a seemingly immemorial right to wheedle money from mourners at the graveside. Well might Thomas Lewis, in his 1721 pamphlet *Seasonable considerations on the indecent and dangerous custom of burying in churches and church-yards* inveigh against interment in and around churches as a practice 'begun through Pride, improved by Superstition, and encouraged for Lucre'. But such protests were isolated. Despite the opening of a number of burial-grounds for dissenters, mentioned earlier, and the provision of some additional churchyards in London, the eighteenth century saw no significant change in the means available for the disposal of the dead. But it did see a significant change in consciousness, a critical shift in attitudes towards personal mortality.

Graveyard Gothick and the Domesticated Dead

The eighteenth-century changes in attitudes to the dead derive from the growing economic importance of the merchant and commercial classes, 'the middling sort', generating a new bourgeois individualism, an enhancement of the sense of self-value. Among much else, this found expression in the creation of the affectionate family, in new attitudes towards children, in the kind of personal benevolence found in Addison's Sir Roger de Coverley and in the novels of the Sentimental School, in the reanimated sense of personal sin and salvation that fuelled Methodism. The emergence of new attitudes towards mortality is signalled by the Graveyard School of poetry, with its thrilled and horror-struck concentration on the details of death. Just as Methodism's insistence on individual sinfulness, particularly under Whitfield, harked back to sixteenth- and seventeenth-century Calvinism, so also the ghoulishness of the Graveyard poets recalls a Baroque sense of 'the skull beneath the skin'. But however lurid the early seventeenth-century's imagination, the death of the individual, as Donne reminds us, enforced the lesson that no man is an island, and Hamlet's gravedigger, surrounded by a promiscuous clutter of bones, was working in democratic ground. A century later such a scattering of the physical self was viewed with less equanimity. Edward Young's *The Last Day*, written in 1710 and one of the earliest poems to bear the stamp of the Graveyard School, addressed with solemn literalness the problem of the bodily resurrection, and, significantly, the need for the resurrected body to be individually intact.

> Now monuments prove faithful to their trust,
> And render back their long committed dust.
> Now charnels rattle: scatter'd limbs, and all
> The various bones, obsequious to the call,
> Self-moved advance; the neck perhaps to meet
> The distant head, the distant legs the feet.
> Dreadful to view, see through the dusky sky
> Fragments of bodies in confusion fly,
> To distant regions journeying, there to claim
> Deserted members, and complete the frame.

The desire to hang on to the personal uniqueness of the body, here made wonderfully and ludicrously explicit, is directly associated with the importance of the individual monument, as indeed it is in the opening lines quoted above. For the Graveyard poets, 'the ghastly ruin of the mould'ring tomb', however universal its message of mortality, was also an object of concentration in its own right, a macabre cynosure to which the mind's eye constantly returned. In *The Grave*, published in 1743, Robert Blair fixes on the material stuff of commemoration with an agreeably horrid enthusiasm.

> Night's foul bird
> Rook'd in the spire screams loud: the gloomy aisles
> Black-plaster'd, and hung round with shreds of 'scutcheons
> And tatter'd coats of arms, send back the sound
> Laden with heavier airs, from the low vaults
> The mansions of the dead.

Here, the churchyard has subsumed the church which, 'Black-plaster'd', has become a standing assemblage of graves and monuments.

With Blair we are, of course, in the realms of the Gothick. But though the graveyard and its mortuary church continued – and continues – as part of the sensationalist stock-in-trade, it was to be tears rather than terror that effected the decisive change in attitudes towards death. Nor is this surprising. The desire for the body to remain intact, to retain physical integrity after death was, as has been suggested already, an expression of a newly won and still vulnerable valuation of the self. As a necessary corollary, the idea – indeed, the reality – of bodily dissolution had to be warded off. Richardson's Clarissa Harlowe, saint and martyr of the morality of the middling sort, is only one of many sentimental heroines whose bodies show no sign of corruption after death. If the corpse was to be thought of as intact, held secure and discrete in or under its monument, was not the dear departed there to be addressed, in imagination at least? As Philippe Ariès has pointed out, personal visits to the tombs of loved ones were unknown before the eighteenth century. As early as 1746, James Hervey's *Meditations among the Tombs* provided visits by proxy, with appropriate reflections.

> Yonder white stone, emblem of the innocence it covers, informs the beholder of one, who breathed out its

> tender soul, almost in the instant of receiving it. There, the peaceful infant, without so much as knowing what labour and vexation mean, *lies still and is quiet; it sleeps and is at rest.*

The italics are Hervey's own. Though, elsewhere among the tombs, he can think that the 'crumbling bones mix, as they moulder' – although only to make a moral point about reconciliation through death – here, faced with the key sentimental image of the dead babe, Hervey conjures the child into continuing existence underground, permanently there even if permanently asleep. The child is 'peaceful', '*still*' and '*quiet*', '*it sleeps and is at rest*'. More than a century later, in *Great Expectations*, Dickens's Pip was to play the same game, though to more complex and ironic effect.

> To five little stone lozenges, each about a foot and a half long, which were arranged in a neat row . . . and were sacred to the memory of five little brothers of mine – who gave up trying to get a living very early in that universal struggle – I am indebted for a belief I religiously entertained that they had all been born on their backs with their hands in their trousers-pockets, and had never taken them out in this state of existence.

From Hervey's *Meditations*, it is only a short step to treating the tomb as a spur to imaginatively resurrecting the dead: sentiment's graveside contemplation can bring back the departed, their image softened by tears. This is precisely what happens in the most famous of all such meditations, Thomas Gray's 'Elegy in a Country Churchyard'.

> For them no more the blazing hearth shall burn,
> Or busy housewife ply her evening care;
> No children run to lisp their sire's return,
> Or climb his knee the envied kiss to share.
>
> Oft did the harvest to their sickle yield,
> Their furrow oft the stubborn glebe has broke:
> How jocund did they drive their team afield!
> How bow'd the woods beneath their sturdy stroke!

Even as transience is acknowledged, imagination and memory recreate the dead as actors in an idyll of rustic life. Effectively in this passage, the affectionate family, that central creation of eighteenth-century middle-class values, is extended to include the departed: the dead have been domesticated. The pattern is set for a whole tradition of Romantic and Victorian graveside reveries: naively direct in Wordsworth's 'We are Seven', where a 'little maid' insists to the dim poet that her brother and sister, buried 'Beneath the churchyard tree', are still part of the family; serio-comic in Arnold's arch doggy elegy 'Geist's Grave' – 'We stroke thy broad brown paws again'; wryly subversive in Hardy's 'Friends Beyond', where the village dead are returned only to express their indifference to the living.

Sentiment, the City, and the Body-snatchers

Gray's churchyard was in the village of Stoke Poges; Hervey's tombs were in the parish churchyard of Kilkhampton, Cornwall: both, that is, were rural, as indeed all the locations for similar sentimental musings seem to have been. If they were to retain even a semblance of verisimilitude, they needed to be. As has already been argued, their creation depended upon a sense of the body as still intact, either sleeping underground or imaginatively recoverable, and a sense of the grave as secure and discrete, so that a particular grave or tomb could be identified with a particular person or type of person. These requirements simply were not met in the burial grounds of London or the provincial cities, where the conditions deplored by Evelyn, Wren and Lewis continued to worsen, particularly after 1750, when the massive population increase of the nineteenth century had its beginnings. In 1700, the population of London was some 600,000; in 1750, still only 650,000; in 1800, as we have seen, it was nearly a million. In the vaults below the urban churches and chapels, the lead coffins of the better-off were stacked in their hundreds, and even thousands; in the burial-yards outside, bodies were continually disturbed, coffins broken up, graves violated, to make way for fresh interments. As if this were not bad enough, the second half of the eighteenth century brought a new, and peculiarly melodramatic threat to the security of the grave and the integrity of the corpse. In 1777 occurred the first indictment for body-snatching in London: at night, in the churchyard of St George the Martyr, Southwark, an attempt had been made to steal a newly interred corpse for the purposes of dissection. Though the first prosecution, it was by no means the first case: the trade of the resurrection-men had been well-established in Edinburgh and Dublin, as well as in London, since the mid-century.

From the time of Henry VIII, the bodies of executed murderers had been made available for medical dissection. The growth of empirical science in the seventeenth and early eighteenth centuries meant that demand began to outstrip supply. In 1747 the first systematic courses of anatomy in London were offered by William Hunter, who opened a school for dissection in the same year; in 1748 he was joined by his younger brother, John, who was to become the leading anatomist of the eighteenth century. St Thomas's Hospital established a regular dissection-room in 1780, an example soon followed by Guy's and St Bartholomew's. By the early 1790s there were about 200 anatomy students in London. At the beginning of the 1820s, there were 1000, working their way through some 800 corpses a year. The sensational character of body-snatching in part explains the particular *frisson* of horror with which it was regarded. But only in part, for dissection itself was viewed with similar abhorrence. No doubt the stigma attaching to an operation that was only legally carried out on the bodies of murderers was a reason for this, but again only a partial one. It was the middling sort who seem to have been most appalled by body-snatching and dissection. Certainly, the grim work of the resurrection-men became a staple of sensationalism in Victorian middle-class fiction, from Dickens's *A Tale of Two Cities* (1859), to Robert Louis Stevenson's short story 'The Body Snatcher' (1881), to R.D.Blackmore's *Perlycross* (1894) – all written long after the last resurrectionist had hung up his dark lantern. Why was middle-class abhorrence so intense and so persistent ? Surely because body-snatching and dissection outraged the very bases of the new attitudes towards mortality and remembrance. They constituted a sacrilegious attack upon the pieties of sentiment, upon the contemplative tomb, upon the domesticated dead. Body-snatching violated the security of the beloved grave, and dissection violated the intactness of the beloved body. Moreover, both body-snatching and dissection were urban: so also, of course, were the values they violated. Based, as we have seen, in the emergent economic and cultural importance of the middling sort, these values were, in the full sense of the word, bourgeois. However countrified the churchyard in which the sentimental tomb was set, the core of the audience that read about it lived in the towns. In the towns were the printers, the booksellers, and the circulating libraries; it was here that the novels and, even more important, the literary miscellanies that catered for sentimental taste were published and distributed. And the towns, London in particular, were where the church-vaults were packed, where the graveyards were choked, and where the resurrection-men went about their business. In short, the very class that had cultivated the new sensibility towards death, for whom sensitivity towards the dead and the remembrance of the dead was of major cultural importance, lived where those sensibilities and sensitivities were most likely to meet continual affront.

The Making of Père Lachaise

Outside England, precedents for dealing with the urban dead were already available. As early as the seventeenth century, a European cemetery had been established outside Surat, on the Gulf of Gambay in north-west India, then the chief Mogul trading port with the infant colonial powers of the West. Other mercantile and administrative centres made similar provision as the European nations increased their hold on the sub-continent. Probably the most important for the British, certainly one of the most grandiose, was in Calcutta. The victory of the East India Company at Plassey in 1757 had given them control of Bengal: as a result, by 1773, Calcutta had replaced Madras as the Company's principal town. The provision of the South Park Street Cemetery, founded in 1767, was an essential step in Calcutta's development, and was integral, at a significantly early stage, to the planning of the city that was to become the capital of British power in India. The contrast with the kind of provision being made – or rather not made – in cities back in England is striking. Even more so as urban cemeteries made their appearance in Scotland and Ireland in the early 1770s: Calton Hill in Edinburgh, and Clifton Graveyard in Belfast. Both provided alternative interment to the crowded burial-grounds of the city centres – Clifton was specifically designed to relieve the churchyard of St George's – and both attracted fashionable patronage. Neither was particularly closely tied in to any more comprehensive scheme of urban development, though Calton Hill had a tangential relationship to plans, largely unexecuted, for the laying out of the south east part of Edinburgh. Although close at hand, neither Edinburgh nor Belfast seems to have been regarded as a significant precedent for the English cemetery movement as it emerged in the early nineteenth century. Instead, the critical lead, repeatedly acknowledged by the cemetery reformers, came from Paris, and was an example not only of a remedy for the congested and offensive churchyards, but also of urban strategic planning on the grand scale.

In 1784 the great burial-ground of central Paris, the Cimetière des Innocents, which had been in continuous use since the middle ages, was closed. In the next couple of years, the municipality forced upon the church authorities the closure of almost every other ancient graveyard in the city. It was decided that all the burying-grounds should be cleared: the age-old heterogeneity of the dead, exemplified by Les Innocents, was to be decisively removed from the midst of the living. Throughout the winters of 1786-7 and 1787-8, the accumulated bones of centuries were carted away to subterranean limestone quarries beyond the Barrière d'Enfer, from whence the Romans had first dug the building stone for Paris. These became The Catacombs, a nether world entered beneath a grand classical portico, with underground chapels and endless ossuaries in which the bones of an estimated three million Parisians were neatly stacked and artistically displayed. The year following this mass clearance of the human debris of the *ancien régime*, the storming of the Bastille signalled a start to clearing away the *ancien régime* itself. As a means of coping with the dead, The Catacombs were not a preparation for the future. Quite literally, they were a putting away of the past. What kind of provision was to be made for the Parisian dead? In 1793, under the auspices of the National Convention, plans were prepared for a huge crematorium outside Paris, the scale of which clearly showed the influence of Etienne-Louis Boullée's pre-revolutionary designs for funerary architecture, all of which were imaginary and none of which was built. The crematorium proved equally impractical. In the following year the Prefecture proposed an alternative, far more workable but, in its own way, no less ambitious. Paris was to be provided with four 20-acre cemeteries outside the city walls, one at each of the cardinal points. The scheme lapsed until Napoleon's Consulate, when it was revived by the Prefect of the Seine, Nicolas Frochot. He decided that only three cemeteries were needed: in the north, the Cimetière Montmartre; in the south, the Cimetière Montparnasse; and in the east, popularly named after the original owner of the land, the Cimetière du Père Lachaise. Père Lachaise was the largest of the three, the first opened, and from the beginning the most important. The cemetery was securely enclosed within a high wall, and the hilly grounds laid out by the architect Alexandre-Théodore Brongniart, whose design combined formal avenues on the main axes with serpentine walks that brilliantly exploited the picturesque terrain. The first burial took place on 21 May 1804.

Instead of the old, packed burial-grounds of central Paris, Père Lachaise offered a landscape setting that was consciously Elysian, the Neoclassicism of its early monuments and mausolea wholly appropriate to the imperial rhetoric of Napoleonic France. But the cemetery's success, and much of its significance as a precedent, rested on its economics as much as its aesthetics: indeed, its aesthetics were a direct function of its economic organization. Plots for burial were offered for sale in perpetuity. Here was one of the simplest, yet one of the most fundamental shifts in the development of attitudes towards death. The right to burial in a family vault had existed for many years in the churchyards and burial grounds of France, as they had in Britain. Although such burial could be claimed by right of ownership, in both countries it was a privilege that remained within the grant of the church authorities. Now, at Père Lachaise, perpetual possession became available to anybody with the money to invest. Ownership of land, what English politicians liked to call 'a stake in the country', could extend itself beyond the grave, because the grave itself could become real property. Though the property owner was mortal, the fact of ownership went on for ever. What arrangement could be better suited to accommodate the new sensibility towards death that had emerged, in French sentimentalism as well as English in the eighteenth century? Ownership simultaneously guaranteed both the security and the discreteness of the tomb. Perpetual possession ensured that, just as the individual body would remain undisturbed, so the larger body of the bourgeois family would remain intact. These guarantees of continuity had a further meaning as well. Because permanent ownership was expensive, Père Lachaise offered the comforting assurance that social rank would be maintained; indeed, that it would be fossilized, literally turned into the stone of a thousand family mausolea. The cemetery was highly segregated, its regime quite different from the rough equality that had ruled over the dead of Les Innocents. For those who could not afford perpetuity, the cemetery authorities offered five-year leases and common graves, each of which contained seven corpses. In the early years of the cemetery these remained undisturbed, but after the mid-century, with space at a premium, the poor were buried in mass graves, the *fosses communes*. After five years any memorials were removed, fresh earth was tipped on top, and they were used again. If the poor are always with us, Père Lachaise ensured that their graves, at least, need not be.

The Earliest English Cemeteries

Despite the eighteenth-century precedents of Edinburgh and Belfast, the example of Paris generally and Père Lachaise in particular, there was no articulated campaign for the provision of cemeteries in England until the 1820s. The long years of the Napoleonic War were not conducive to social thinking, while the working-class distress and agitation that followed the peace made any proposals for social reform suspect. Indeed, it may well be that establishment hostility towards any ideas emanating from France, whose people had 'killed their King and denied their God', acted as an impediment. In this context it is not surprising that the cemetery movement in England got off to a stuttering start; so much so that, in its early years, it may hardly be regarded as a movement at all. The first burial-ground in England which may properly be called a cemetery was The Rosary in Norwich, which was licensed in 1819. It was built on five acres of market garden outside the crowded medieval city, it was unattached to any parish or district, and it offered burial to anybody who could pay for it, regardless of denomination. As a result, the dead, or their relatives, could prescribe whatever form of burial service they wished. Dissent had a long tradition in Norfolk, and it had been sharpened in Norwich itself by the periodic bouts of semi-authorized persecution that were characteristic of many eighteenth- and early nineteenth-century cathedral cities. The disabilities to which nonconformists were subject when it came to burial under the auspices of the Church of England have already been described; in Norwich these were exacerbated by the fact that most of the dissenting burial-grounds in the city were only leased from the Corporation. Unsurprisingly, the founder of The Rosary was a nonconformist minister, the Reverend Thomas Drummond, and its non-denominational character, its guarantee of religious equality and freedom of conscience, seem to have been the critical factors in its establishment. Certainly, the cemetery largely catered for non-Anglicans. In many ways, then, The Rosary was a further step in the process whereby dissenters had provided their own burial-grounds. Any relief it afforded to the tiny, if numerous, churchyards of the city was incidental, and it was certainly not part of any larger urban plan: indeed, as the Norwich Corporation was notorious for inefficiency and corruption, there was no civic authority capable of any such planning. Even its appeal to the nonconformist community was, during the early years, remarkably limited: only two burials in 1822, none in 1823, three in 1824, eight in 1825. This was not

St James's Cemetery, Liverpool, opened in 1829; west end of the quarry site, with chapel designed by John Foster.

the kind of support on which national campaigns could be launched. The Rosary seems to have been largely unknown outside Norwich. But the role that nonconformity played in its foundation recurred in other early cemeteries – and these, crucially, were in the new cities. By the 1820s, Norwich was in economic decline: it was the booming industrial towns and their mushrooming populations that were increasingly absorbing the attention of social reformers. Here, the setting-up of cemeteries would become part of the whole nineteenth-century debate about urban conditions; about how the towns were to be managed, organized, disciplined; about how the people of the great cities were to lead every step of their lives, from the cradle to the grave.

In 1821 a cemetery open to all sects and denominations was established at Chorlton Row on the Rusholme Road, south-east of the centre of Manchester. The city had a Quaker ground that had opened in 1813 and which seems to have catered for a wider community than that which set it up, but Chorlton Row was the first general cemetery in Manchester specifically established as such. Its prime movers were nonconformists, as is evidenced by the label it had attracted within a few years: The Dissenters' Cemetery. Chorlton Row was also bourgeois, sited in what was then a suburb, and one that was beginning to attract the villas of the Manchester manufacturers, among whom nonconformity was strong. Less obviously middle-class was the Every Street Cemetery in Ancoats, east of the centre of the city and considerably closer in. Opened in 1824, it was, like Chorlton Row, non-denominational: more local research is needed to establish how it functioned and what social class it served. No clues are forthcoming from the cemetery itself, which was closed in 1943 and disappeared beneath a playground for the Manchester University Settlement. Both these early Manchester cemeteries were relatively modest. Although only five acres in area, Low Hill Cemetery, west of the centre of Liverpool, was a far grander affair. Opened in 1825, it was entered between two substantial Greek Revival lodges joined by a Doric screen, on the architrave of which was carved the single word 'NECROPOLIS'. Restrainedly dramatic, the design of Low Hill – by Liverpool's leading architect John Foster – was also stating its identity as civic improvement in the best late Georgian manner. This awareness of the cemetery's functional relationship to the city in whose architectural display it joined, at once useful and ornamental, embodied, for the first time in England, the self-consciousness that marks a new building type. From this point the cemetery began to acquire its own architectural identity. But it was an identity that was not to become fixed to any one model. Even as Low Hill was opening, only a mile to the south schemes were being laid for a cemetery that would more clearly express those affective qualities that originated in sentimental and Romantic attitudes towards the dead, and to which the layout of Père Lachaise was in part a response.

If Low Hill was dramatic, the Cemetery of St James, first opened for burials in 1829, was theatrical. Nonconformists had taken a leading part in establishing Low Hill; at St James's – as its name, taken from a nearby parish church, indicates – the motive force came from the Anglicans. The cemetery fills some twelve acres of an abandoned stone quarry, immediately to the east of the platform on which Giles Gilbert Scott's Anglican Cathedral now stands. The architect of the cemetery was John Foster, whose free-standing chapel – Doric externally, Ionic internally – perches above a sheer cliff at the north end. Landscaping was designed by John Shepherd. Ramps slope down to the floor of the cemetery, paths wind through tunnels amidst informal planting, rock-cut catacombs are terraced into one of the quarry faces. Intriguingly, the picturesque vies with the sublime in a setting that is both beguiling and heroic. Significantly also, Foster's and Shepherd's handling of the quarry emphasized enclosure, a quality that, variously achieved and expressed, was to become a major element in English cemetery design of the first half of the nineteenth century. For all its spatial intricacy, Père Lachaise, by comparison, was open, public; the enclosure of St James's nurtured the personal and private. It was, in fact, perfectly tailored to that particular sentimental inwardness which created the contemplative tomb, that intimacy between the bereaved and the dear departed whereby the dead were retained within the affectionate family. In this there is evident a substantial difference of emphasis between French and English middle-class commemoration of the dead. In St James's, as in Père Lachaise, burial plots were available for sale in perpetuity: the affectionate family, like the bourgeois family in which it had its origins, could go on for ever. In Père Lachaise, however, the continuity that was, and still is asserted by the row upon row of house-tombs was primarily dynastic, and their assembly *en masse* – quite unlike anything in English

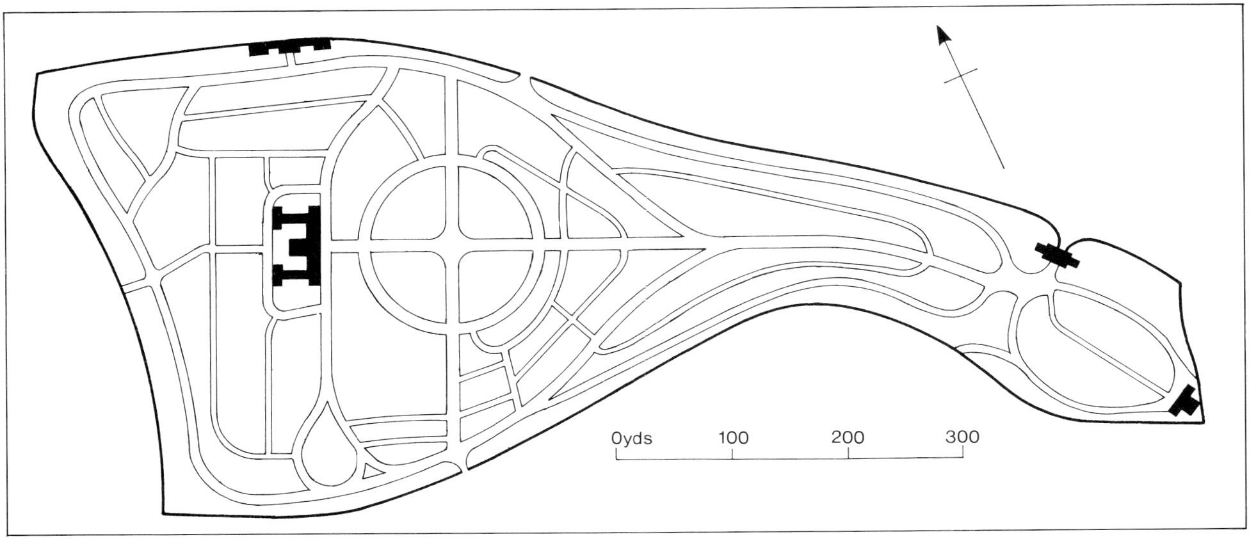

Plan of Kensal Green Cemetery, London, as finally carried out 1833-7; path widths not to scale.

cemeteries – implies a public demonstration of class solidarity. By contrast, memorials to the English middling-sort, a term which accurately expresses a much looser class grouping than that of the French bourgeoisie, were far less disciplined by a sense of belonging to a social order. It is true that catacomb ranges, like those at St James's, could express something of the same sense of uniform dynastic possession, but no English cemetery is dominated by its catacombs. Instead, it was the idea of the family as a domestic entity, living and dead, which tended to prevail, and the inward and self-reflexive quality of much English cemetery design provided the enabling context in which this could happen. None of which, of course, is to suggest that the French bourgeoisie was in fact any less affectionate than its English equivalent, or that the English middle-class family was in fact less dynastic than the French; who, after all, could forget the Forsytes?

The sophisticated architectural and spatial impact of St James's, its particular affective character, had a further dimension, as in its different way had Low Hill's. In both cemeteries, design functioned as advertisement, for both were established by private enterprise, as had been The Rosary and the two Manchester cemeteries before them, and as were the majority of English cemeteries until the various Burial Acts of the early 1850s. Finance was usually provided by setting up a joint stock company. Money was raised by the issue of shares on which dividends were paid when the company's product, the cemetery, began to realize a profit. Planning, planting, architecture and design were all employed to attract custom, for cemeteries like St James's and Low Hill were commercial concerns. Other, less tangible, elements were also commercially important. The idea of civic improvement and the idea of individual sensibility, variously expressed through both cemeteries, were marketable commodities. This is not to be cynical, for the fact that a market for them existed, as it did not in contemporary Norwich, says much for the public and private enlightenment of the middling-sort in early nineteenth-century Liverpool. And, in economic terms, it worked: by 1830 the Cemetery of St James was paying a dividend of 8%.

Kensal Green

Meanwhile, what was happening in London? From the mid-1820s, the barrister George Frederick Carden had conducted a campaign in magazines and periodicals decrying the inadequacies of burial provision in the metropolis and urging the building of cemeteries on the Parisian model. But land in London was expensive and difficult to obtain, and the financial interests vested in the parish churchyards were intricate and well-entrenched. It was not until 1830 that Carden managed to organize the first public meeting to discuss the provision of a general cemetery for London, and not until 1832 that proposals took final form with the incorporation of the General Cemetery Company. In 1831 some 54 acres of land had been purchased at Kensal Green by one of the founders of the Company, Sir John Dean Paul, who was a banker and was to become its first Chairman. Although the first burial took place early in 1833, Kensal Green Cemetery was not finished until 1837, the delay having been occasioned largely by disagreements within the Company about the style of its buildings. Paul was an advocate of Neo-classicism; Carden, who was the Company's first Secretary, favoured Gothic. Paul won: elaborately detailed Gothic designs by H.E.Kendall were rejected despite their having obtained first prize in the public competition that was held; the Company Surveyor, John Griffith, drew up designs in an austere Greek Revival manner instead. Carden lost his Secretaryship and his place on the board. Whatever the aesthetic merits of the argument, there seems no doubt that it was Paul's weighty financial commitment to the Company that proved decisive. Certainly, the adoption of Greek was commercially astute. In the early 1830s, despite the distant cries of the gathering Goths, Neo-classicism still commanded the field of polite architecture – and it was at a polite market, or one that aspired to politeness, that Kensal Green was aimed. Significantly, Kendall's design for its layout derived from Nash's layout of Regent's Park: although this scheme was subsequently amended the executed plan carries the signs of its lineage. Strongly axial, its straight Central Avenue runs through a quadrated circle before arriving at the Anglican chapel, which is also reached by perimeter drives that swing round the outside of the circle. If such design, like that of its Liverpool predecessors, was couched in the language of urban improvement, it was a language that consciously quoted the aristocratic formality of late Georgian planning in the West End, particularly that of the Crown estate, amplifying its quotations in the long colonnades flanking the Anglican and nonconformist chapels – the latter now demolished. The leases on the best houses around the Park were beyond the pockets of most of the middle class; at Kensal Green, however, the availability of burial plots in perpetuity offered a permanent stake in a development that consciously expressed a cognate gentility.

But if the middle-class clientele of Kensal Green were to be allowed to aspire, they were also to be allowed to express themselves. The Company had considered exercising control over the design of monuments in the cemetery – which would not have been dissimilar to the aesthetic restrictions on alterations that the Crown estate imposed upon its tenants. But the idea was abandoned in favour of complete freedom: anybody who bought burial ground in Kensal Green could erect whatever memorial they liked. Only the catacombs below the Anglican chapel imposed a certain conformity upon the dead. Above ground, the results of the Company's policy were allowed to run counter to the formality and discipline of the cemetery's buildings and layout: the image of class uniformity presented by Père Lachaise, or indeed by the terraces around Regent's Park, was dispelled by Kensal Green's funerary variety. The *laissez-faire* policy that the Company adopted towards monuments was a version of, and perfect match for, the *laissez-faire* doctrines generated by the accelerating economic activity of the late eighteenth and early nineteenth centuries. The aggressive individualism inseparable from such doctrines had its basis in precisely the same middle-class commercial success that, as was argued earlier, produced the affectionate family. The apparently contradictory impulses towards aggression and affection that resulted, were in practice, in the history of the Victorian middle-class family, often complementary. The more a husband strove to become that capitalist hero, the Carlylean Captain of Industry, the more a wife needed to become, in Patmore's phrase, the Angel in the House. Each role gave form and definition to the other: the corollary of the king in the counting-house was the queen in the parlour. The patterns that shaped middle-class life also shaped its commemoration. So it was that at Kensal Green, liberated by a management policy of non-intervention, the celebration of individualism joined the contemplative tomb and the domesticated dead as part of nineteenth-century cemetery rhetoric.

But Victorian individualism, however middle-class its birth and lineage, could produce unorthodox offspring. In this context, no monuments are more suggestive than

those to Andrew Ducrow and John St John Long, both in prime positions on the junction between the main avenue and the circular drive. Long died in 1834 and is commemorated by a statue of Hygieia standing within an Ionic peristyle atop a tall podium – a design derived from the Choragic Monument of Lysicrates. Where Long had chosen Greek, Ducrow opted for fantastically elaborated Egyptian: his mausoleum, designed in 1837 and costing £3000, has recumbent sphinxes and lotus capitalled shafts at each of its corners, angels hovering in low relief on its sides, and a great draped urn with horse's head handles crowning its roof. Though one is *svelte* and the other showy, both monuments are highly self-assured, both characteristic of individualist celebration. Yet Ducrow and Long were hardly typical members of the middling sort. Long pedalled a patent medicine of his own invention and, four years before his death, had been found guilty of manslaughter when he managed to kill one of his own patients with the stuff. His monument was posthumous vindication, erected, to quote the inscription, 'by those who knew his worth, and the benefits derived from his remedial discovery'. Ducrow, the son of a circus strong man from Southwark, was a celebrated trick rider who ran successful equestrian shows, attracted the patronage of William IV and finished up as proprietor of Astley's Circus. His mausoleum, 'erected by Genius for the reception of its own remains', was posthumous congratulation.

Their monuments and their histories provide one of the keys to understanding Kensal Green's appeal to the nineteenth century. In a rapidly changing society, the prizes of individualism also brought the penalties of unstable rank and uncertain status. Kensal Green granted full freedom of individual expression, whether through assertion like Ducrow's or excuse like Long's: but a memorial in Kensal Green, particularly a substantial one, was also a badge of belonging, an expression of middle-class membership – made more so by the fact that

membership was expensive. Ducrow may have been a circus performer and Long a confidence trickster, but they were also, respectively, a successful entrepreneur and a man of science. Did not the very fact of their monuments prove as much? Their monuments guaranteed membership and, as the epitaph of Long's memorial reminds us, he was just 'one of the many who will rest here'. The 'many' stretch down Central Avenue to either side of Ducrow and Long – the generals and diplomats, doctors and lawyers, bankers and speculators. In front of the Anglican chapel, the expanse – and expense – of it all finds consummation in two memorials to members of the royal family, no less: Augustus Frederick, Duke of Sussex, who died in 1843, and Princess Sophia, daughter of George III, who died in 1848. Their arrival in Kensal Green made the cemetery's reputation: after all, if a circus showman and a convicted quack could command grand monuments only a hundred yards or so from the blood royal, what miracles of social acceptance could the cemetery not achieve ? By

Kensal Green Cemetery, London, 1833-7; panoramic view of the Anglican chapel, designed by John Griffith, and its associated monuments; including the bollarded tomb of the Duke of Sussex, d. 1843, and the sarcophagus on podium in memory of Princess Sophia, d. 1848.

1840 shares in the General Cemetery Company had more than doubled their original value of £25 and, in 1843, Clark's *Hand-book for visitors to the Kensal Green Cemetery* could boast that it contained 'members of more than two hundred of the first families in the kingdom'. It was all very satisfactory.

Other elements, alongside those already discussed, amplified Kensal Green's appeal to the middle class. As we have seen, fear of intrusion had been a significant element in forming attitudes towards the grave. Although the Dissection Act of 1832 effectively removed any real threat that the resurrection men posed towards the middle-class corpse, Kensal Green still made a display of security. The immense, almost unbroken length of its boundary wall

Kensal Green Cemetery, London; Andrew Ducrow's mausoleum, built to Dawson's designs in 1837, and the monument to John St John Long, d.1834, sculpted by Robert Sievier.

along Harrow Road was a sufficient demonstration of purpose. Equally important – perhaps more so as the fear, though not the *frisson* of body-snatching diminished – it functioned as a powerful expression of enclosure: despite the size of the cemetery, the visitor's sense of the high wall, emphasized by the flatness of the enclosed ground, is pervasive. Reassuringly circumscribed, Kensal Green could be created as its own world, and in this the cemetery's planting played a decisive role. It will be remembered that a rustic setting was the invariable accompaniment to the sentimental tomb: contemplation required countryside, and the domesticated dead inhabited wooded ground. When Kensal Green was established it lay beyond the brick and mortar of the outer suburbs, but the cemetery itself was far from providing ideal terrain. Its flatness, already referred to, gave scant opportunity for the picturesque landscaping that was conducive to sentimentalism, and doubtless contributed to the adoption of a formal layout. Even so, early designs and an aerial perspective of *c.*1832, now in the London Museum, show that elements of formal planting are subordinated to informal groups of evergreens and broadleaves, mixed copses that cluster round junctions and mark the beginnings of drives, or casually punctuate areas of open ground and the long line of the boundary wall. In all this there was a marked change of emphasis from the tomb-lined streetscape of Père Lachaise, despite the latter's exploitation of picturesque landscaping. The particular quality achieved by Kensal Green is all the more evident when it is compared to the immediately contemporary Glasgow Necropolis, for which the Glaswegian doctor, John Strang, had campaigned in much the same way as had Carden in London. James Stevens Curl has rightly pointed out the decisively urban character of the great Glasgow cemetery, laid out on a bare hill opposite the cathedral, its Greek monuments and mausolea coursing round the slopes below the commanding presence of John Knox, whose giant statue tops a Doric column on the summit. Here, as Curl says, 'is literally a city of the dead'. Not so at Kensal Green, for, amidst the complex urban references of its planning and architecture it also quotes the visual characteristics of a traditional English churchyard, with its informal planting and its scatter of tombs. What was in creation at Kensal Green in the first years of the 1830s was the garden-cemetery. As early as 1830, in a letter to the *Morning Advertiser* supporting the establishment of cemeteries outside the metropolis, John Claudius Loudon had urged that they be 'planted with every sort of hardy trees and shrubs' so that the London cemeteries 'and every other burial ground in the country, might be made . . . botanic gardens'. Interested in every aspect of urban planning and landscape design, an outstanding horticulturalist, Loudon had a personal preference for formal planting and a rationalist approach to the organization of burial space. His ideas gained currency during the 1830s and 1840s, particularly after 1843 when he published *On the laying out, planting, and managing of Cemeteries*. Influential as his theories were, however, they were secondary, in the early years of cemetery-planning, to the central idea of the garden and rural park, and to its interpretation through the picturesque tradition, which had largely invented the English country churchyard as a major visual property. As we have already seen, the churchyard was the *locus classicus* for the new middle-class attitudes towards the dead, a synthesis of sentimentalism and the picturesque. At Kensal Green this coextended with the cemetery's appeal to class status and aspiration. Quite literally, it was what the middling sort were looking for, determining not only what they expected, but what they actually saw.

All the key constituents in Kensal Green's hold on the middle-class imagination are remarkably clear in the illustrations to Laman Blanchard's article 'A visit to the General Cemetery at Kensal Green', published in *Ainsworth's Magazine* in 1842. At the top of the last page a funeral procession moves up Central Avenue, between the Long and Ducrow monuments (significantly enough), towards the Anglican chapel: the avenue is as wide as Whitehall, the monuments tower several storeys above the mourners, the chapel hangs in the far distance like a vast Palladian mansion. The illustration that runs down the side of the same page presents quite another version of the cemetery. A different funeral procession finds itself on a narrow path which meanders through a clearing fringed with trees, winding past scattered monuments and leaning headstones: visitors straggle along the path – a woman holding the hand of a child, a couple arm in arm, an elderly man with a walking stick. Yet there are no serpentine paths in Kensal Green: as a representation of the cemetery's actual appearance, this second image is as discrepant as the exaggerated scale and perspective of the first. But neither illustration, of course, was concerned with literal truth. Both were fantasies, the one imaging the pomp of an imperial prospect, the other picturing the familial intimacy of a rustic churchyard. The illustrations to Blanchard's article gave visual form to impulses that were at the very heart of the bourgeois dream: the one impulse sought to celebrate power and prestige, while the other longed to cherish sensibility and domestic life. We are back with the Captain of Industry and the Angel in the House. Public and private, urban and rural, they were, as was suggested earlier, complementary, as are all good heroes and heroines. And both, of course, were personifications from that middle-class complex of aspirations, attitudes and feelings towards which Kensal Green was addressed.

Lady Mary Wortley Montague describes the burial-places about Constantinople as appearing more extensive than the city itself: and Mr. St. John, remarks—"I know of few spots on earth so productive of calm thoughts, and hushed and delightful feelings as that mysterious valley, where the dust of the Egyptian kings reposes." Our cemeteries, yet in their first bloom and verdure, have less of magnificence, less of space, less of solitude; yet in them will these calm thoughts and elevated feelings spring up, and blossom under the eye of Heaven. To erect a monument to desert, is a deed, says Godwin, "the more entitled to commendation, as it is refined, and remote from the grosser conceptions of the majority of the species;" and the same authority decides that his heart must be "made of impenetrable stuff," who does not attribute a certain sacredness to the grave of one he loved, and feel peculiar emotions stirring in his soul as he approaches it!

The final page from Laman Blanchard's 'A visit to the General Cemetery at Kensal Green', Ainsworth's Magazine, *1842.*

Provincial Cemeteries of the 1830s: the Greek Monopoly

The first general cemetery in London, and the largest in England at the time, Kensal Green was also the best-known and the most publicized. The frequent accounts of it in popular journals and the publication of guide-books indicate the extent to which it was visited and its importance in giving shape to early nineteenth-century sensibilities about death. Having said as much, it must also be said that the chronology of other cemeteries from the first years of the 1830s means that direct design influence from Kensal Green was often slight; in some cases, indeed, impossible. With the exception of Kensal Green, all English cemeteries of the early 1830s were in provincial towns and cities. In the metropolis itself, to be discussed subsequently, a second cemetery was not begun until 1836. The provincial towns, particularly in the industrial areas, were frequently the centres of vigorous regional cultures and economies; their sense of local identity was strong, and recently acquired civic pride ensured that independence from London would be jealously guarded. The marked similarities that these provincial cemeteries shared with one another were not the simple consequence of copying: rather, they were the result of similar responses to similar demands – the middle-class expectations and sensibilities that, as we have already seen, produced Kensal Green.

Cheltenham, wealthy and fashionable, was provided with its first cemetery in 1830. Its single chapel, by the local architects Rowland Paul and Sons, was Greek Revival, as had been the buildings of Low Hill and St James's in Liverpool, and as all cemetery buildings up to the mid 1830s seem to have been. In Greek, the provincial promoters of cemetery-building clearly found a conducive and marketable style – civic, elevated, and, thanks to Kensal Green, upper-class in its associations. Cheltenham cemetery was turned into a public park in 1966, and the character of its original planning and planting is now difficult to guess at. More informative is Key Hill Cemetery in Birmingham. The Birmingham General Cemetery Company was incorporated in 1832, ostensibly to provide interment for all denominations, but in practice a nonconformist enterprise. Key Hill, which opened in 1835, was partly laid out in a sand quarry, a setting that immediately recalls St James's in Liverpool. In Birmingham, however, the quarry continued to be worked periodically until the mid twentieth century. Whatever one's notions of propriety, the arrangement made sense: the same site supported two commercial operations, burying and quarrying, and as the wall of the quarry receded so fresh ground was made available for burials. The layout of Key Hill shows similar economic shrewdness: formality and informality are juxtaposed, thus balancing, in terms of the cemetery's market, the two impulses in middle-class demand that were analysed earlier. In the lower part, the Doric chapel, designed by Charles Edge and demolished in 1966, was raised on a platform in the middle of the main carriage drive, which runs up from Icknield Road and forms the principal axis of a rectilinear grid of paths. The higher ground, against the irregular quarry face that forms the long eastern boundary of the cemetery, was given full picturesque treatment. Paths meander from the Key Hill entrance to

Key Hill Cemetery, Birmingham, 1834-5; view over the catacomb hollow.

The General Cemetery, Newcastle, 1834-6; the Jesmond Road entrance, designed by John Dobson. Royal Commission on Historical Monuments.

the lip of the L-shaped hollow that houses the catacomb range; on the floor of the hollow, little tracks curl around groups of free-standing monuments. The planting is dominated by plane trees, lining the main carriageway and boundary wall near the chapel, but informally scattered in and above the catacomb hollow, so the whole of this side of the cemetery is lightly wooded. No part of Kensal Green is so self-consciously countryfied. In the same year that Key Hill made its debut, Woodhouse Cemetery in Leeds was opened by the Leeds General Cemetery Company, which had been established in 1833. Compared with Key Hill's leafy enclosure, Woodhouse seems public and urban: John Clark's weighty Graeco-Egyptian gatehouse and lodges are deliberately imposing, the chaster Doric of his chapel, decidedly smart. There is now no way of telling how these buildings related to the original planting: as at Cheltenham, this has been destroyed by the cemetery's conversion into a park, which has seen off most of the monuments as well.

As in many cemeteries set up by joint stock companies, we may read the buildings of Woodhouse as an attempt to translate capitalist enterprise, albeit enlightened, into the terms of civic improvement. Certainly the Leeds of the 1830s needed public-mindedness, for its booming mills had created some of the worst urban conditions in England. In Newcastle, by contrast, the architectural language of civic development was further advanced, and in John Dobson the city had one of the nineteenth-century's most accomplished exponents of urban design. Newcastle's first cemetery, Westgate Hill, had opened in 1831, though its origins were as early as the mid 1820s. Designed by John and Benjamin Green, it was a relatively modest affair. The establishment of the Newcastle General Cemetery Company in 1834 signalled a move towards something far more ambitious. John Dobson was engaged as the Company's architect, responsible not only for buildings but also for layout and planting. The Newcastle

The General Cemetery, Nottingham, 1837-40; the gatehouse and almshouses, designed by S. S. Rawlinson.

General Cemetery opened in 1836: it is among Dobson's finest works, and is one the great architectural achievements of nineteenth-century cemetery design. Dobson concentrated architectural focus upon the two entrances which pierce the enclosure of the high stone boundary wall: a deep semi-circular arch between square towers, tightly flanked by the two chapels, forms the main entrance from Jesmond Road; the secondary entrance, from Sandyford Road, has pedestrian gates through massive piers capped by sarcophagi. Everything is Greek, stylistically pure to the point of austerity. Unbending slightly, the main carriage-drive curves gently, and the planting includes weeping willows, the horticultural favourite of the sentimental muse. Loudon, ever formal in his tastes, disliked the willows but was impressed by the whole conception and thought the Jesmond Road entrance 'the most appropriate cemetery lodge he knew'. If appropriateness, for Loudon, principally meant the maintenance of funerary dignity, it also included, as we have seen, a consciousness of civic improvement. The entrance range of Nottingham General Cemetery expresses this consciousness with surprising gusto. The joint stock company that built the cemetery had been incorporated by Act of Parliament in 1836; as at Low Hill in Liverpool, and Key Hill in Birmingham, its prime movers were nonconformists. Facing what was always a busy junction on Alfreston Road, and thus in a setting that was distinctively urban, the cemetery's main entrance was designed by S.S. Rawlinson, and built between 1837 and 1840. The heavily detailed gatehouse, with its two-storey belfry tower, is the massive central accent of a complete terrace, which stretches symmetrically to either side and accommodates almshouses financed by the Freeman's

Rights Committee. The treatment of the entrance as the main feature in a larger unit of townscape identified the cemetery with the very fabric of the city. It also effectively associated the idea of the cemetery with the charitable activity represented by the almshouses. Where Key Hill combined two commercial activities on the same site, the design of Nottingham General managed to imply an identification between private enterprise and philanthropy – not altogether unjustly, of course, for the entrepreneurship that promoted the cemeteries was consciously directed at the public welfare, even if that welfare was defined in terms of middle-class interests.

In the same year that the Nottingham General Cemetery Company was founded, Sharrow Vale General Cemetery in Sheffield was opened. The hilly terrain dropped down to the bank of the River Porter, according to a contemporary account 'thickly shadowed over with oak, and ash and elder', and leant itself to Romantic landscaping. This was managed by the Sheffield architect, Samuel Worth, who also designed the Doric chapel and Graeco-Egyptian gates. Manchester, meanwhile, was adding to the modest cemetery provision it had acquired in the 1820s. The first shareholders' meeting of the Ardwick Cemetery Association was held in April 1836; the following month, the Trustees of Manchester General Cemetery were incorporated. Both cemeteries opened in 1837, both with Greek Revival chapels, gateways and lodges. Occupying 12 acres at Harpurhey, well north of the central area, Manchester General was considerably the more ambitious, and indeed the first cemetery in the city to attempt to provide burial space on a substantial scale: by the time it was finished, it had cost £18,000. Ardwick is now a playing field; all Harpurhey's buildings were demolished in the 1960s and its weeping wych elms now mourn over an expanse of derelict and vandalized monuments. In the same year that saw the inception of the two Manchester cemeteries, the Bristol General Cemetery Company was formed. Land was purchased at Arno's Vale, about a mile from the city centre, and the cemetery laid out between 1837 and 1840. The architect was Charles Underwood, who provided a pair of studiously correct Doric lodges and two chapels, Ionic for the nonconformists and Renaissance Corinthian for the Anglicans. Pursuing a pattern that is by now familiar, he set the formality of his buildings amidst informal planting, with paths curving up into the wooded high ground that rises behind the chapels. In fact, the synthesis of elements at Arno's Vale suggests considerable sophistication, and one is tempted to see the conception of the cemetery as a carefully contrived series of settings, an affective sequence tuned to the nuances of sensibility that could be expected from the cemetery's middle-class patrons, and which were doubtless shared by its proprietors. In as far as the lodges represent the point of demarcation between the open world of the city and the closed world of the city's dead, they mediate between the public and the private: classically severe, their Doric would have been understood by the nineteenth century as masculine, and they belong to the male world of commercial Bristol. From there to the chapel and to the gentler elegance of Ionic, an architectural unbending that symbolizes the emotional shift which accompanies physical removal from the city. From the chapel to the graveside and the tender associations of the rustic and the picturesque, to the realm, that is, of the feminine and domestic. If the public exterior of Arno's Vale is characteristically male, its heart belongs to mummy.

The London Joint Stock Cemeteries: the Advent of Gothic

Whatever the expressive qualities of Arno's Vale, however its planting sought to woo the softer emotions, the cemetery was nevertheless and necessarily the product of Bristol commercial enterprise. It is not coincidental that joint stock cemetery companies in Bristol, Nottingham, and Manchester were all established in 1836. A series of fine harvests from 1830 to 1835 had produced an accumulation of purchasing power that had benefited industrial enterprises as well, and led to surplus monies in the banks available for investment. Since 1830 a large block of government war debt, the most popular means of investment, had been converted from 4% to 3%, so the yield to the individual investor from 'the funds' had decreased. With more money in the economy other investments were sought, and 1835–6 saw the first speculative boom in the nascent railway industry, which promised lucrative returns. The commercial success of cemeteries such as St James's in Liverpool and Kensal Green made them attractive propositions as well. The ambitious scale of Kensal Green had made it a substantial speculative venture: if other metropolitan cemeteries were

Arno's Vale Cemetery, Bristol, 1837-40; panoramic view from the entrance lodges to the chapels; buildings designed by Charles Underwood.

to follow suit then they would need to raise funds on a similar scale. The hiatus between the incorporation of the General Cemetery Company and the establishment of the next London cemetery company probably resulted from speculative caution and the need to ensure that shares were offered to a market with enough money to invest. That situation arrived in 1836, when, as well as the provincial companies already mentioned, two London cemetery companies were incorporated. The earlier was the Southern Metropolitan Cemetery Company. In 1837 the company opened its cemetery on a broad, sloping site in what is now West Norwood but was then the relatively rural suburb of Lower Norwood. Norwood Cemetery, as it became known, occupies 39 acres and cost £75,000 to complete. The architect, responsible for the layout as well as the buildings, was William Tite, then in the early stages of a highly successful career that would include designing the Royal Exchange, the Presidency of the RIBA, and a knighthood.

All the architecture of Norwood was Gothic, from the massive railings of the enclosing wall to the two chapels that topped the hill at the cemetery's highest point. Kendall had of course provided Gothic designs for Kensal Green, and, in 1836, J.A. Picton had designed a little Tudor lodge and chapel for the churchyard of St Mary's, Kirkdale, Liverpool, which he laid out as an Anglican cemetery. But Norwood seems to have been the first general cemetery to employ Gothic, and certainly the first to employ it on such a scale. As we saw earlier, the decision to build Greek at Kensal Green – and the corollary rejection of Kendall's Gothic – sprang from the hegemony enjoyed by Neo-classicism in the field of polite and public architecture. By the time Tite designed Norwood, there had been a change. The contribution of Gothick taste to the new attitudes towards death and commemoration that emerged in the the eighteenth century has already been discussed. That taste, of course, had its architectural as well as its literary expressions: the monkish ruin glimmered in the picturesque landscape of sentiment alongside the contemplative tomb. The story of how the Gothic Revival grew from the stylistic naughtiness of Strawberry Hill into the serious historicism of the nineteenth century is a favourite of architectural historians and need not be

told again here. Tite's use of Gothic at Norwood is undoubtedly part of the larger tale, but two elements seem particularly important. In 1835 the great competition for the new Palace of Westminster was held, and the style specified was Gothic or Elizabethan: in the most important public building of the first half of the century, the building that was to embody the legislative heart of the nation, the Goths had dished the Greeks. Despite the classical thunder of C.R.Cockerell, Charles Barry's Tudor elevations established a new paradigm for civic architecture, and gave Gothic a public status and identity it had previously enjoyed only in the dreams of enthusiasts. What style could more commend itself to the board of the Southern Metropolitan Cemetery Company? Gothic combined the glamour of recent success with the patriotic feelings that clustered round the Mother of Parliaments. Tite's Gothic was Tudor and Barryesque, his Anglican chapel quoting – even if a long way off – from that of King's College, while the great catacomb arcade on which the chapel stood, and which stretched along the crest of the hill to either side, was a *coup de théâtre* thoroughly concordant with the visual taste that produced the Westminster river front.

If the first influence on Norwood's Gothic was the style's newly found civic authority, the second was its growing identification with religious sentiment. In 1836 the young A.W.N.Pugin published *Contrasts*, which made the most uncompromising claims for the high religious seriousness of Gothic, which spoke of Pointed Architecture and Christian Architecture as if they were synonymous: in Gothic alone was 'the faith of Christianity embodied, and its practices illustrated'. If Tite, steady man of business that he was, had known *Contrasts* – and its immediate notoriety makes that quite likely – he would doubtless have deplored the intemperateness of its attacks on the architectural profession as heartily as he distrusted its Roman Catholic proselytizing. But *Contrasts* was one sign of the architectural times. From John Carter's authoritative drawings of English cathedrals in the 1790s, the work of antiquarians had increasingly familiarized public and architects alike with the ecclesiastical Gothic of the middle ages. Even the Commissioners Churches had popularized the association of Gothic with churches – though largely on grounds of cost. For all that Pugin inveighed against the prevalence of 'pagan' Classical memorials, Gothic had been increasingly familiar in funerary monuments since the beginning of the century. Edward Blore's *Monumental Remains*, first published in 1824, was perhaps the best known of a number of works illustrating major medieval tombs in Britain. *Contrasts* claimed Gothic for the Roman church; a few years later the Cambridge Ecclesiologists – their architectural ideas derived from Pugin and their theology from the Oxford Movement – tried to appropriate it for High Anglicanism. Although, throughout the 1840s, protestantism continued to find Gothic dangerously Papist, the general religious associations of the style were too strong and too widespread to permit of its being monopolized by any one Christian grouping. Gothic articulated much of the growing religious consciousness, and self-consciousness, of the early Victorian middling sort, and that consciousness directly informed the burial of the dead. To the range of associations which had accrued around middle-class commemoration was added the need to demonstrate Christian belief. Although monuments derived from Classical models continued to be erected, Gothic tombs, Gothic details and Gothic forms proliferated, alongside overt and often elaborate Christian iconography. From the 1840s onwards, Gothic became the universal style for cemetery buildings, their stylistic connotations coming close to actually denoting Christian burial. If Tite's Gothic at Norwood was contemporary in drawing upon the civic celebrity of Barry's Westminster, it also anticipated the religious sentiments and associations of a whole generation.

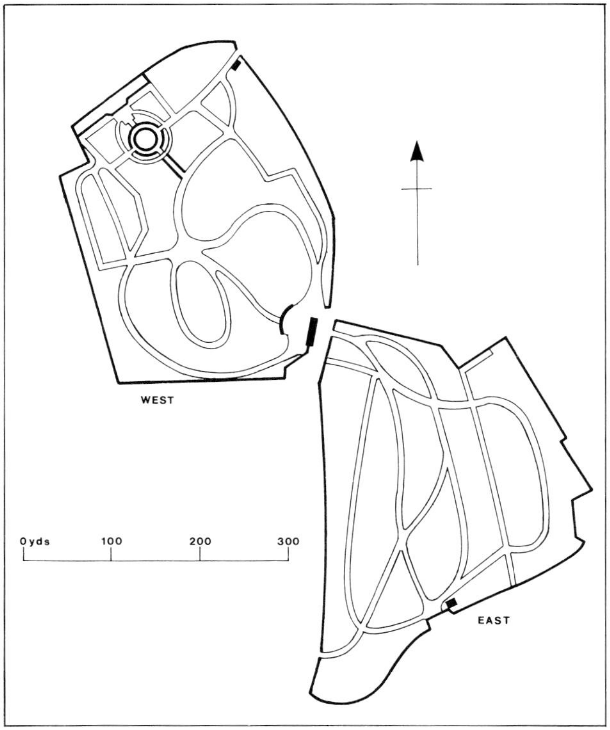

Plan of Highgate Cemetery, London; the west cemetery laid out to the design of David Ramsay 1837-9, the east cemetery 1855; path widths not to scale.

Like the Southern Metropolitan, the London Cemetery Company was set up in 1836. Its scope was ambitious: in the wording of its Act of Incorporation, the Company proposed 'establishing cemeteries for the Interment of the Dead, Northward, Southward and Eastward of the Metropolis'. Such a scheme takes us back to the 1794 proposals for cemeteries at the cardinal points around Paris – though in the case of London, the west side was already catered for by Kensal Green. The motive force behind the company was Stephen Geary. Geary was the architect of the colossal – and much-mocked – statue of George IV that gave its name to King's Cross, had designed buildings of public entertainment – including an early gin palace – and had patented several inventions. Above all, as his range of activities suggests, he was an entrepreneur and his role in the building of cemeteries seems to have been more developmental and managerial than architectural. The London Cemetery Company established two cemeteries: the northern, at Highgate, opened in 1839; the southern, at Nunhead, in 1840. Stylistically, their architecture was eclectic: at Highgate, the catacomb avenue and circle were built in the Egyptian style, and quickly became famous; at Nunhead, J. B. Bunning, employed as the Company's surveyor in 1839, designed a delightfully cranky pair of Greek lodges. Significantly, both cemeteries used Gothic for the chapels. At Highgate, small chapels are tucked neatly either side of the main gatehouse, the whole range, in an attenuated and symmetrical lancet style, possibly designed by Geary himself. Far grander is the octagonal Anglican chapel at Nunhead, designed by Thomas Little, its over-scaled *porte-cochère* – all crockets, turrets and tracery – providing a theatrical closure to the perspective of the broad drive that

Highgate Cemetery, London, 1837-9; the entrance to the Egyptian Avenue.

runs uphill from the main gates. However, it is not style that is the most important consideration in the architecture of Highgate and Nunhead: it is much more the particular integration of architecture and landscape. At Norwood Tite's Gothic buildings had been been set on an open hillside, with broad paths curving up through informal planting: to quote Hugh Meller, 'a wonderfully spacious design,with clumps of deciduous trees and concentrations of tombs'. It was a design that belonged in the tradition of the landscape park, picturesque in some of its effects but also relaxed. At Highgate and Nunhead, buildings and layout combine to create landscapes that are more dramatic, more wholeheartedly Romantic. Highgate in particular, landscaped by David Ramsay, brilliantly exploits those effects of enclosure and spatial intimacy that we first noticed at St James's in Liverpool, simultaneously pushing further the kind of rural evocation so important at Birmingham's Key Hill. Highgate is relatively small, its original area only some 20 acres, but the careful disposition of the paths that turn and wind up the steep gradient on which the cemetery is laid out make it seem much larger. At the same time, the high, unbroken boundary wall to Swain's Lane, the planning and planting, envelope the visitor – or the mourner – emphasizing the inwardness that establishes the cemetery as its own world. To all this, architectural features are strictly contributory. The Egyptian Avenue, with its stage-managed perspective, and the catacomb circle strung round the Cedar of Lebanon, though formal features in their own right, are subordinate phases in the cumulative effect of Highgate as a whole. Despite Loudon's complaint, in 1843, that Norwood in particular, and the London cemeteries in general, were planted and laid out 'too much in the style of a common pleasure ground', they were tailored precisely to the early Victorian middle-class market: sharp men like Geary made sure of that. Highgate especially was a great success: set in a more fashionable area than Nunhead, less formal than Kensal Green, less public than Norwood, it became the definitive cemetery of the London bourgeoisie in the nineteenth century.

The joint stock cemeteries were, as we have seen, major speculative ventures. As such, they presented complex problems of funding, management, and marketing – all of which, of course, affected and even determined the nature of their layout and design. The problems of getting this mix wrong are revealingly demonstrated by the fifth of the metropolitan private enterprise cemeteries. The West London and Westminster Cemetery Company was incorporated by Act of Parliament in 1837, and empowered to raise the very large sum of £100,000, half of it in shares of £25 each. Seemingly, the 'projector' of the enterprise was again Stephen Geary, who was also appointed as the Company's architect. In practice, however, affairs were run by two lawyers among the Directors, most of whom never met. Forty acres of ground, lying between Fulham Road and Old Brompton Road, were bought, but disputes over the ownership of the land ensued: the property was not finally conveyed to the company until the summer of 1839, and the first burial in the cemetery, which became known as Brompton, did not take place until 1840. By this time Geary had left. Never really involved in the management of the company, he had been replaced as architect early in 1839 when a competition for the cemetery's buildings had been won by Benjamin Baud, who had been Wyatville's assistant in the remodelling of Windsor Castle. The land at Brompton was a flat rectangle: eschewing any attempt at the picturesque, Baud opted for high formality. In its original conception, Brompton was the antithesis of Highgate. Where Highgate was enclosed, irregular, intimately personal, Brompton was open, rational, emotionally neutral. Where Highgate was romantically countrified, Brompton was urban. Baud planned the cemetery around an undeviatingly axial layout, the principal drive running straight through the centre of the site from the main gatehouse to the domed Anglican chapel, which was framed up between parallel, two-storey catacomb ranges and approached across a great circle, ringed by more arcaded catacombs and intended to have nonconformist and Roman Catholic chapels balancing the Anglican one on the main axis. All the buildings were designed in a consistent Italianate Renaissance manner: such a choice of style was significant. The influence of Charles Barry's Palace of Westminster on Tite's adoption of Gothic at Norwood has already been suggested. In the early 1830s, Barry had also successfully introduced an Italianate *palazzo* style for the design of London clubs. It seems highly likely that the West London and Westminster's selection of Baud's Renaissance designs was prompted by a desire to catch a fashionable architectural idiom – and, of course, the clientele that went with it. If so, the company miscalculated. In Brompton's first years the number of

Brompton Cemetery, London, 1839-42; the Anglican chapel, designed by Benjamin Baud.

burials was small: a handful in 1840, only 89 in 1841, 285 in 1842. Undoubtedly, part of the trouble lay with the initial financing. Baud's designs were expensive and the delays occasioned by the disputed ownership of the land meant that the company was attempting to raise money in the economically straightened years after the disastrous harvest of 1838, the years that gave birth to the tag 'the hungry forties'. As a result, Brompton was always undercapitalized. Eventually, in 1844, Baud was replaced as architect: having lost the ensuing court case in which he claimed some £4000 in unpaid fees from the company, he largely abandoned architectural practice. The West London and Westminster struggled on until the early 1850s when, as we shall see, the cemetery was taken over by central government and the company wound up: in its last years, it was paying a mere 1% on the capital investment. Critical as these economic factors were, however, it seems likely that the nature of Brompton's layout and buildings contributed to its comparative commercial failure, that the cemetery's aesthetics were mistaken in terms of the market, particularly when contrasted to the financial success of its emotional opposite, Highgate. Baud's designs – smart, rational and public – made insufficient provision for the domesticity, the inwardness and intimacy, which had become essential elements in the business of middle-class mortality, and which were so skilfully exploited by Highgate. Moreover, Brompton made no appeal to the kind of synthesis of family affection and religious piety expressed through the combination of Gothic architecture and Romantic landscaping at Norwood and Nunhead. Renaissance urbanism, and indeed urbanity, were all very well for a London club, but not for a London cemetery.

The Early 1840s: Abney Park, Equality, and the Urban Poor

At present, developments in the provision of cemeteries outside London during the economically critical years of the late 1830s and early 1840s are far from clear. More work is needed, but it seems that the same slump that made commercial life so difficult for the proprietors of Brompton also inhibited cemetery-building as a speculative venture elsewhere in England. As well as his London enterprises, Stephen Geary was involved in 'projecting' cemeteries at Peckham and Brighton; the first was never built and the second, despite its catacomb range, was essentially an extension to an existing Anglican churchyard. However, he was also one of the principals behind establishing a cemetery at Gravesend, for which an Act of Parliament was obtained in 1838 and which was opened in 1841. The architect was Amon Henry Wilds, whose design included an impressively grand gatehouse, which has twinned lodges either side of a central arch with pairs of Doric columns, and a Greek chapel. Proposals to develop Gravesend as a watering-place in the Brighton fashion had been put forward earlier in the 1830s, and a plan had been drawn up by Wilds, who himself came from Brighton. Little came of the scheme, but the architecturally aspiring cemetery seems to have been an element in it.

If the cemetery at Gravesend was provided for a smart town that never happened, Reading Cemetery, somewhat similar in its scale, was more directly responsive to economic realities. Picking up on the commercial advantages of the newly arrived Great Western Railway, the town was expanding steadily; its population, 19,000 in 1841, had more than doubled since the beginning of the century. Laid out and built between 1842 and 1843, the cemetery has – or had, for some of the buildings have been demolished – a Tuscan entrance lodge and classicizing chapels, all designed by the local architect William Brown. The cemeteries at Gravesend and Reading, both of which have genuine architectural pretensions, are exceptions in the general picture of reduced activity. Other immediately contemporary cemeteries are few in number and decidedly limited in ambition. Acts of Parliament passed in 1840 enabled cemeteries to be established at Winchester and Shrewsbury; in the same year a half-acre cemetery was laid out by a private company in Truro; in 1841, the north Devon town of Bideford acquired a small interdenominational cemetery complete with a chapel in the lancet style. Such modest amenities doubtless gave relief to the crowded little towns to which they were attached. In the industrial cities, however, no new cemeteries were added to those provided in the 1830s until the middle of the following decade brought an upturn in the general economic situation. Hard hit by the recession, the potential investors of the manufacturing towns had no surplus capital for new entrepreneurial schemes. It is striking that, apart from the rather anomalous case of Gravesend, all our examples of cemeteries founded in the years following 1838 are from market and county towns, and all, with the exception of Shrewsbury, are from the south of England. Among the northern towns only Derby was provided with a new cemetery, and Derby, with a population of some 35,000 by 1841, was both relatively small and – compared to the manufacturing giants to its north and west – growing relatively slowly. Even so, a mere 4 acres, opened in 1842 on the New Uttoxeter Road, was all that was felt necessary – or alternatively, all that could be managed.

The early 1840s did see, however, two new joint stock company cemeteries open in London: Abney Park at Stoke Newington in 1840, and Tower Hamlets, just off the Mile End Road, in 1841. They differ in character both from each other and from their metropolitan and provincial predecessors. Abney Park, established by the Abney Park Cemetery Company, the nine trustees of which were all Congregationalists, is particularly instructive. As we have seen, nonconformity was involved with the very inception of cemetery building in Britain. From the Rosary onward, cemetery companies sold burial to all comers regardless of denomination. But such ecumenism had to confront Anglican Canon Law, which stipulated that any burial ground for members of the Church of England had to be consecrated by the diocesan. In the big London cemeteries, with their massive capital outlay, the desire to attract members of all religious persuasions was motivated as much by the need to target as large a middle-class market as possible, as by any interdenominational idealism. As a result, cemeteries were subdivided: a consecrated section with its own chapel received the Anglican dead; their dissenting brethren found rest in the unconsecrated section, which normally had its own chapel as well. In provincial cemeteries, however, frequently established under direct nonconformist auspices, the Anglican consciousness of schism and of superior legitimacy often led to ostracism. Good members of the Establishment shunned dissenting ground, and a separate cemetery was the result. We have already seen this at Liverpool, where St James's was the Anglican entrepreneurial answer to Low Hill. In Birmingham, Key Hill remained a nonconformist place of interment and the Church of England opened its own cemetery a few hundred yards away at Warstone Lane in 1845. Even consecration did not always allay Establishment suspicion: although a portion of the General Cemetery in Nottingham was consecrated, Anglican distrust was such that they made their own provision, firmly known as the Church Cemetery, in 1848. At Abney Park, the Congregationalist founders had little patience with what they saw as Establishment divisiveness and discrimination. But then, Abney Park itself was not the kind of ground that could meekly be made subject to episcopal authority. The cemetery, 32 acres in extent, was laid out on the old Fleetwood-Abney estate, home territory for a dissenting élite whose credentials went back to the heroic days of the Civil War and the Commonwealth. More important still, it was to Fleetwood House that Dr Isaac Watts had come as tutor in 1696, and his intimate association with the house, its family and its grounds lasted for the rest of his life. Pious, learned, accomplished, and a major religious poet, Watts was a figure of central significance in the cultural mythology of dissent, and Abney Park was little short of holy ground. Watts was credited with having had a hand in designing the estate's early eighteenth-century layout, and there in the grounds was his favourite seat, a tree-shaded hummock that became known as Watts' Mound. Fantasy, or a culturally exiled community's need for its own myths of continuity, had even identified the Mound as the grave of none other then Oliver Cromwell, his body reverently hidden there by his sister, Bridget Fleetwood, to protect it from the vengeful spite of Charles II. If dissent could not take a stand against Establishment arrogance here, in the haunt of Dr Watts and on the bones of the Lord Protector, where could it? The company decided from the very beginning that there would be no Anglican consecration at Abney Park. As Paul Joyce has said, 'Conscience dictated that no humiliating demarcations, such as had cordoned off the exiles in earlier cemeteries, should be allowed to mar this silent assembly of equals'. The cemetery's single chapel epitomizes this ecumenism: designed by William Hosking,

Abney Park Cemetery, London, opened in 1840; the chapel, designed by William Hosking.

its eclectically assembled Gothic may have made every ecclesiologist wince, but its style strikes the right note of generalized religious feeling, and its 120 foot spire points heavenward just as surely as the most correct of catholic fanes. In the event, Abney Park did succeed in attracting some Anglicans with Broad Church sympathies, but its clientele remained overwhelmingly nonconformist throughout the nineteenth century.

The persistence of division even in death was not the only point at issue, however, between Anglicans and nonconformists. In all the joint stock cemeteries established by Act of Parliament, compensation for loss of burial fees was liable to the Anglican clergy from whose parishes the dead had come. Predictably, such a levy was objectionable to the Congregationalists of Abney Park and, in order to avoid it, the cemetery went ahead without an Act of Parliament. In eliminating burial fees, the company seems to have been concerned with more than asserting denominational independence. Anglican fees significantly increased the cost of interment: at Norwood, for example, a guinea was charged on every burial. Though insignificant in the overall cost of a middle-class funeral, such a sum represented a fifth of the average total cost of the least expensive working-class funerals. And it was for the burial of the working classes that the trustees of Abney Park seem to have felt a particular concern. As we have seen, private enterprise cemeteries established in London and the provincial cities were aimed at the middling sort, their buildings, their planting and planning designed to accommodate and express middle-class attitudes towards death and commemoration. Such attitudes were expensive to maintain, and providing for them was lucrative. The Court of Chancery, responsible for vetting executors' accounts, accepted without question undertakers' bills of between £60 and £70, exclusive of fees, for the funerals of clergymen, officers of the armed forces, and members of the professions; gentry funerals started at about £150 and went up to £400; burying the nobility cost anything from £800 to £1500. None of these expenses included the cost of buying a place of interment in a cemetery. At Highgate, the cost of perpetual lodging in the terrace catacombs ranged from £10 to £94, and a brick-lined family grave cost £21. As for the monument, that was as expensive as piety, affection or aggrandizement wanted it to be: at Kensal Green, as we saw earlier, Ducrow's mausoleum cost £3000. Ducrow was of humble origins and there can be no doubt that the extravagence of his monument was one means of celebrating his triumph over obscurity. It was an opportunity that fell to exceedingly few working-class people, and it was they, the humble and obscure, who formed the vast majority of the population and thus the great bulk of its mortality.

In the 1860s, lower middle class families and above formed 20% of the population, and the families of skilled workers 10%, leaving the unskilled labouring classes and the labouring poor, the agrarian and urban proletariat, to make up 70% of the British people. With the expenses of middle-class mortality in mind, comparative figures are revealing. In 1834, when the directors of the General Cemetery Company were anxiously watching the early progress of their investment at Kensal Green, agricultural labourers at Tolpuddle in Dorset were transported for combining to resist a proposal to cut their weekly wage below 7s 6d. Around 1850, the date of the charges for interment at Highgate quoted above, Henry Mayhew found that tailors working in the sweated trade of the East End slop shops that provided cheap middle-class clothing were earning between 1d and 2d an hour. How could working-class families, their whole lives passed in a poverty that varied only in its degree of intensity, afford burial when even a common grave at Highgate cost £2 10s? This is the context in which the trustees of Abney Park Cemetery resisted the imposition of Anglican burial fees. Their doing so was an attempt to mitigate the usually prohibitive costs of cemetery interment for working-class families, and was indicative of the company's inclination towards a more general equality. The company's prospectus stated quite specifically that its object was to provide a cemetery which not only was available to all denominations, but 'which shall be open to all classes of the community'. Consistent with this, the trustees ordered their architect, William Hosking, to separate the catacombs from the chapel and to make them as limited and undemonstrative as was compatible with minimum business interest because they identified catacombs with social élitism. Within its limits, Abney Park was successful in attracting labouring-class burials, which took place in common graves between the perimeter paths and the boundary walls – all decent enough, even if firmly demarcated from the bodies of the better off.

What Abney Park provided was, of course, chronically inadequate. Even so, it shows to advantage against the

Highgate Cemetery, London; the view from the terrace; a print of c.1850 by R. Hind. Camden Library Services.

policies adopted by other joint stock cemeteries towards the burial of the poor. Though burial in Tower Hamlets Cemetery was relatively cheap, its excellent financial returns derived from a policy of filling common graves as full as possible and packing them together as densely as possible. In its Annual Report of 1842, the directors of Kensal Green suggested a scheme for the long-term disposal of the bodies of London's paupers: 'It has been found that seven acres will contain about 133,550 graves; each grave will receive ten coffins; thus accommodation may be provided for 1,335,000 deceased paupers . . .' If Tower Hamlets was exploitative, this was merely callous. But whether adopted policies were opportunistic or unfeeling – or indeed philanthropic like that of Abney Park – it was increasingly clear that the London private enterprise cemeteries could not deal with the burial of the working-class people of the metropolis. The reasons, of course, were inherent: the joint stock cemeteries catered for a middle-class market. High prices and social discrimination made them peripheral to the needs of the mass of the labouring population, and it was in that population that the real crisis lay. Oddly, emblematically, dawning bourgeois awareness of that crisis began to express itself through the cemeteries themselves – or, at least, in the way they were experienced in relationship to the urban world that their walls excluded but that, increasingly, surrounded them. The inwardness and enclosure of the private enterprise cemeteries, their cultivation of both domesticity and individualism in response to the psychology of middle-class mortality, fostered insularity. This was one expression of a prevalent and, at times, almost absolute class segregation, the result of which was profound ignorance among the early nineteenth-century bourgeoisie about the lives and living conditions of the proletariat. From the middle of the 1830s that ignorance was under attack, from parliamentary reports on industrial conditions, from the writings of socially conscious novelists and journalists, from the vocal distress of working-class people themselves in the harsh years after 1838. The moral and, ultimately, the political ambience of the cemetery began to change. At Highgate, the broad terrace constructed along the northern perimeter of the cemetery was a favourite place of resort for visitors and residents of the neighbourhood. Yet, whereas the grounds themselves provided the middle-class funerary setting *par excellence*, the terrace looked over and beyond the cemetery's class enclave to the whole of London spread below. Here, as contemporary commentators recommended, was the place for the thoughtful to reflect and meditate: not, however, upon the individual grave or the family tomb, but – to quote the telling phrase of an 1839 newspaper account – upon 'the modern Babylon'. Though the 'Age of Great Cities' celebrated the technological prowess of urban growth, what was offered for contemplation here was the city's other identity: Babylon the Great, Bunyan's City of Destruction, the City of Man that St Augustine contrasted to the City of God. For the thoughtful middle-class man or woman on the terrace of Highgate in the last year of the 1830s, the city was much more than a backdrop: as Babylon, it was the location, visibly and palpably present, of what the unsettling Thomas Carlyle in *Chartism* had just labelled 'The Condition of England Question'. In as far as Highgate and the private enterprise cemeteries were expressions of middle-class values, those values and their insularity were part of what England's crisis brought into question.

"*Gatherings from Graveyards*": *the Burial Crisis*

The view from the terrace at Highgate, contemplating the modern Babylon, meant that the relationship between cemetery and city, necropolis and metropolis was redefined. That the cemetery could no longer continue as a place of privilege and class refuge was clear from G.A. Walker's *Gatherings from Graveyards*, published in the same year as *Chartism*, the year that Highgate opened, and a report from Babylon to the people on the terrace if ever there was one.

In 1837 Dr George Alfred Walker had set up his surgery in Drury Lane. He was in the middle of a densely built-up area, its populace crammed into a maze of courts and alleys behind the buildings that fronted the main thoroughfares. Walker was interested in cemeteries and in the problem of managing the dead of a great city: he had visited Paris and Père Lachaise; he was familiar with the difficulties of urban burial in his home town of Nottingham. In the tight huddle on either side of Drury Lane, at the back of The Strand, around Covent Garden and Long Acre, Walker found some of the worst of the London burial grounds, hemmed in by buildings, tight up against houses and tenements. As we saw earlier, the majority of these London grounds belonged to Anglican parishes and many were churchyards, particularly in the City itself. Supplementing these were those that had been established by nonconformist congregations, along with a number of private burial grounds set up as commercial enterprises though often claiming connection with one or other of the dissenting churches. Many of these grounds, particularly the Anglican ones in the City, were tiny, a matter of a few hundred square yards. Even the largest, several of which were in the congested working-class districts of East London, were pitifully small given the size and rate of expansion of the populations they were supposed to serve. Among the Anglican churches, St George's-in-the-East had 3 acres for a population of 40,000; St Matthew's, Bethnal Green, had 2 acres for more than 70,000; St Mary's, Whitechapel, had under an acre for nearly 35,000 people; while the three burial grounds of St James's, Clerkenwell, totalled less than an acre between them, which was all the Church of England could manage for 50,000 souls. The largest of the speculative grounds were also in the East, positioned to take advantage of the demand for cheap burial: the three biggest were Cambridge Fields in Bethnal Green, with an area of 5 acres, Spa Fields in Clerkenwell, with 3 acres, and Sheen's New Ground in Whitechapel, with 2. Bunhill Fields, on the edge of the City, was by far the biggest of the nonconformist burial grounds, but even then was only 3¾ acres in extent and had been constantly in use since the middle of the seventeenth century. Only a handful of forty or so burial yards belonging to individual nonconformist communities, including those of the Roman Catholics, were larger than half an acre, and the great majority were less than 1000 square yards in area. With the notable exception of the far more strictly controlled Jewish and Quaker burial grounds, all these grounds – Anglican, nonconformist and private – were grossly congested, unseemly and insecure. We have seen how new sensibilities towards death and commemoration, cultivated among the middle class but untenable amidst the sordid realities of urban interment, created a market for the cemeteries of the 1820s and 1830s. Effectively, the joint stock cemeteries, particularly in London but also in the great provincial towns, allowed the bourgeoisie to buy an alternative to a place in the burying grounds.

What private enterprise did not do, of course, despite the philanthropic rhetoric of cemetery projectors and prospectuses, was deal with the problem of urban burial itself – the mounting crisis that came from trying to push the bodies of tens of thousands of men, women and children into the same little spaces of earth year after year. *Gatherings from Graveyards* placed that crisis before its middle-class readership in unrelentingly physical terms. As a whole, the book is unsystematic, even disorganized; but in its central section, Walker's horror-struck eyewitness accounts of the conditions actually prevailing in the burial yards are unforgettable. At Whitechapel church, 'the ground is so densely crowded as to present one entire mass of human bones and putrefaction'. At St Anne's churchyard, Soho, 'rotten coffin wood and fragments of bone are scattered about . . . the ground is very full . . . considerably raised above its original level . . . [and] . . . overlooked by houses thickly inhabited'. In the corner of the St Giles ground

> is the 'bone house' which is a large round pit; into this had been shot, from a wheelbarrow, the but partly-decayed inmates of ... smashed coffins. Here, in this place of 'Christian burial', you may see human heads, covered with hair; and here, in this 'consecrated ground', are human bodies with flesh still adhering to them. On the north side, a man was digging a grave; he was quite drunk, so indeed were all the grave diggers we saw ... a child's coffin, which had stopped the man's progress, had been cut, longitudinally, right in half; and there lay the child ... wrapped in its shroud, resting upon the part of the coffin which remained. The shroud was but little decayed . . .

In ground after ground Walker saw graves violated, bodies dismembered and exposed, simple human dignity ignored and outraged. But these were ordinary horrors compared to what he found in the burial place under Enon Chapel, Clement's Lane, established as a private speculation in 1823. In a space 59 feet long, 29 feet wide and some 6 feet in depth, separated from the chapel above by nothing more substantial than floorboards, Walker estimated that 12,000 bodies had been interred.

> Soon after interments were made, a peculiarly long narrow black fly was observed to crawl out of many of the coffins; this insect, a product of the putrefaction of the bodies, was observed on the following season to be succeeded by another, which had the appearance of a common bug with wings. The children attending the SUNDAY SCHOOL, held in *this chapel*, in which these insects were to be seen crawling and flying, in vast numbers, during the summer months, called them 'body bugs' – the stench was frequently intolerable . . . Vast numbers of rats infest the [surrounding] houses; and meat exposed to the atmosphere, after a few hours, becomes putrid.

Walker was moved by pity and by anger, but he sought to move his readers by fear as well. According to the pythogenic theory from which he argued, the gases given off by human putrefaction could be deadly to anybody who inhaled them; the filth and corruption of the urban burial yards generated poison and disease; the very atmosphere filling the close courts around the worst of the grounds, thick with the 'mephitic vapour' of decomposition, was a primary source of universal contagion. And the burial grounds were just one element in a cumulative urban emergency: beside the yards were the open sewers, the reeking water supplies, the undrained tenements, the overflowing cesspits and middens of the unregulated city. Just as Carlyle argued that the Condition of England Question confronted the whole population and not just the distressed labouring classes, so also Walker argued that the vilely insanitary conditions inflicted upon the urban proletariat, living and dead, 'to which their poverty and not their will consents', involved everybody. And if the prosperous and complacent ignored the crisis, it would involve them whether they wished it or not:

> Let those who at present supinely look on and disregard the dangers threatening their poorer neighbours from

> the vast sources of disease, remember that pestiferous exhalations arising from the numerous infecting centres of the metropolis, are no respecters of persons.

What was needed was 'the enforcement of efficient "Sanatory [*sic*] Regulations" throughout every department of the kingdom, and the ENTIRE REMOVAL OF THE DEAD FROM THE IMMEDIATE PROXIMITY OF THE LIVING'. Legislative action must be taken, Walker concluded, to close the urban burial grounds and provide instead cemeteries sited outside cities and available to all classes.

The Public Health Campaign: Cemeteries, Sanitation, and Edwin Chadwick

Although campaigners like Carden, Strang and Loudon had emphasized the sanitary role of cemeteries, though ideals of civic improvement and religious duty had contributed to their foundation, the cemetery movement's principal achievement and expression, from the founding of The Rosary onward, had been the provision of middle-class burial by means of private enterprise. *Gatherings from Graveyards* signalled the integration of the movement with the broader aims of Early Victoran public health agitation – itself a critical part of the Condition of England debate. In the process, the cemetery movement, or at least its objective, was democratized. That this should happen was inevitable: the key issues of public health were expressed through the lives and deaths of working-class families, people who could not defend themselves against insanitation, who could not buy their way to a healthy home and a decent grave. We are back with the blind demographic forces that, as was discussed earlier, shaped the whole development of nineteenth-century Britain, and the argument of *Gatherings from Graveyards* effectively acceded to that reality. Walker's acknowledgement of the indiscriminate equality of contagion, of the fact that while disease may start with the impoverished and undernourished it ultimately spared no class, was painfully pertinent. On 21 October 1831, the first case of Asiatic cholera, *cholera morbus*, had been diagnosed in Sunderland. The disease had taken from 1817 to make its deadly journey from the plains of Lower Bengal, along the shores of the Mediterranean and across the long reaches of European Russia and Germany, to Britain. By the autumn of 1832, 52,000 people had died of the disease, and while the rule of King Cholera had been at its most severe in the homes of the labouring poor, his edicts had lain upon the middling sort and their betters as well. After the terrible first epidemic of 1831–2, cholera became the most feared of Victorian killers, and in London and the great towns it did not want for murderous company: typhus, typhoid, smallpox, diphtheria and dysentery were all endemic. In the crowded working-class districts of London slightly more than one death in five was from epidemic, endemic or contagious diseases; in Liverpool the figure was one in four; in Manchester nearly one in three. While class segregation provided a significant measure of protection, particularly for the upper strata of the middle-classes and for the gentry, there was no enclave, however privileged, that was finally immune. After all, it was typhoid fever that was to kill Prince Albert in 1861. Although we now know, with a century of bacteriological medicine behind us, that Walker's pythogenic theory and the parallel miasmatic theories that ascribed the spread of sickness to aerial infection were wrong, they were unerring in identifying the social sources of disease and contagion: the terrible living conditions of the labouring classes, the polluted water they drank, the unsewered and unventilated buildings they inhabited ('called houses by courtesy', as Walker said), the physical debility they suffered. It was against these enemies that the early Victorian warriors of sanitary reform pitched themselves, and among their foes, thanks largely to Walker, were the urban burying grounds and those who profited from them.

The campaign against burial in towns, intramural interment, was fought on several fronts. Walker continued to expose prevailing conditions in a sequence of books that were essentially compendia of abuses: *The Graveyards of London*, published in 1841, *Interment and Disinterment*, of 1843, *Burial-Ground Incendiarism*, published in 1846, and taking its title from the practice adopted by undertakers at the Spa Fields ground of secretly burning corpses and coffins in the bone-house to make more room for interments. The Metropolitan Association for the Abolition of Burials in Towns, founded by Walker, pursued the same objects, which were supported after 1844 by the influential Health of Towns Association. The arguments against intramural burial were taken up by the *Lancet*, then a radical reforming journal under the direction of

Cobbett's friend, the great Thomas Wakley, and by the *Builder* which, after 1844, was under the crusading editorship of George Godwin. In both, the battle against the burial grounds was co-ordinated with a broad campaign not only against insanitary conditions, but also against the ignorance, jobbery and incompetence that continually frustrated reform. As member for Finsbury, Wakley carried the fight into parliament, where he drew particular support from William Mackinnon, Robert Slaney and the ubiquitous Anthony Ashley-Cooper, later the Earl of Shaftesbury. 'Graveyard Walker', as he became known, had demanded 'the interference of the Legislature to abolish or reform' the whole baleful system of urban burial, and it was towards parliament and legislation that the principal efforts of the reformers were increasingly directed.

In 1837, a more than usually virulent outbreak of fever had caused great distress in the working-class districts of London, and a steep increase in applications for relief had driven up the poor rates. Financial repercussions were felt across the divide between proletariat and bourgeoisie, where mere misery was not. An inquiry was demanded and the Poor Law Commissioners appointed Thomas Southwood Smith, physician to the London Fever Hospital, to investigate Bethnal Green and Whitechapel. The subsequent report was the first systematic account of the sanitary crisis confronting the metropolis, and its first acknowledgement by official sources. The man directly responsible for commissioning the report had known full well what horrors it would reveal and had planned it accordingly: he was the Secretary to the Poor Law Board, Edwin Chadwick. With the publication of the report, Chadwick assumed effective leadership of public health agitation, and was to impel its vanguard until the early 1850s. Trained as a lawyer, Chadwick had been the disciple and personal friend of Bentham in the latter's final years. In 1832 he had been appointed assistant commissioner to the inquiry into the administration of the Poor Law, and had become chief commissioner in 1833. His energy transformed the inquiry into a Benthamite crusade, and it was through him that utilitarian principles were injected into the very marrow of the Poor Law Amendment Act. The Act established a unified and uniform system of poor relief and its central organization came to form a structural model for much subsequent social legislation. And, of course, the Act was detested, loathed for its authoritarianism, its impersonality, and its seeming desire to punish the poor rather than help them. Not all of this was Chadwick's fault, though it highlights a persistent paradox in his character: selflessly committed to the public good, he seemed incapable of fellow feeling. That there was great human misery he knew, but he seemed to know it only as a logistical problem. Yet his utilitarianism was not over-theoretical and he showed little interest in philosophical abstraction *per se*: rather, he brought the mental habit of abstraction to the practice of public administration, and to that he gave his life. So absolute was his dedication that for him the practical metamorphosed into the ideal, became an inspiration, an encompassing dream of efficiency and order. As Secretary to the Poor Law Commissioners he was tireless; from the centralized power he exercised on their behalf he forged a formidable weapon of inquiry; and in the nexus between public health and poverty he found his field. Emotionally chilly, apparently humourless, authoritarian in temper, he was, nevertheless, a zealot, whose passions burnt amidst endless committees and countless memoranda, and whose fervour expressed itself through numerical tables. The reeking cities were the Augean stables to his statistical Hercules. To use a Carlylean formulation that Carlyle would have thought utterly contradictory, Edwin Chadwick was the Hero as Bureaucrat.

"Interment in Towns"

Following the revelations of the 1838 report of the Poor Law Commissioners, the government ordered them to undertake an inquiry into working-class sanitary conditions throughout Britain. Chadwick drew up the letters of instruction to the assistant commissioners across the country, emphasizing that the inquiry could lead 'to the removal of the causes of prevalent and fatal diseases, and of consequent destitution and suffering'. From their evidence, Chadwick compiled the monumental *Report on the Sanitary Condition of the Labouring Classes of Great Britain*, which was published in 1842. In the same year, William Mackinnon introduced a parliamentary bill designed to ban intramural burial in London and to empower vestries to establish cemeteries outside the city. The timing was appropriate, for Walker and his associates had already ensured that the burial crisis would be perceived as integral to the debate about urban sanitation. In the year following his main report, Chadwick brought out a supplementary report, commissioned by the Home Secretary, *On the Results of a Special Inquiry into the Practice of Interment in Towns*. Like the main report itself, the supplementary report not only gave new authority and impetus to the agitation for reform, but also redefined the nature and objectives of the argument. Broadly speaking, *Interment in Towns* demonstrated that the existing situation was medically and morally intolerable, that urgent and comprehensive remedies were needed, and that these could only be provided by the state. Many of Chadwick's specific recommendations as to how cemeteries should be planned and organized were drawn directly from Loudon, who occasionally had published material on cemeteries in the *Architectural Magazine* and the *Gardener's Magazine* during the 1830s, and whose treatise *On the Laying Out, Planting and Managing of Cemeteries* appeared in the same year as Chadwick's report. For Loudon, cemeteries presented problems that were primarily practical. His concern was how best to design and run a given cemetery, not how to develop a strategy that could deal with the burial crisis, and his work ranges accordingly from recommendations about drainage and planting to observations on efficient grave-digging. Chadwick's scope was far grander.

Interment in Towns starts by summarizing and accepting the argument, based upon miasmatic and pythogenic theories, that gases and fluids from human decomposition were toxic. Atmospheric and water pollution originating from the choked burial grounds was widespread, poisoning whole areas of working-class London, and an overcrowded and rapidly expanding population was making an already insufferable situation horrific.

> In the metropolis, on spaces of ground which do not exceed 203 acres, closely surrounded by the abodes of the living, layer upon layer, each consisting of a population numerically equivalent to a large army of 20,000 adults, and nearly 30,000 youths and children, is every year imperfectly interred. Within the period of the existence of the present generation, upwards of a million of dead must have been interred in those same spaces.

Chadwick reached his initial conclusion rapidly enough: 'all interments in towns, where bodies decompose, contribute to the mass of atmospheric impurity which is injurious to public health'. Thus far Chadwick followed and confirmed Walker's findings. But the scope of the report was far wider than *Gatherings from Graveyards*, developing into an investigation of the whole field of urban mortality, and particularly into the arrangements made for death and burial among the labouring classes. What Chadwick found and recorded still appals. Throughout the working-class areas corpses were kept, often uncoffined, usually for ten days, frequently for a fortnight or more, in the same room with the living. How could they be kept anywhere else when four out of five labouring families had only one room to live in? How could they be removed for interment more quickly when the survivors had to find ways of raising money they did not have for undertakers' charges, funeral costs, and burial fees? One of Chadwick's witnesses, Mr Wild, an undertaker with a large proletarian clientele around the Blackfriars Road, decribed the result.

> In cases of rapid decomposition of persons dying in full habit there is much liquid; and the coffin is tapped to let it out. I have known them to keep the corpse after the coffin has been tapped twice, which has, of course, produced a disagreeable effluvium. This liquid generates animal life very rapidly; and within six hours after a coffin has been tapped, if the liquid escapes, maggots, or a sort of animalculae, are seen crawling about. I have frequently seen them crawling about the floor of a room inhabited by the labouring classes, and about the tressels on which the tapped coffin is sustained. In such rooms the children are frequently left whilst the widow is out making arrangements connected with the funeral. And the widow herself lives there with the children. I frequently find them altogether in a small room with a large fire.

Here was the reality of death among the urban poor in early Victorian Britain, and of those poor, as Chadwick pointed out, an average of one in four died of a contagious or epidemic disease. In such cases, he argued, the corpse of father, mother or child, kept for days or even weeks in the midst of the surviving family, became the means of further infection. Here is the evidence of Mr Jeffreys, an undertaker in Whitechapel:

> ... when the corpse is uncovered, or the coffin is open, females will hang over it. A widow who hung over the

> body of her husband, caught the disease of which he died. The doctor told her he knew she must have kissed or touched the body: she died, leaving seven orphans, of whom four are now in an orphan asylum. A young man died not long since, and his body rapidly decomposed. His sister, a fine healthy girl, hung over the corpse and kissed it; in three weeks she died also.

Although there was some danger of continuing contagion from a corpse, the aetiology of disease to which Chadwick subscribed, here a variant of the pythogenic theory, was, as we saw earlier, incorrect. Grimly enough, the living were far more infectious than the dead. But what is really striking about these narratives, beyond their obvious horror, is the way in which they suggest a macabre parody of mourning and remembrance in the affectionate family of the middling sort. In the single rooms occupied by working-class families, the dead were literally, not metaphorically, domesticated, and continuity between the living and the dead was forged not by affection but by infection. Though he was the last man one would think of as a sentimentalist, Chadwick's class had inevitably sensitized him towards death and determined many of his attitudes towards the physical corpse. As if sensing the grim burlesque of his own class perceptions, Chadwick was as much concerned by the psychological as by the physical consequences of the situation working-class families were facing every day. In contrast to the middle-class experience of death in the family, he believed that the experiences of working people desensitized them, left them brutalized or, at best, apathetic: 'the wretchedness being greater than humanity can bear, annihilates the mental faculties – the faculties distinctive of the human being'. At the root of it all, of course, was poverty. Burying the dead cost money, and, to Chadwick's mind, a lot more than it needed to. Some of the harshest criticisms in *Interment in Towns* were reserved for the London funeral business. The trade generally was exploitative and unregulated: Chadwick found undertakers who fleeced working people through semi-fraudulent burial clubs, employees of private grounds who masqueraded as officiating clergy, grave-diggers who grubbed up and destroyed recently buried remains to make room for more. Perhaps even worse, in Chadwick's view, the funeral business was grossly inefficient and its prices exorbitantly high: as he concluded, succinctly, 'the supplies of funeral goods and services are ... a multiform monopoly'.

Quite rightly, Chadwick recognized that the objective of burial reform was to enable the labouring classes to bury their dead decently, safely, efficiently, and at prices they could afford. He also realized that establishing suitable places for burial was only one element – even if the major one – in the arrangements that would be needed. Consequently, the recommendations of *Interment in Towns* were radical and comprehensive. Firstly, the existing urban burial grounds should be closed, intramural interment forbidden by law, and cemeteries established outside the towns. Basing his recommendations on Loudon, Chadwick specified that the sites chosen should be well-drained, preferably with a gravelly or sandy soil, and should, where possible, be on rising ground to the east of the towns which they were to serve. But who was to establish these new places of burial? Not, Chadwick argued, the joint stock companies that had laid out the cemeteries of the 1820s and 1830s. He found the cemeteries already established in London inadequate and objectionable, perpetrating in the suburbs many of the abuses found in the burial grounds of the city centre. They had been set up without any 'precedent examination of the evils affecting the public health ... incident to the practice of interment' and without any 'new precautionary measures or improvements' having been introduced. Praising Loudon's recommendations for how cemeteries should be planned and organized, Chadwick affirmed:

> there is scarcely one of the new cemeteries in which one or other of the well established principles of management, in the choice of the site, or the preparation of the soil, or in the drainage, or in the mode of burial, or in the numbers interred in one grave, or in respect to the precautions to prevent the undue corruption of the remains and escapes of dangerous morbific matter, or in the service and officers, or in jurisprudential securities, is not overlooked.

In consequence, as the metropolis spread and its houses surrounded them, the new cemeteries could become just as harmful to public health as the old burying grounds. Chadwick's judgement on them is tellingly sceptical: 'the practice of burial has in general been simply removed to better looking, and in general, better situated places'. His critique, general and specific, led him to a more fundamental conclusion about the role of the joint stock companies. In the words of one of his witnesses:

' "However disinterested may have been the motives which have induced some to become shareholders ... the primary and effective character of their association is undeniably that of trading associations" '. By the agency of the joint stock companies, ' "Christian burial is made an article of traffic" ', and a traffic, Chadwick noted, in which the shareholders would be reluctant to sanction sanitary improvements when change 'does not promise an immediate return for the expense incurred'. In short, *laissez-faire* would not answer the burial crisis: public welfare could not be entrusted to the market decisions of private enterprise. But nor, Chadwick thought, should it be left to the parochial organization of the established church. This was the core of his objection to Mackinnon's bill, before parliament as *Interment in Towns* was being completed. The bill proposed establishing parochial boards of health, formed by incumbents and churchwardens, empowered to build cemeteries outside London, with allowance made for parishes to group together into unions for the purpose. Chadwick believed that this would create too many boards competing for too little space, that inefficiency and duplication of effort would result, inevitably increasing costs and pushing up the price of interment. Furthermore, because Mackinnon based his proposals on the local administration of the Anglican church, other denominations would feel – and could actually be – excluded: as a result, the church rate through which it was proposed to raise funds, and which was already a major grievance among dissenters, would be resented and resisted. Neither private enterprise nor the Church of England would do. Chadwick wanted national cemeteries provided by central government. Moreover, he wanted them as part of a complete legislative programme by means of which the state would make provision for every stage of a body's progress from the death-bed to the grave.

The idea of national cemeteries was nothing if not ambitious. Financed directly by the state, they would be sited well outside urban concentrations, their area calculated according to the size and rate of growth of the population they were intended to serve. Loudon, always rationalistic in his views on disposing of the dead, had argued that it was safe to reuse ground for burial after a certain period, and had devised a system of rotation involving a tightly-managed grid plan of graves to allow this to be done. Chadwick proposed a similar scheme for the national cemeteries, working on a ten-year cycle, any bones remaining after that time to be carefully reinterred in common graves, as was the German practice. The cemeteries would offer rationalized funerals, simpler than those sold by the private trade but, according to Chadwick, more dignified: greater probity and efficiency would make them 60% cheaper than their commercial equivalent, and charges could be scaled according to the degree of elaboration required – an idea taken over from Parisian practice. Information about the national cemeteries, their charges and their funerals would be taken to labouring class families – the people most in need of them – by district officers of health, who would also be responsible for registration of death and for giving advice to the bereaved. If bodies needed to be removed from families, receiving houses would be provided on the German model, where corpses could be kept in sanitary conditions and prepared for burial. By preference, the national cemeteries should be sited on the navigable waterway system, 'The Great Silent Highway', with steam barges being used to transport coffins from collection points in the cities: as the railway network developed, special lines could also link the cemeteries with centres of population. Formal landscaping and evergreen planting on the principles suggested by Loudon would be developed, not only for aesthetic reasons but because a well-managed cover of greenery was the most effective way of absorbing and dissipating the gases of decomposition. But aesthetics would be important as well, for 'places of public burial demand the highest order of art in laying out the sites, and decorating them with trees and architectural structures of a solemn and elevating character'. Because the cemeteries would receive so many dead, the churches could develop appropriate and impressive services to be performed 'over great numbers at once', 'the aggregation of burials ... only ... limited by the effective power of the human voice', the effects 'heightened to a thrilling degree by music'. Within the cemeteries, parishes, communities and congregations would be able to apply for specific areas to be set aside for their use. Crafts, trades and occupations could be grouped together, perhaps with their own funerary customs and in association with inspirational monuments to the great and good:

> There are few occupations which could not furnish examples for pleasurable contemplation to the living who are engaged in them, and claim honour from the public. The humblest class of artisans would feel

> consolation and honour in interment in the same cemetery with Brindley, with Crompton, or with Murdoch, the artisan who assisted and carried out the conceptions of Watt; or with Emerson, or with Simpson, the hand-loom weaver, who became professor of mathematics at Woolwich; or with Ferguson, the shepherd's son; or with Dollond, the improver of telescopes, whose earliest years were spent at a loom in Spitalfields; or with others who 'have risen from the wheelbarrow' and done honour to the country ...

The idea of such emulation seems to come directly from Carlyle's *Heroes and Hero-Worship*, published in 1840: not inappropriately, for Heroism was Carlyle's recipe for curing England's ills, and the importance of the Condition of England Question in formulating the early Victorian debate about sanitation has already been suggested. More remarkably, the secular and industrial hagiography Chadwick outlines in the passage above strongly suggests parallels with the ideas of Auguste Comte, and anticipates by several years the *Positivist Calendar*, with its Religion of Humanity and its list of those who have advanced Civilization and who are to be commemorated in place of the Catholic saints. There is also, in Chadwick's scheme as in the theories of Carlyle and Comte, a strong impetus towards direct social management – an idea of management, moreover, that rested upon strong bureaucratic centralization and that foreshadowed the military analogies of the corporate state. Otherwise anonymous workers, the industrial infantry, fallen on the great economic battlefront, were to be given mass obsequies in acknowledgement of their corporate heroism, then buried in occupational regiments around the tombs of their social and political role-models – the sergeants rather than the captains of industry. Effectively, the cemeteries advocated by the Secretary to the Poor Law Commissioners were to be instruments of state policy. Nevertheless, in all this there was a genuine concern for the proletariat of the great cities; indeed, there was a clear sense in which Chadwick wished to celebrate working people. Given the degree to which the Victorian working class was submerged, their lives hidden from the cognizance of their social betters, Chadwick's desire for their monuments to be major features in his imagined cemetery, has subversive implications.

What Chadwick proposed was a comprehensive and coherent strategy for dealing with the burial crisis that confronted London and the great towns – and dealing with it on an heroic scale. His analysis of the crisis was acute; his suggested remedies, impossible. Impossible not because the idea of national cemeteries was in any way absurd, or theoretically unworkable, but because it envisaged a quite different society from that which existed in Britain in the early 1840s. It presupposed a high degree of social cohesion, and a strongly developed and centralized sense of social direction: neither was apparent in the years around 1843. Chadwick's great report on sanitary conditions, and his supplementary report on urban interment, attracted considerable attention: but legislatively nothing happened. Mackinnon's bill was withdrawn, perhaps partly as a consequence of Chadwick's criticisms, more because the government promised legislation of its own. No such legislation emerged. A Royal Commission on the Health of Towns reported in 1845, its findings largely informed by the labours of the indefatigable Chadwick. But by then parliamentary interest was wholly absorbed elsewhere – in the agitation for Free Trade, in the repeal of the Corn Laws, and in the splitting of the Tory party. More important than these political distractions, the economy took a marked upturn from 1842: despite the appalling human consequences of the Irish famine of 1845–6, expansion in the rest of the economy was sustained, albeit unevenly, for the remainder of the decade.

Sanitary agitation, as we have seen, had its source in the grim days of 1838-9 and continued against the fiery backcloth of Chartism. The quickening of commercial activity after 1842 brought some alleviation to working-class distress, though of course, no cure for its causes. Relative prosperity quieted the conscience of the better-off, and a lull in Chartist unrest allayed the alarm of the legislators. In 1843-4, with money unprecedentedly cheap and substantial surplus capital available in the banks, investors began looking for their 5%, and investment followed a pattern similar to that of the mid 1830s. The result was the second railway boom, generated from unfettered speculation which reached the proportions of mania in 1846, before collapsing in the following year, bringing a sharp, though temporary, financial crisis. Just as investment in cemetery companies had attended the first railway boom, so the period of the second brought a new wave of commercial cemetery-building – doubtless a dull business compared to the frenzy of the railway market, but also a lot safer. The cemeteries of the second half of the 1840s were widely spread geographically, built in several smaller towns as well as in the great manufacturing centres, several of which acquired new cemeteries in addition to ones established in the preceding decade. Most important, this second period of private cemetery-building also saw a small number of cemeteries established by local government and financed by public money; set up, that is, not as a commercial speculation but as a public utility genuinely available to all. It is highly probable – though it is difficult to be sure – that the handful of publicly funded cemeteries established in the mid 1840s were a first consequence of the arguments Chadwick had put forward in *Interment in Towns* – a manifestation at a local level of what he had advocated on a national scale.

The Later 1840s: Private Enterprise and Public Utility

Among the earliest of the new cemeteries were three whose designs originated with Loudon: Bath, Cambridge and Southampton. They form an intriguing group, both for what they tell us about aesthetic developments and because they happen to have been funded, and thus to have functioned, in three different ways. Abbey Cemetery in Bath was for the Church of England and was privately financed, the land on which it was laid out having been bought by the Rector of Bath; Cambridge General Cemetery was established by a joint stock company; Southampton General Cemetery was set up by the town council. All were designed in 1843, the year of Loudon's death; the first two opened in 1844, the third in 1846. Of the three, only Cambridge was carried out much as Loudon had planned it. The site was flat and rectangular, some three acres in area. Loudon's design, which he illustrated in *On the Laying Out, Planting, and Managing of Cemeteries*, was strictly regular, the chapel placed centrally at the intersection of the principal carriage drives which quarter the ground. Parallel subsidiary paths ran across the cemetery, neatly dividing the burial space into oblong strips. Planting was as formal as layout, and undeviatingly evergreen: Cedars of Lebanon at the corners of the carriage turn around the chapel, clipped pines and yews along the main drives, holly for the boundary hedge. Although the chapel has now been demolished and much

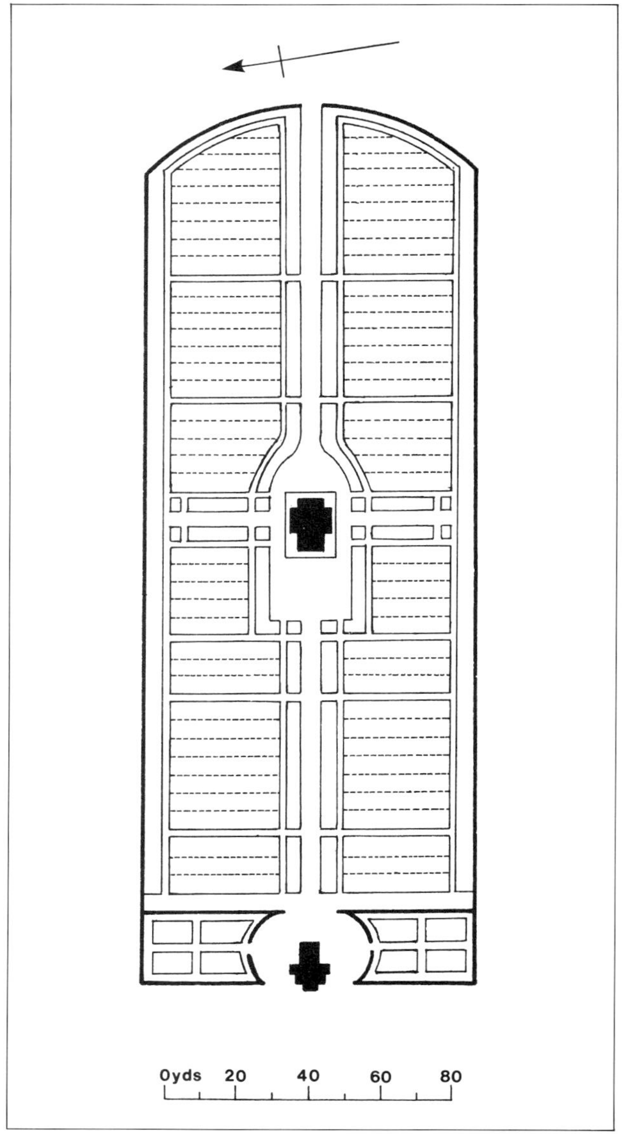

Plan of Histon Road Cemetery, Cambridge, based on the plan given in J. C. Loudon's On the Laying Out, Planting, and Managing of Cemeteries, *1843.*

of the ground cleared of monuments, Cambridge still shows the outlines of Loudon's scheme. At Abbey, it is now difficult to determine the relationship between the existing cemetery and Loudon's original design, which seems not to have survived. Nevertheless, the pronounced axiality of the main pathway, running straight uphill and bisecting an oval drive in front of the chapel, expresses Loudon's formal preferences clearly enough. Southampton, significantly, as we shall see, was eventually completed to radically altered designs. In fact, Cambridge was the only cemetery of the 1840s to adopt Loudon's aesthetic: no matter how much he might have condemned the 'pleasure-park' planning of cemeteries like Norwood, their design offered something more than rationalism. As James Stevens Curl has pointed out, Loudon's approach 'was hygienic and essentially utilitarian' – hence, of course, the attraction of his ideas for Chadwick. But the rationalism that reduced mortality to a problem of sanitation and orderliness, though essential to any strategic attempt – such as that of Chadwick's – to deal with the burial crisis as a whole, offered cold comfort to the bereaved, who had to confront death and burial as an intensely personal experience rather than as a statistic. Loudon's logic and the aesthetic that derived from it, were antipathetic to the whole complex of sensibility that had developed from the sentimental and the picturesque, and could even be construed as unChristian, almost irreligious. At Cambridge, indeed, the cemetery company had tempered Loudon's secularism by choosing Gothic rather than the Italianate he preferred for the lodge and chapel – designs in both styles having been prepared by the architect, Edward Buckton Lamb.

No doubt much of the rejection of Loudon's ideas in the 1840s stemmed from commercial considerations: for a cemetery to make a profit for its shareholders, design had to respond to the prevailing tastes of the market. But this is not the whole explanation: whereas Cambridge, where his proposals were executed, was the product of private enterprise, Southampton, where his original designs were totally changed, was set up by Southampton Town Council with funding from public sources, and directly commercial considerations were not a necessary part of its planning. Most of the alterations to Loudon's design for Southampton were by W.H. Rogers. All were in the cause of the picturesque: curving paths, informal planting, varied deciduous trees among the evergreens. Consonant with this was the medievalizing variety of the cemetery's buildings: Tudor for the lodge, Early English lancets for the nonconformist chapel, Norman – enjoying a revival in the 1830s and 1840s – for the Anglicans. As we saw earlier, the logic of Chadwick's rejection of private enterprise led directly from a redefinition of how cemeteries should work to a redefinition, *via* Loudon, of what they should look like: newly rationalized form was to follow newly rationalized function. Southampton, however, showed that the assumption of public responsibility for burial did not necessitate the adoption of utilitarian planning and design – or, indeed, of any substantially new aesthetic at all. Largely laid out in the familiar manner of the landscape park, Christian in architecture, countryfied in character – though with views beyond to the town it served and from which it was funded – Southampton General Cemetery simply took the middle-class vocabulary of the private enterprise cemeteries and redeployed it for public use. Southampton was not the only town council in the 1840s to make public provision for burial, though more research is needed to ascertain how widely this happened. One of the most ambitious schemes was in Leeds, where the Town Council established a Burial Grounds Committee which expended £25,000 in setting up three cemeteries in 1845: at Holbeck, Armley and – substantially the largest – at Burmantofts. The Leeds cemeteries, like that at Southampton, took over the existing aesthetic: all three adopted medieval architectural styles, their planting, as far as one can now judge, mixed deciduous and evergreen, their layouts combined formal with informal features.

The majority of the cemeteries contemporary to Southampton and Leeds, however, were established by private enterprise. A selection from the second half of the 1840s will sufficiently indicate their range. The Hull General Cemetery Company was established in 1845, the public competition for its buildings was won by some Gothic designs from the young Cuthbert Brodrick in 1846, and the cemetery was opened at Spring Bank in 1847. In Plymouth, rapidly expanding around the booming naval dockyard, the Plymouth, Stonehouse and Devonport Cemetery Company was incorporated in 1846, raised £15,000 capital in £25 shares, and opened its 10 acre cemetery north of the centre of the city in 1848. Also incorporated in 1846, the Northampton General Cemetery Company completed its Billing Road cemetery in 1847 at a cost of £5250. In 1848 the Leicester General

The Church Cemetery, Nottingham, 1848-53; monuments in the sandstone quarry.

Cemetery Company was established after protracted wrangling between dissenters and Anglicans over the interdenominational character of the enterprise, and a cemetery opened in 1849. Also opened in 1849 was Overleigh Cemetery in Chester, one of the most striking of early Victorian cemeteries and, instructively enough, entirely unaffected by Loudon's ideas. Occupying a hilly site that was fully exploited by serpentine paths, its buildings, all by the local architect T.M. Penson, rang the changes on medievalism in much the same way as Southampton had done: a Norman chapel for Anglicans, a quaintly gabled Elizabethan chapel for nonconformists, and a Tudor entrance lodge. The design of the cemetery drew upon the whole tradition of the landscape park. Planting was highly varied, picturesquely arranged in informal clumps and thickets. Setting off the dissenters' chapel there was even an ornamental lake, complete with a little island, some suitably melancholy willows, and – if contemporary engravings are to be believed – a complement of swans. Alas, contemporary engravings are almost all we have left, for Overleigh's lake has been drained, its buildings demolished and many of its monuments cleared. Also taking advantage of the improved economic situation after the middle of the 1840s, several specifically Anglican cemetery companies were established to provide cemeteries for members of the established church in towns where nonconformity had been first in the field. The Birmingham Church of England Cemetery Company was founded in 1845, a site was secured off Warstone Lane, and a cemetery opened in 1848. Its chapel by J.R. Hamilton, now demolished, had a 116 ft steeple with a Perpendicular cloister range stretching for five bays to either side, its scale and elevated position lording it over the dissenting neo-Greek of the nearby Key Hill. The year after the incorporation of the Birmingham Company, the misleadingly named Sheffield General Cemetery Company was established and set up an Anglican cemetery immediately adjoining that which had opened in 1837, its Gothic chapel, complete with spire, in even closer competition with the Greek chapel of its earlier neighbour. In Nottingham, a 4 acre site on the Mansfield Road was acquired in 1848 and further extended in 1853 to form the Nottingham Church Cemetery, its grounds incorporating a whole series of sandstone caves with a picturesqueness that rivals the contemporary General Cemetery at Chester.

Meanwhile, as companies of different complexions built cemeteries up and down the country, what was happening in London? After the opening of Abney Park and Tower Hamlets, only one other cemetery was added to those of the metropolis in the whole 1840s, and that was an example of commercial opportunism at its most cynical. The Victoria Park Cemetery was established in Bethnal Green in 1845 by C.S. Butler who, as member of parliament for Tower Hamlets, must have known of the desperate need for burial space – as, indeed, any other kind of space – among the East End working class. If so, then all he saw in that necessity was a market opening. Situated by a canal wharf north of the Mile End Road, the wedge-shaped cemetery, flat, sodden, and virtually bare of trees, totalled 11 acres: by the early 1890s, when it was closed and converted to a public park, 300,000 bodies had been crammed into it, almost all in common graves. Clergy who had to officiate at funerals there carried earth in their pockets for scattering on the coffin so that they would not have to pick up the noisome soil. Victoria Park was nothing more than Spa Fields on a bigger site, an urban burying ground little different from those anathematized by Walker.

The increase in the rate of cemetery-building in the second half of the 1840s gave rise to the first central government legislation specifically dealing with cemeteries. The Cemeteries Clauses Act of 1847, 10 & 11 Vict. c.65, was a consolidatory Act, one of several such measures passed by Russell's ministry in 1847: others included the Markets and Fairs Clauses Act, the Gasworks Clauses Act, the Waterworks Clauses Act, the Harbours, Docks and Piers Clauses Act, and the Town Improvement Clauses Act. These Acts were essentially exercises in administrative housekeeping, designed to speed up and tidy up the cumbersome business of obtaining a private Act of Parliament for works of a public nature, whether carried out by public authorities or private enterprise. The Cemetery Clauses Act empowered any company establishing a cemetery under its terms to compulsorily purchase land for that purpose, as set out in the Land Clauses Consolidation Act of 1845, which allowed for such a procedure in the case of works recognized as being of public benefit. The company had to drain and sewer the cemetery, which was to be enclosed by walls or railings at least eight feet in height, and no part of it was to be within 200 yards of a dwelling. The company could be sued for fouling water supplies by any person who had the right to use the water that had been polluted. Any cemetery established under the Act had to have one part set aside for Anglican burial, consecrated by the diocesan bishop, and provided with an appropriate chapel. The company was also empowered to keep one part of the cemetery unconsecrated and to build a chapel there in which burial services could be performed 'according to the rites of any church or congregation other than the Church of England'. The company was to pay an agreed sum to the incumbent of any parish from which a body came as compensation for his loss of the burial fee. No burials were allowed under any chapel within the cemetery, 'or within fifteen feet of the outer wall of any such chapel'. Burial-plots could be sold either for a limited period or in perpetuity, in which case an exclusive right of burial, which was to be considered as personal estate, was conferred on the purchaser. Registers of all interments were to be kept, keyed to a grid plan of the cemetery. As will be clear from its provisions, the Cemeteries Clauses Act standardized the terms on which many of the joint stock cemeteries that have already been considered were established. As a result, the Act was intensely conservative. It carefully defined the right to sell burial-plots in perpetuity which, as was discussed at length earlier, was of major importance to the middle-class families who were the principal customers of the private enterprise cemeteries. But these bourgeois interests were maintained while the Act did nothing to address the burial crisis that afflicted the urban labouring classes, or even to encourage the cemetery companies to do so. Similarly, its sanitary provisions were minimal. The impact of the reformers was evident in the restriction on proximity to houses, and in the prohibition of burial under chapels. But there was no regulation of density of burial and no specification as to depth. There was no attempt to link cemetery provision with wider issues of public health: even the drainage requirement left prosecution for water pollution to aggrieved individuals. Nor was there any provision for a system of inspection – that central plank of other early Victorian social legislation. If such features of the Act were unenlightened or merely timid, the attitude towards nonconformity it embodied was positively reactionary. From a prospective company's point of view, the great advantage of obtaining an Act under its provisions was the power it conferred to compulsorily purchase the necessary land. In return, the provision of Anglican burial ground and its consecration, the building of an Anglican chapel, and the payment of burial fee compensation, were made mandatory – all, of course, potentially offensive to dissenters, and all quite specifically objected to by the founders of Abney Park. Under the Act, indeed, it was not even obligatory for cemetery companies to provide unconsecrated ground or a nonconformist chapel: the 'public benefit' that was the justification for powers of compulsory purchase was defined in exclusively Establishment terms.

State Intervention: the General Board of Health

The Cemeteries Clauses Act was plainly inadequate. It did nothing to enable cemeteries to be built by local administrations, as Mackinnon had wanted, and certainly nothing to initiate the kind of national provision recommended by Chadwick. At best, it smoothed the parliamentary path for private enterprise. But, in the quarter of a century or so since The Rosary had been founded, private enterprise, whether enlightened or simply opportunist, had signally failed to provide an answer to the urban burial crisis. Dissatisfaction with the joint stock companies as arbiters of public welfare had been increasing since Chadwick had first argued against them in 1843. As an opponent of the Torquay Extra Mural Burial Company said in 1851:

> ... he was quite inclined to give every credit to the patriotic gentlemen who had made a move for the benefit of the public, but he could not help thinking that the object partly was to put something in their pockets ... all persons who entered into joint stock companies expected to get something out of it ...

Since the Royal Commission on the Health of Towns had reported in 1845 there had been several abortive attempts to introduce public health measures in parliament. In 1848 events conspired to support the persistent efforts of the reformers: the miseries suffered by Ireland in the wake of the famine; the resurgence of Chartism, with the physical force party bidding fair to make working-class distress more than just vocal in its expression; above all, the re-emergence of cholera in the middle of the year gave the sanitary questions that had been canvassed for a decade a sudden urgency. On the last day of August 1848, the first Public Health Act, 11 & 12 Vict c.63, received the Royal Assent. It laid the foundations for all subsequent public health measures, up to and beyond the First World War, and it was the beginning of the legislative process that would establish public cemeteries throughout Britain.

The framing of the Public Health Act shows Chadwick's direct influence. It sought to establish a central authority for the supervision of public health, similar to that which existed for the administration of the Poor Law. This was the General Board of Health, with the first Commissioner for Woods and Forests as President and two other Commissioners nominated by the Privy Council: Chadwick and the redoubtable Lord Ashley were appointed, to be joined by Southwood Smith in 1850, when a fourth Commissioner was added to Act as medical adviser. The Board itself was empowered to appoint officials as required, and these included inspectors. As a result of vested interests, particularly the influence of the City, London was exempted from the authority of the Board, coming instead under the Metropolitan Commission of Sewers. The powers of the Commission were substantially increased by an Act passed within a few days of the Public Health Act itself, though its membership was carefully arranged to include the Lord Mayor and representatives of the Corporation. Outside London, the General Board was empowered to create local boards of health on the petition of 10% of the ratepayers, and to enforce the creation of such boards in places where the annual death-rate exceeded 23 in 1000. The Act obliged every local board to assume a range of powers over the sewage and drainage of the district for which it was responsible, and permitted it to undertake a number of more general public health functions – street cleaning, providing water supplies, regulating lodging houses, controlling offensive trades. Among these permissive functions were included powers relating to the burial of the dead which derived directly from Chadwick's report of 1843. In order to prevent 'the manifold Evils occasioned by the Retention of the Dead in the Dwellings of the Poor', local boards were empowered to provide receiving-houses for the dead and 'to make all necessary Arrangements for the decent and economical Interment of any Corpse which may have been received'. After due inspection, the local boards could report any burial ground or churchyard deemed dangerous to health to the General Board, which could prohibit further burial provided there were 'sufficient Means of Interment … within a convenient Distance'. Any new burial ground had to have the express consent of the General Board. All burials within the walls of churches and chapels were prohibited. As far as it related to the disposal of the dead, the Act's most significant achievement was to establish that issue legislatively as part of general public health policy. But the practical operation of the Act was uneven, and more detailed research is needed on its various local applications. Did any local board establish receiving-houses, for example, or set up a scheme for 'the decent and economical' burial of the working-class dead? Certainly, intramural interment was stopped, and a number of urban burial grounds were closed. But the Act omitted positive and specific measures to enable local boards to establish cemeteries, and no burial ground could be closed, no matter how pestiferous it was thought to be, unless a convenient alternative was available.

Burial in London at the Mid-century

The Public Health Act, as we have seen, did not apply to London, where the influence of the City magnates on the Commission for Sewers made radical sanitary measures unlikely, and the City's general reputation for jobbery and incompetence further attracted accusations of time-serving and wilful obstruction. While the General Board, driven on by Chadwick's zeal, was tireless in its inspections, reports and recommendations up and down the country, the Metropolitan Commissioners seemed culpably inactive. By 1849, the cholera that had appeared in the previous year had assumed epidemic proportions and was particularly severe in London. At its height, it trebled the capital's average weekly death-rate. In the midst of it all, quite literally, were the urban burial grounds, not only incapable of coping with the victims of the very diseases they were thought to generate, but actually making a profit out of the process: most of the commercial burial-yards were still at their ghastly business; Anglican clergy continued to demand their burial fees; vestries, beadles, parish clerks and sextons claimed their cut as well. The General Board insisted that action should be taken by the Metropolitan Commissioners and Chadwick made no secret of his belief that shameless vested interests were blocking the cause of reform. With an unerring feeling for the key sensibilities of its readership, *Punch* published 'An Elegy, written in a London Churchyard' in the autumn of 1849. In lampooning Gray, *Punch* presented the burial crisis not just as a problem of public health, but as a grotesque moral and psychological threat to the whole complex of middle-class attitudes towards death and remembrance, of which the original 'Elegy' is such a prime document.

> The sexton tolls the knell till parting day,
> The latest funeral train has paid its fee,
> The mourners homeward take their dreary way
> And leave the scene to Typhus and to me.
>
> Now fades the crowded graveyard on the sight,
> But all, its air who scent, their nostrils hold,
> Save where the beadle drones, contented quite,
> And drowsy mutes their arms in slumber fold.
>
> Save where, hard by yon soot-incrusted tower,
> A Reverend Man does o'er his port complain,
> Of such as would, by sanitary power,
> Invade his ancient customary gain.
>
> Beneath those arid mounds, that dead wall's shade,
> Where grows no turf above the mouldering heap,
> All in their narrow cells together laid,
> The former people of the parish sleep ...
>
> For them no more the chamber-light shall burn,
> The busy doctor ply his daily care,
> Nor children to their sire from school return,
> And climb his knees the dreaded pest to share ...
>
> No doubt in this revolting place are laid,
> Hearts lately pregnant with infectious fire;
> Hands, by whose grasp contagion was conveyed,
> As sure as electricity by wire.
>
> Full many a gas of direst power unclean,
> The dark o'erpeopled graves of London bear,
> Full many a poison, born to kill unseen,
> And spread its rankness in the neighbouring air ...

The final verses, parodying the epitaph on Gray's rustic swain, point both the miasmatic moral and the way towards a remedy.

> Long was his illness, tedious and severe,
> Hard by a London Churchyard dwelt our friend;
> He follow'd to the grave a neighbour's bier,
> He met thereby ('twas what he fear'd) his end.
>
> No longer seek Corruption to enclose
> Within the places of mankind's abode;
> But far from cities let our dust repose,
> Where daisies blossom on the verdant clod.

Public opinion is at any time difficult to define, and is a particularly slippery concept in discussing Victorian England. But the combination of revulsion, compassion and fear evident in the *Punch* parody does seem an accurate expression of middle-class feeling as the cholera epidemic of 1848–9 exhausted itself: whatever the interests of and in the City, something had to be done to get rid of the urban burial grounds in London and to provide public cemeteries.

In fact, the Metropolitan Commissioners had not merely been doing nothing. In October 1848 they had appointed John Simon as the first medical officer of health for the City of London. Simon was to become probably the most distinguished of all medical authorities on public health in the nineteenth century, and this was his first major post. In November 1849 he presented his first annual report to the Commission. It was a brilliant and appalling analysis of the whole foetid muddle of the City's sanitation; *The Times* printed it in full. With an epidemic just ended and no knowing when it would return, with all the evidence about the transmission of disease assembled by miasmatists and pythogenists, supported by middle-class opinion, urged on by the findings of the City's own medical officer, the government decided on the wholesale reform of burial in London. In February 1850, the General Board of Health put forward an appropriately comprehensive scheme, clearly based upon Chadwick's recommendations of 1843. It proposed establishing a Metropolitan Interment Commission empowered to close all the urban burial grounds and buy up all the existing joint stock cemeteries. Those cemeteries deemed inappropriate would be closed, but Kensal Green would be retained and enlarged to form the Great Western Cemetery. Additionally, the Commission would build a Great Eastern Cemetery which 'would not have its parallel in the whole world': no site was specified, but Erith was thought to be the most likely location. The

Commission would also introduce a rationalized system of funerals available for all the inhabitants of the metropolis and graduated so as to bring decent burial within the range of even the poorest families. The cost of buying the existing cemeteries, of extending Kensal Green and of building the Great Eastern Cemetery was estimated at £700,000; thereafter, running the cemeteries would cost £112,000 annually. A model for reforming every stage in the disposal of London's dead was now available, and in Chadwick and the General Board of Health there existed a willing agent. In August 1850, 'An Act to make better Provision for the Interment of the Dead in and near the Metropolis', 13 & 14 Vict c.52, became law.

The Metropolitan Interments Act and the Defeat of Chadwick

The Act constituted the whole area of metropolitan London as the Metropolitan Burial District and, for the purposes of the Act, brought it under the authority of the General Board of Health. The Board was directed to build 'either within or without the Limits of the District, Burial Grounds of sufficient Extent for the decent Interment of the Bodies of the Persons dying within the District'. The cemeteries so provided were to be divided into sections, one to be duly consecrated for Anglican burial, the other to remain unconsecrated; individual parts could also be appropriated to the sole use of particular sects or denominations. A chapel for the performance of the Anglican burial service was to be provided for the consecrated section, and the Board was empowered to build a chapel or chapels in the unconsecrated section. Additionally to providing new cemeteries, the Board was empowered to 'purchase and take by Agreement or otherwise all or any' of the existing joint stock cemeteries in the Metropolitan District, and these were listed in a schedule to the Act. Any churchyard, chapelyard or burial ground in the District where the Board considered that interment should be discontinued could be closed by order of the Privy Council on the Board's recommendation, and any future burial prohibited. The inhabitants of parishes where the burial grounds had been closed, whether Anglican or nonconformist, were to have full right of interment in whatever new cemetery was provided under the Act. In compensation for the loss of burial fees, the Board was to pay 6s 2d to any Anglican incumbent whose churchyard had been closed for each interment of his parishioners in the consecrated section of the cemetery. The same fee of 6s 2d was also to be paid, if the family requested it, to any minister performing a burial service in the unconsecrated section. The Act also allowed for compensation to parochial vestries, clerks and sextons for loss of fees, and to the owners of commercial burial grounds for loss of income resulting from closure. As well as providing for 'the Maintenance, Planting, Decoration, and Care' of the cemeteries built under the Act, the Board was to fix charges for interments and to make regulations governing every aspect of the management of the cemeteries, including the depth, formation and density of graves. The Board was also permitted to build receiving-houses for the dead, establish a system for conducting funerals at fixed costs 'according to Classes arranged with reference to the Nature and Amount of Matters and Services to be furnished', appoint medical officers who could advise bereaved families on funerary provisions, and even to contract with railway companies 'for carrying out of Bodies in properly constructed Carriages' from London to the new cemeteries. In order to finance all the various works the Act enjoined, the Board was empowered to order increases in the Poor Rate in the parishes of the Metropolitan District and to order the levying of a Burial Rate, and to borrow from the Commissioners of Public Works against the security of these rates and of the fees and payments that would accrue to the cemeteries. However, the Board could not make any purchases, issue any contracts, or undertake any other financial arrangements, where expenditure exceeded £100, without the permission of the Treasury.

Essentially, the Metropolitan Interments Act empowered the General Board of Health to carry out the scheme it had proposed a few months before for a Metropolitan Interments Commission, adding to it a number of provisions drawn from Chadwick's *Interment in Towns*. The Act was one of the most radical measures of nineteenth-century social legislation. It envisaged substantial state investment in public welfare, and, consequently, a major role for the state in the lives and deaths of the people of London. In empowering the Board to buy out the owners of the joint stock cemeteries, it also constituted what was effectively a programme for nationalizing a whole class of private enterprise concerns within the metropolitan area. Especially enlightened, particularly when compared to the Cemeteries Clauses Act, was the even-handedness with which the Act tried to deal between Anglicans and nonconformists: the provision of unconsecrated ground in the new cemeteries was mandatory, special areas could be reserved for individual denominations, the members of non-Anglican congregations could ensure that their own officiating minister received a fee equivalent to that paid to Church of England clergy. Yet the Act's radicalism was hedged by constraints that effectively placed the whole measure on probation: any purchase of existing cemeteries had to take place within two years of the Royal Assent; at the same time, as has been indicated, all the Board's financial dealings above £100 had to have the express approval of the Treasury. In operation, these limitations on time and money made the Act look over-ambitious, and the Treasury's sustained resistance to providing the necessary funding made it all but unworkable. In immediately practical terms, all that the Metropolitan Interments Act achieved was the purchase of one London cemetery.

The month after the Act came into force, the Board approached the directors of the London cemetery companies, but found none of them willing to sell their cemeteries. It was not until March 1851 that the Board managed to obtain the Treasury's sanction for compulsory purchase, and that was only given on the condition that the cemeteries would be bought successively. The only two purchase orders issued were for Brompton and Nunhead. The Board's estimate of how much the cemeteries were worth differed widely from those of the companies. The negotiations went to arbitration in July 1851, which was eventually decided very much in the Board's favour: in October, Brompton was valued at £75,000, Nunhead at £42,000. But, by this time, any element of compulsion had disappeared. In July, at the time of the arbitration hearing, the Treasury was already seeking ways of withdrawing and the arbitrator's final award became subject to the consent of the companies. The owners of Nunhead turned it down. At Brompton, however, the shareholders saw in the settlement a means of extrication from the financial difficulties that had dogged the cemetery, as we saw earlier, from the beginning. In January 1852, against the advice of the directors, a shareholders' meeting voted to accept the arbitration offer. The legislation gave protection to either party in negotiations against the withdrawal of the other and, despite the Treasury's grumbling, Brompton became the only metropolitan cemetery owned directly by the state. By this time, the Metropolitan Interments Act was already a dead letter. Early in 1851, the General Board's attempt to buy land at Abbey Wood, Erith for the proposed new cemetery there had failed. Assurance companies would not advance the necessary money because the Public Health Act had set an initial five-year term on the Board's existence; the government refused to issue Exchequer Bills as an alternative means of funding. Effectively, the Board had been prevented from building any new cemeteries just as surely as it had been frustrated in its attempts to buy the existing ones. The whole history of the Metropolitan Interments Act strongly suggests that the government in general, and the Treasury in particular, never had any intention of allowing it to work. In fact, within months of its being passed, measures to replace it were already being considered.

The Great Eastern Metropolitan Cemetery remained a paper dream, as did the purchase and enlargement of Kensal Green: with them went Chadwick's vision of national cemeteries. Without them, all the carefully integrated arrangements of the Metropolitan Interments Act evaporated – the receiving-houses, the rationalized funerals, the whole centralized system by which the dead of the metropolis would be managed. Decisive in the Act's failure was the decision that it should be implemented by the Board of Health, for that meant Chadwick. Bossy and inflexible as the man undoubtedly was, the real cause of opposition to him was the undiplomatic vigour with which he pursued the cause of public health. Chadwick, quite simply, was dangerous. As Dickens's arch time-server, the smooth Ferdinand Barnacle, was to say a few years later in *Little Dorrit*, ' "You have no idea how many people want to be left alone. You have no idea how the Genius of the country ... tends to being left alone" '. The General Board did not come under direct parliamentary control, and this gave opponents the opportunity to attack it and all its works as unconstitutional, particularly with reference to its power of creating local boards by fiat. Doubtless, some grievances were legitimate, but often enough the constitutional argument was mere camouflage for the defence of vested interests – commercial, professional and political. The Board survived the demise of the Metropolitan Interments Act, but not for long. In November 1852, Lord

Shaftesbury wrote in his diary: 'the Board of Health is to be destroyed, its sin is its unpardonable Activity'. In August of the following year he listed the forces of darkness, as he sincerely thought them, who had eventually succeeded in tearing down the Board's bright banner of public hygiene. It included: civil engineers; water companies; the Poor Law Guardians; the Commissioners for Sewers; the College of Physicians, because the Board had 'proved that many a Poor Law medical officer knew more than all the flash and fashionable doctors of London'. Most significantly, for the fate of the Metropolitan Interments Act, Shaftesbury's catalogue of foes included the Treasury: 'for the subalterns there hated Chadwick: it was an ancient grudge, and paid when occasion served'. In 1854, the powers of the General Board of Health were merged in those of the Local Government Board, and Chadwick pensioned off. He never held another major administrative post.

The Burial Acts: the Provision of Public Cemeteries

Meanwhile, as Whitehall was settling its old bureaucratic scores, how were London's dead to be buried? Ironically, a cemetery on the scale of those imagined by Chadwick was actually established – by private enterprise. Incorporated in 1852, the London Necropolis and National Mausoleum Company bought 2000 acres of heathland at Brookwood, near Woking in Surrey, and, over the succeeding years, laid out and planted what is still the largest cemetery in Britain. It was connected to London by railway, with a terminus in Westminster Bridge Road, and the company arranged to take burials from parishes on southern and eastern districts of the metropolis – from middle-class Westminster and Bloomsbury, from dockside Wapping and Deptford, and from the crowded working-class areas of Whitechapel, Shoreditch and Southwark. Although the conception of the cemetery derived from Chadwick, and his ideas, with those of Loudon, informed much of its organization, it was, necessarily, a commercial enterprise. By far the most ambitious of the joint stock cemeteries, Brookwood was also one of the last. For though the Metropolitan Interments Act had been wrecked, and Chadwick, with the Board of Health, brought low, the reformers had won the argument for the establishment of public cemeteries funded from public money. In London there could be no return to the situation that had prevailed before 1850: the doctrines of the free market were too entrenched to allow any direct interference with the private enterprise cemeteries, but, as long as they were the only alternative to the choked churchyards and burial grounds, it was at last apparent that intramural interment would not cease. As early as the winter of 1850–51, commercial burial grounds in the centre of London, closed during the cholera epidemic, had reopened surreptitiously. The vibrant indignation with which this was reported in the *Builder* sufficiently indicates the depth of public feeling.

> What a merciless, remorseless pursuit is that of money-making! How loathsome is the hollow show of reason with which the unseemly actual motive is glossed recklessly over. This is winter: the cholera-agitation has subsided: now is the time to mount again on the municipal shoulders off which we were shaken in the time of fear! Such is the secret thought of the traffickers in corruption. That the bodies so trafficked in will only be ripe, rotten, and ready for the stew and distillation of the coming summer, is nothing to them. That thousands and tens of thousands will be tainted with the fever-poison, and themselves fomented into rotten leaven of corruption to poison and foment still more and more, – what is all that to them? Let us eat, drink, and be merry, whoever may die. *Sauve qui peut.*

Though it might get rid of the Metropolitan Interments Act, and shackle the troublesome Chadwick, the government had to find a workable system of public burial. This was done by adopting and adapting Mackinnon's bill of a decade before.

On the first day of July 1852, 'An Act to amend the Laws concerning the Burial of the Dead in the Metropolis', 15 & 16 Vict c.85, received the Royal Assent. The Metropolitan Burial Act, as it became known, repealed the Act of 1850, thereby abolishing the Metropolitan Burial District and the jurisdiction of the General Board of Health over burial in London. The Privy Council was empowered to prohibit further interment in any place of burial in the metropolis, or in any part of the metropolis, if advised by the Secretary of State that such action was necessary for the protection of public health. It was also enacted that no inhabitant of a parish where the burial ground had been closed could be buried in the ground of another parish. The only exceptions to these provisions were St Paul's Cathedral, Westminster Abbey, and the joint stock cemeteries in the metropolitan area, including Brompton, the purchase of which the Act confirmed. No new burial ground could be opened in London or within two miles of it without the Secretary of State's permission. The vestry of any metropolitan parish could be convened, on the requisition of ten ratepayers, to consider providing a new parochial cemetery. If this was thought necessary then the Secretary of State was to be informed and the parish was to appoint a Burial Board, consisting of not fewer than three and not more than nine ratepayers; elections to the Board were to be held periodically. If desired, parishes were allowed to unite in providing a single burial ground for their common use. The Act enjoined every Burial Board, once established, to proceed 'with all convenient speed' to make provision for the interment of the dead of their parish or parishes, either by building new cemeteries or by arranging for parish burials to take place in an existing cemetery. The Boards were empowered to meet their expenses out of the Poor Rate, to borrow any monies they needed against the security of the rate, and to purchase land compulsorily if necessary. Part of any new cemetery provided by a Burial Board could be consecrated for Anglican use by the bishop of the diocese when it appeared to him 'to be in a fit and proper condition', provided that another part of the cemetery remained unconsecrated: the Board could erect appropriate chapels on both sections. In building a cemetery, a Burial Board was empowered to contract for whatever work was needed, provided that public notice was given of all intended expenditure over £100. Once a cemetery had been opened, the Board was to manage it, with powers to fix charges, to pay fees to clergy, sextons and churchwardens, to sell burial plots either 'in Perpetuity or for a limited Period', and generally to make whatever regulations were deemed appropriate. In addition, the Act empowered Boards to build receiving-houses for the dead and to make any arrangements thought necessary for conveying bodies from the parish to the cemetery. The provisions of the Act extended to all of what had been the Metropolitan Burial District, with the exception of the City of London. Here, the Act empowered the Mayor and Corporation to appoint the City's Commissioners of Sewers as the Burial Board for the hundred or so parishes within the City and its Liberties, any money expended by the Board to be met out of the consolidated rate.

In August 1853, the arrangements that the Metropolitan Burial Act had made for London were extended to the rest of England and Wales, 16 & 17 Vict c.134. The Secretary of State was given power to prohibit further interments in any given place within the two countries, and the same provisions were made for establishing new public cemeteries by means of parochial Burial Boards. In August 1855, the same measures were extended to Scotland, 18 & 19 Vict c.68, where the Act was to be carried out by the Parochial Boards for the Maintenance of the Poor, and, in July 1856, to Ireland, 19 & 20 Vict c.98, where variations in local administration were incorporated into the legislation and where each cemetery established by a Burial Board was to contain a section for Roman Catholics as well as Anglicans and nonconformists. In the years immediately following the Acts of 1852 and 1853, various amendments passed through Parliament as need arose, the whole sequence coming to be known as the Burial Acts. Finally, in August 1857, a consolidatory Amendment Act, 20 & 21 Vict c.81, brought together the most important changes that had been made in the legislation since 1852. Town councils, local Boards of Health and local Improvement Commissioners could all be constituted as Burial Boards where circumstances warranted it, and councils were empowered to levy a separate Burial Rate if needed for the purposes of the Acts. Where a Board was acting for more than two parishes, the decision of a majority of the constituent vestries was to be binding on all of them – a provision necessitated by the impossibility of getting unanimity out of the plethora of vestries covered by the City of London Burial Board. Any Board was empowered to build more than one cemetery and, if desired, grounds for Anglicans and nonconfrmists could be established separately. Where a Burial Board decided that a new burial ground was to be used in the same way as the old churchyard – that is, wholly consecrated to Anglican use – then it was not mandatory to leave part of the ground unconsecrated for nonconformists. Where a cemetery contained consecrated and unconsecrated sections, they should be demarcated by 'such Boundary Marks of Stone or Iron as may be sufficient'. Division by means of a wall or fence was specifically stated as unnecessary – a clarification that resulted from the refusal of Henry Philpotts, Bishop of Exeter, to consecrate the Anglican sections of the Burial Board cemeteries at Tiverton and Great Torrington because they were not separately walled off. Philpotts claimed, not without reason, that he was only following Canon Law, but nonconformists deeply resented what they took as Establishment arrogance. Other instances of divisive discrimination lay behind the Amendment Act's stipulation that cemetery charges had to be the same in both consecrated and unconsecrated sections. Finally, the Secretary of State was empowered to appoint inspectors, and the Privy Council to issue Orders, to ensure the maintenance of public health in any place of burial, whether parochial or otherwise, whether established by a Burial Board or by private enterprise.

The Burial Acts of 1852–7 provided the answer to the burial crisis of the 1830s and 1840s, and established a system of public interment that, in its essentials, has survived to the present day. Yet the Acts resulted from compromise and improvisatory adjustment. Arguably, it was precisely because of this that they worked: they were the product of circumstances and existing practice rather than theory. Where Chadwick, good utilitarian that he was, had sought to return to first principles and had created, on paper at least, a brave new bureaucratic world as a result, the Burial Acts were based on the administrative *status quo* and its traditional local unit, the parish. Although so much of the legislation was only permissive, the Privy Council's power to prohibit all intramural burial, combined with the existing legal obligation on parishes to bury their dead, gave the Acts a force that was practically mandatory – particularly where reform was most needed, in London and the great towns. Remarkably, the Acts created a national system of public cemeteries without any national bureaucratic structure. Both the working and the funding of the Acts were decentralized: the power to build cemeteries was fixed firmly at a local level, with Burial Boards financially accountable not to the Treasury but to the parish ratepayers. Although the parish was, of course, Anglican, the fact that the rate was payable by nonconformists as well gave them authentic power in parishes where there were substantial dissenting communities: in practice, where this was the case, nonconformist interests were reflected in the membership of the Burial Board. Moreover, the provisions of the original Acts of 1852 and 1853 contained a number of safeguards for non-Anglican denominations, and these were bolstered by the subsequent amendments. That resulting from Philpotts' recalcitrance, in particular, gave a Board the means of overriding opposition from the diocesan bishop by appeal to the authority of the Privy Council – an appeal from the ecclesiastical to the civil power that marked a significant step in the progressive secularization of administrative authority in the nineteenth century. The retention of authority at a local level, the devolution of funding, denominational equality, were all matters of middle-class concern: by their very nature, the Burial Acts ensured that the provision and regulation of public cemeteries would rest in middle-class hands. The availability of vaults and burial plots in perpetuity, so significant a factor in the attraction of private enterprise cemeteries for the middling sort, was also an important feature of the Burial Board cemeteries.

But what of the urban working class, whose dire need, as Chadwick recognized, burial reform had to meet? Shaftesbury noted critically that though the Board of Health had 'devised a long and intricate scheme to lower, for the poorer sort, the expense of interments', the Burial Acts ordained extramural burial 'and leaves the artisan to meet the increased cost as well as he can'. There was some justice in this criticism, though more work needs to be done on the costs of working-class funerals, about which very little seems to be known, to see how significant a factor was the increased distance from home parish to place of burial. Despite Shaftesbury's doubts, however, it seems clear that Burial Board cemeteries did manage to provide interment cheaply as well as decently. For example, the charges at Toxteth Park Cemetery in Liverpool, opened in 1856, were significantly lower than at Tower Hamlets, which made a dubious specialty of cheap working-class burials, and much lower still than those in *haut bourgeois* Highgate. In Toxteth, the highest charge for exclusive right of interment was 15guineas, and that bought a grave 9ft x 9ft x 4ft 6in. in the best of the reserved sections of the ground: there were graduated charges for smaller and less well-positioned sites down to a Class 3 grave, the cheapest in the reserved sections, which was £2 10s. These were predominantly middle-class interments, and all would have been likely to have had monuments. Burial without an inscription or memorial, but including all fees apart from that to the minister, could be had for 9s 6d for an adult, 7s 6d for a child, and 4s 6d for an infant. These were working-class prices, and though the interment they bought was anonymous, it was decent and secure, and in surroundings the same as those enjoyed by the better-off.

The Burial Board Cemeteries

The great majority of Victorian cemeteries were established by Burial Boards. Once public authorities were given the power to provide decent places of burial, the building of new joint stock cemeteries ceased to be commercially viable. Virtually no private enterprise cemeteries were set up after the 1850s. Well-established concerns such as Kensal Green and Norwood in London, Key Hill and Warstone Lane in Birmingham, St James's in Liverpool and Harpurhey in Manchester, continued with reasonable prosperity. Convenience, personal taste, family associations, and a degree of social élitism, all contributed to their continuity, but essentially they became ancillary to the public cemeteries – usefully so, in fact, considering the ceaseless pressure exerted by the ever-growing urban populations. The rapidity with which parishes adopted the Acts is remarkable, and indicates just how long they were overdue. In London, almost as soon as the Metropolitan Burial Act was passed, the St Pancras vestry elected a Burial Board which promptly bought an 88 acre former farmstead on Finchley Common. Opened in 1854, it became the first Burial Board cemetery in London: when a further 94 acres were added in 1877 to make the St Pancras and Islington Cemetery, it also became the largest. Close by, and also opened in 1854, was the St Marylebone Cemetery, its chapels designed by the same firm that had been employed at St Pancras, Barnett and

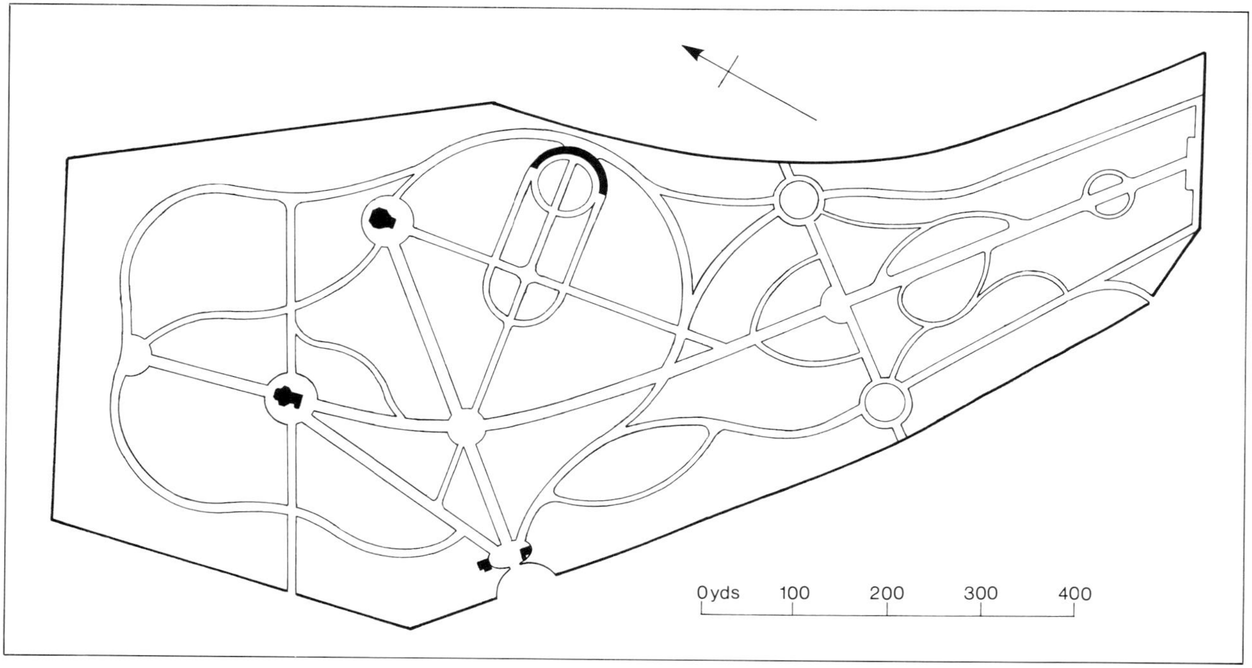

Plan of the City of London Cemetery, Little Ilford, based on the plan by William Haywood published in 1856; the cemetery has since been extended to the east; path widths not to scale.

Birch. The Burial Board of St George's, Hanover Square – whose several urban burial grounds had a particularly noxious reputation – also acted quickly. They purchased a 23 acre site on the Uxbridge Road to the west of London, equipped it with a massive lodge and £1000 worth of planting, and opened it as the Westminster Cemetery, again in 1854. South of the river, in the same year, Lambeth acquired its first public cemetery, some 40 acres in extent, to add to the private provision made by Norwood. Over the next couple of years, as the inner London churchyards and burial grounds were closed and intramural interment discontinued, parishes throughout the metropolis established new public cemeteries: in 1855, Paddington, Putney, and Kensington – where the Burial Board had to go all the way out west to Hanwell to acquire a site; in 1856, Tottenham in north London, Woolwich, Greenwich and Camberwell in south London – this last with Anglican and nonconformist chapels by no less a man than George Gilbert Scott, whose early career had been decisively advanced by his design for the parish church of St Giles in Camberwell. Unusually, the Camberwell Burial Board also provided a Roman Catholic chapel. Unfortunately, but not at all unusually, all three chapels have been demolished in the twentieth century. In 1857, the West Ham Burial Board opened the first public cemetery specifically designed to serve the working-class population east of the City parishes. It had been delayed by wrangling over land, and the difficulties experienced by the Board foreshadowed many similar problems, often the result of disagreements between Anglicans and dissenters, that were to retard the provision of cemeteries in east London for the rest of the century. In 1858, adjacent cemeteries were opened for Deptford and Lewisham, and have since been amalgamated as Brockley Cemetery.

Of all the metropolitan cemeteries established in the years immediately following the 1852 Act, the most imposing, and perhaps the most influential, was the City of London Cemetery, laid out on a 130 acre site at Little Ilford, then on the very edge of the capital's north-eastern suburbs. Landscaping was by Robert Davidson, and the architect, in overall charge, was William Haywood, surveyor and architect to the City's Commissioners for Sewers, who constituted the Burial Board. Asymmetrical in its overall disposition, Hayward's and Davidson's plan has as its core straight carriage-drives radiating out from the main entrance to the Anglican and nonconformist chapels, and, *via* a centrally placed *rond-point*, to the catacombs, which curve round one end of a formally laid out oval that had been the site of a pond. Lodges, chapels and catacombs are all Gothic, as is the mausoleum that Haywood designed for himself and his wife, beside the drive to the Anglican chapel. Planting exploits a whole range of effects and connotations: weighty avenues of chestnut trees, sombre conifers around the chapels, bushes of azalea, laurel and rhododendron, flower beds by the entrance lodge. There is much that is picturesque; much that derives from the tradition of the landscape park; much that has its source in Loudon. But the character of the City of London Cemetery is more than the sum of its influences, and quite different from that of any predecessor. At Little Ilford, the Victorian cemetery is redefined: the key factor is the enhanced scale on which it is conceived and planned. This is more than a mere function of size. Haywood's cemetery has a consistent and proportionate breadth of design that sets grandly formal features – the wide principal drives, the carriage-turns about the chapels, the sunken oval of the catacombs – in a more relaxed, essentially open landscape with long, curving paths and informally planted trees, standing alone or grouped into copses. Both rural and urban in its connotations, both personal and public, the large coherence of the City of London Cemetery was an expression of the new corporate identity taken on by the hundred and more parishes it served. At Little Ilford, the Victorians created a model for the municipal cemetery.

Once the Burial Acts applied outside London, vestries throughout the country established Burial Boards. As in the metropolis, this happened with remarkable speed: it also happened in a wide variety of places – in the new urban centres of industry, in the old market towns of the shires, in seaside resorts, even in agrarian parishes. In the first decade of its existence, from 1843 to 1853, the *Builder* advertised eight public competitions for the design of cemeteries and cemetery buildings: from 1854 to 1856, as the first two Burial Acts took effect, it advertised no less than sixty-two. In addition to these were many that did not go to open competition. Of the sixty-two published, eight were for London cemeteries. A simple list of those outside the metropolis will indicate the range. In 1854: Tiverton in Devon; Rochdale in Lancashire, the first of the textile towns around Manchester; Boston, Grimsby, Holbeach and Louth in Lincolnshire, where parishes seem to have

The City of London Cemetery, Little Ilford, 1854-6; the main drive to the Anglican chapel, designed by William Haywood.

been particularly eager to take advantage of the legislation; Newport in Monmouthshire; Bridgnorth in Shropshire; Bury St Edmund in Suffolk; Doncaster in Yorkshire. In 1855, the peak year for such competitions: Soham in Cambrigeshire, scarcely more than a large village; Blandford, Bridport and Weymouth in Dorset; Monkwearmouth in County Durham; Braintree, Colchester, Harwich and Saffron Walden in Essex; Atherton, Burnley, Heywood, Warrington and Wigan, all in the great industrial conurbation of south Lancashire, as well as Toxteth Park, Liverpool, the first public cemetery in the city; Lincoln; Sudbury in Middlesex; King's Lynn in Norfolk; in Northumberland no less than three cemeteries in Newcastle-upon-Tyne, St Andrew's, St John's and St Nicholas's; in Nottinghamshire, Newark and Nottingham itself; Weston-super-Mare, then a fast-growing watering-place on the Somerset coast; Ipswich in Suffolk; Bradford-on-Avon and Salisbury in Wiltshire. In 1856: Windsor in Berkshire; Aylesbury in Buckinghamshire; Chesterfield in Derbyshire; the railway town of Darlington in County Durham; Gloucester; Rickmansworth in Hertfordshire; Bolton and St Helens in Lancashire; South Shields in Northumberland, rapidly becoming part of the Newcastle conurbation; Mansfield in Nottinghamshire; the coastal resorts of Brighton and Hastings in Sussex; Castleford and Scarborough in Yorkshire. There were to be nearly fifty further competitions announced in the *Builder* before 1863, when the number advertised annually began to decline. In its second decade, the magazine contained a total of 108 cemetery competitions, as compared to the eight of its first ten years.

Public cemeteries continued to be provided by Burial Boards until the local government reforms of the last years of the nineteenth century, in particular the Local Government Act of 1894, made cemeteries the responsibility of the newly constituted local authorities at district, town and parish level. In the capital, the London

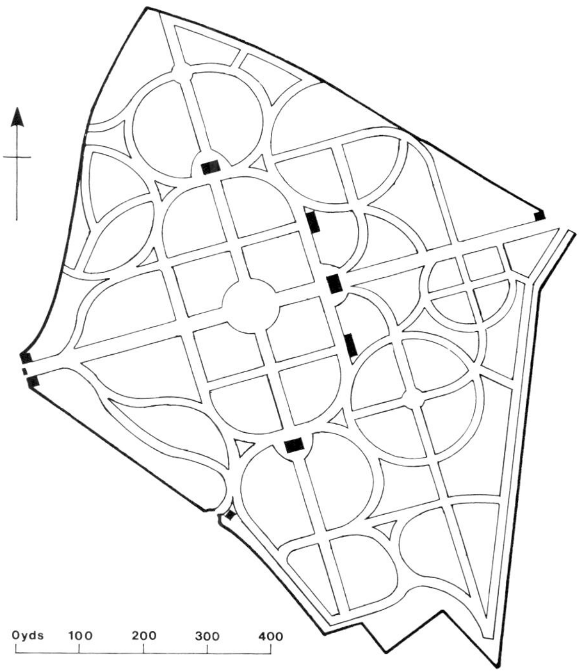

City of Liverpool Cemetery, Anfield, 1860-63; laid out to the design of Edward Kemp, T. D. Barry architect; path widths not to scale.

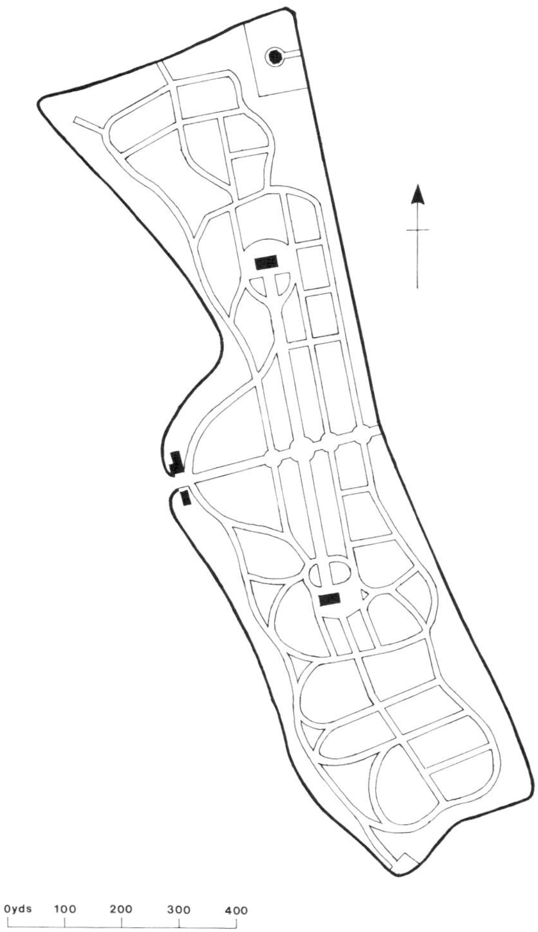

Plan of Witton Cemetery, Birmingham, 1860-64; laid out to the design of Ashwell of Coventry, R. Clarke architect; path widths not to scale.

Stapenhill Cemetery, Burton-on-Trent, Staffordshire, 1865-6; panoramic view of the main promenade and chapels, designed by Lucy and Littler.

Government Act of 1899 created twenty eight metropolitan borough councils which similarly took over responsibility for burial provision, though under the general aegis of the London County Council, set up in 1888. Although the utility and sanitary benefit of the many hundreds of public cemeteries established in later Victorian and Edwardian Britain has always been acknowledged, their visual and architectural qualities have been consistently under-rated. They vary enormously: in overall conception and design, in their relationship to the centres of population they serve, in their planting, in the buildings with which they are equipped, in the style and character of the monuments that fill them. At one end of the spectrum are the great civic cemeteries that adopt the municipal language of the City of London Cemetery: Witton in Birmingham, laid out on an heroic scale in 1860 to designs by Ashwell of Coventry; Liverpool Cemetery, also of 1860, by Edward Kemp and T.D.Barry, its extraordinary road system comprising an interlocking sequence of curving and circular drives; in north Manchester, stretching along the bank of the River Medlock, Philips Park, opened in 1866 and designed by the firm of Paull & Ayliffe; in south Manchester, the Southern Cemetery in Chorlton, dating from 1879 and with H.J.Paull again as its architect. Though smaller, of course, than these expansive exercises in city planning, many of the cemeteries built for medium-sized towns have a similar sense of municipal identity. Characteristic, but each very different and picked virtually at random, are: Burton-on-Trent, founded in 1865, both of its chapels equipped with spires and making the most of its fine position above the river; Exeter Higher Cemetery, opened in 1866, airily set on a broad hilltop east of the city, with excellently detailed chapels designed by Edward Ashworth; Tunbridge Wells, dating from the 1870s and occupying an extensive dog-leg site which includes a magnificent avenue of golden yews. Finally, the largest category of all: the little cemeteries of half-a-dozen acres built for the country towns with their small-scale agricultural industries, for the many ports that supported a fishing fleet or lived off coastal trading, for old market centres that still relied on the local carrier, for suburban villages with their railway line to the city and their growing estates of smart new houses – the cemeteries, that is, for the hundreds of small towns that make up so much of Britain beyond the boundaries of the cities. They are too many for there to be any point in quoting a selection.

The public cemeteries established in the second half of the nineteenth century and in the Edwardian period, for all their diversity, show a number of general developments in layout and planting, in architecture, and in the design of their monuments. What were the common features observable during the period from the Burial Acts to the First World War ?

Later Victorian and Edwardian Cemeteries: Landscape and Planting

When the first cemeteries were being laid out in Norwich, Manchester and Liverpool in the 1820s, the dominant tradition in garden design for nearly a century had been the landscape park. It was a mode of design that incorporated many elements from the picturesque repertoire and that was furthered and developed by the imaginative climate of Romanticism. As we have seen, this was the tradition that produced Norwood Cemetery, calculatedly informal, imitating natural features, with emphasis upon curving paths, rolling terrain and irregular clumps of trees. This was an aesthetic recognized and welcomed by the middle-class clientele which the cemetery company aimed to attract, and it showed remarkable longevity, from the countryfied effects of Key Hill in Birmingham to the artful naturalness of Overleigh in Chester. Challenging the dominance of the landscape park, however, was the far more formal aesthetic with which Loudon was particularly associated. Increasingly, the pursuit of supposedly natural effects was repudiated in favour of the conscious adoption of art and artifice in both planting and overall design. As was discussed earlier, complete formality, as at Brompton and in Loudon's design for Cambridge, was rarely adopted. More often, circles and avenues appeared as detached features rather than as organizing principles of the layout – sometimes to strikingly dramatic effect, as with Highgate Cemetery's sunken Egyptian Avenue and circle of catacombs, or with the two-tier catacomb circle at Warstone Lane, Birmingham. The resulting synthesis of formal and informal features, of artificial and natural, was the basis upon which many of the first Burial Board cemeteries were planned, as is the case with Haywood's influential design for the City of London at Little Ilford. Another means of breaking away from the tradition of the landscape park was by horticultural display. Most of the early cemeteries, while as yet largely unused for graves, filled their grounds with colourful flowerbeds. At Abney Park the great nurseryman George Loddiges created a rosarium with over a thousand cultivated species, and a massive arboretum in which every specimen was conscientiously labelled for the education of an admiring public. Some cemeteries went to the extent of devoting one bed to each of the different botanical families, elevating instruction above the pleasures of purely visual display. Loudon's praise for Abney Park helped to draw attention to its example, and his own plans for Southampton Cemetery included a magnificent arboretum, which was retained in the cemetery's final, much-altered, layout.

By the mid-century, however, this sort of horticultural display was under attack. Loudon himself had criticized Norwood because its layout suggested a private pleasure ground rather than a burial place, and the argument for a

The Higher Cemetery, Exeter, 1865-6; panoramic view, the chapels designed by Edward Ashworth.

distinct landscape character peculiar to cemeteries became an argument against flowerbeds as well. This distinctive character was established by the use of symbolically appropriate planting, weeping and fastigiate trees, yews and dark-foliaged evergreens. Such planting lent itself to both formal and informal effects: thus – to take two examples from the first group of London Burial Board cemeteries – St Pancras features a great variety of conifers modulated by dark clumps of laurel, while Westminster has a principal avenue of cedars. This shift in aesthetic preference coincided with the introduction from America of many suitable species, exploited most notably perhaps at the Brookwood Necropolis in Surrey, which boasts a complete avenue of redwoods.

With such restrictions on planting, much of the emphasis in cemetery design around the mid-century went into the exploitation of differences in ground level. As well as combining a formal and an irregular layout, Joseph Paxton's Coventry Cemetery, dating from 1847, incorporated an architectural terrace and a chapel perched on the edge of a bluff. Paxton's example set the pattern for the next two decades of design, although Highgate had been provided with a viewing terrace for the vista across London as early as 1839 – an important innovation, as we saw earlier, in the relationship between the cemetery and the city it served. A few years after Coventry, William Drummond's Stirling Cemetery was laid out on a plateau between the Castle and Holyrood Kirk, and, in 1867, Paxton's protégé Edward Milner designed what is possibly the steepest of English cemeteries at Stoney Road, Halifax. In Bradford, William Gay designed Undercliffe Cemetery for a private company in 1852, taking advantage of a broad plateau at its highest point to give the town a spectacular skyline of spiky obelisks and pinnacles – a dramatic effect similar to that achieved by the Glasgow Necropolis, opened some twenty years earlier. A fruitful innovation was the sunken, scooped-out plateau exploited by another Paxton protégé, Edward Kemp. At Liverpool Cemetery in 1860 he included both raised and sunken terraces, combining these with the extraordinary road plan mentioned earlier and a striking assymetry in the siting of the avenue. Deliberate asymetry had also been used by William Chater in his design for Saffron Walden Cemetery.

By the 1870s, many of the early cemeteries had begun to decline and were experiencing the first symptoms of neglect. A gradual reaction against the sombre monochrome of evergreen planting set in. There was a return to colour and to flowerbeds, pioneered by Rae at the Dean Cemetery in Edinburgh, with an alpine rockery and spring bulb display, and by Samuel Davis at Maidstone Cemetery, with a floral parterre and fern garden. Quickly, the entire range of contemporary gardening practices appeared in cemetery planting, from carpet-bedding in figures to topiary. Unfortunately, the effects achieved were largely ephemeral, but there are cemeteries in which some aspects of late Victorian horticulture can still be enjoyed. Many northern cemeteries still boast their bedding-out: Arbroath, Sunderland, and Lawns Wood in Leeds are fine examples, the last still preserving its conservatory; topiary can be seen at Windsor; above all, there is the Wimborne Road Cemetery in Bournemouth, opened in 1877, with its avenue of alternating monkey puzzles and standard hollies. At the same time, the uniform reliance on evergreens gradually gave way to the use of flowering deciduous trees. William Falconer, later to become a noted cemetery superintendent in America, and H. E. Milner, son of Edward, were among the early proponents of flowering trees and shrubs, while Milner, in his cemetery at Stoke-on-Trent in the 1880s, revived the pseudo-natural layout of the landscape park used fifty years before at Norwood. When it was opened in 1903, Hendon Park Cemetery was the best London example of this new landscaping: although now sadly shorn of its elaborate original planting, it is still self-consciously rural, crossed by a rivulet with a series of rustic bridges.

By the end of the nineteenth century, however, despite such developments as Milner's revival of the landscape park tradition, grid plans were beginning to emerge as the dominant element in cemetery layouts. The use of a rectilinear grid of paths goes back to Loudon's rationalist theories of the 1830s and early 1840s, and can be found in Burial Board cemeteries from the beginning. Describing Lambeth Cemetery, founded in 1854, the *Builder* noted that the architects, Wehnert and Ashdown, 'divided the whole of the ground into parallelograms, as better adapted to an economical appropriation of the ground for interments'. Similar considerations of efficiency determined the rectilinear layout of West Ham Cemetery, opened in 1857 and, like Lambeth, designed primarily to cater for working-class burials. More usually, however, grid plans were integrated with other, less utilitarian features: hard

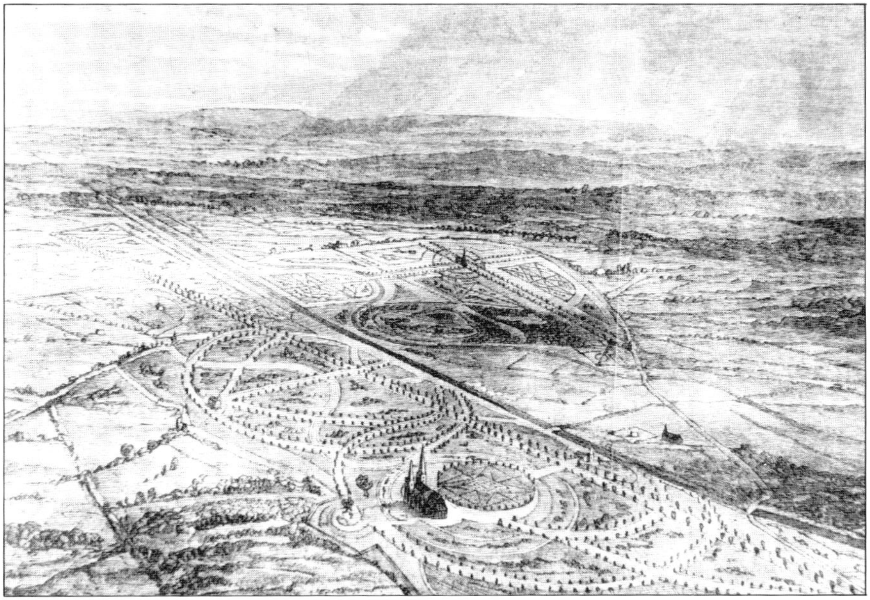

Brookwood Cemetery, Woking, Surrey, 1852-4; aerial perspective from The Illustrated London News, *1852.*

Undercliffe Cemetery, Bradford, 1852-4; the main promenade, laid out to the designs of William Gay.

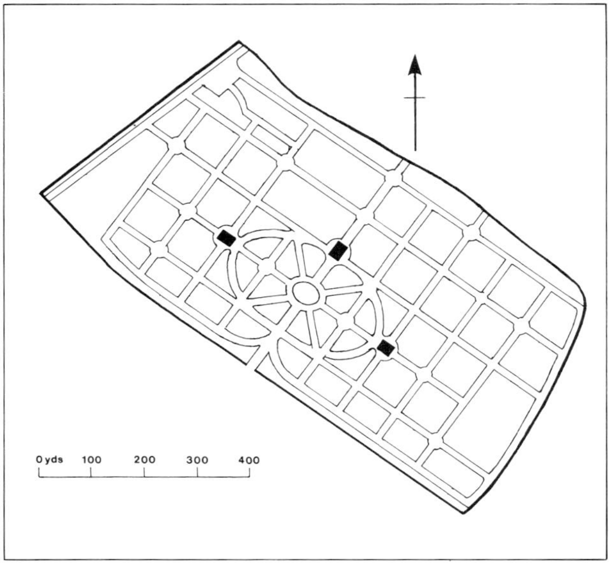

Manchester Southern Cemetery, 1879; H. J. Paull architect; path widths not to scale.

corners were rounded, intersections marked by *ronde-points*, gridded areas encompassed by curving paths. Good examples, which illustrate the progressive development of this mode of planning, are Exeter Higher Cemetery of 1866, Manchester Southern Cemetery of 1879, West Derby Cemetery in Liverpool, laid out in 1881, and Brandwood End Cemetery, opened in 1898 on the south east edge of the Birmingham conurbation. Brandwood End is indeed an outstanding example of how successfully the late Victorians and Edwardians could manage grid plan design: its layout is resolved around a great central avenue, lined with cypresses and variegated evergreen bushes, striking obliquely across the cemetery grounds. At its north end is the pair of chapels in the centre of a carriage turn, *ronds-points* feature the First World War memorial and a splendid oak tree, subsidiary paths crossing the principal drive have avenues of copper beeches, cypresses and – leading to the war memorial – Wellingtonia. It is appropriate that a Great War memorial – the Cross of Sacrifice designed by Sir Herbert Baker and used universally – should be of such importance at Brandwood End. The grid plan, deployed with considerable success at Brandwood End, became the obvious choice for the dignified democracy of the First World War cemeteries of France and Flanders, among the greatest and most moving achievements of Victorian and Edwardian cemetery building.

After the Great War, the inherited components of Edwardian cemetery design were reduced to the grid plan for layout and flowering trees for planting. The latter can be seen to advantage at such inter-war cemeteries as Camberwell New and Grove Park, both in south London. But they are the last flickerings of a great tradition. Over the last fifty years, the British cemetery has become increasingly featureless: laid out on a flat site, mechanically divided up by a grid of paths, primly planted with a few flowering cherries. After a century of inventive, imaginative planning and planting, the ideal of the modern cemetery became an anonymous municipal lawn.

Later Victorian and Edwardian Cemeteries: Buildings and Monuments

Until Tite's Gothic *ensemble* at Norwood, the architecture of the Greek Revival, as we saw earlier, was universal in cemetery design. Similarly, during the first decades of the cemetery movement, classical symbols and styles held a pronounced sway in the choice of monuments. Although examples drawn from the inheritance of medieval monuments were becoming more familiar, attitudes that regarded overtly Christian symbols, particularly those forming part of a Gothic vocabulary, as Papist persisted up to the time of the passing of the Burial Acts. Certainly, broken columns, extinguished torches, urns, and rectangular headstones with acroteria far outnumber crosses or pointed tombstones until after about 1850. Many of the joint stock cemeteries included monuments by leading sculptors. These continued to be erected throughout the second half of the nineteenth century, both in the private enterprise cemeteries and, especially once they became established, in the new public cemeteries founded by the Burial Boards. Kensal Green contains works by John H. Foley – who executed the figure of the Prince Consort for the Albert Memorial – J. G. Lough, M. L. Watson and Robert W. Sievier, who was one of the promoters of that cemetery and whose family memorial is to be found in the

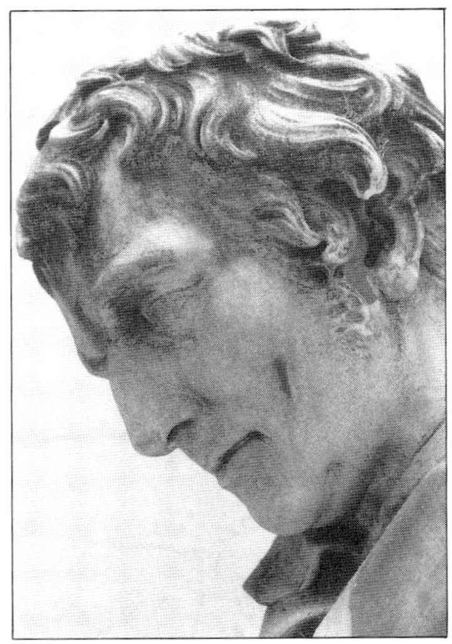

Kensal Green Cemetery, London; Robert Sievier's monument to his parents, probably carved c.1840.

Abney Park Cemetery, London; Edward H. Baily's statue of Isaac Watts, erected in 1845.

chapel range. Works by John Thomas, responsible for the exterior figure sculpture of the Palace of Westminster, can be seen in the Glasgow Eastern Necropolis, as can statuary by the Ritchie Brothers. Similarly, the Dean Cemetery, Edinburgh, contains monuments by John Hutchison, Alexander Munro – who executed much of the statuary for Deane and Woodward's Oxford Museum in the 1850s – and William Brodie, who sculpted the much-loved 'Greyfriars Bobby'. Other cemeteries could feature, as a principal visual focus, a single monument by a major artist, the best example probably being Edward H. Baily's fine memorial to Isaac Watts, erected in 1845 in the centre of Abney Park – the cemetery in which, as we saw earlier, he was the dissenting equivalent of a tutelary deity. Alongside memorials by sculptors with a national reputation are many more – often as ambitious and frequently as accomplished – by local statuaries. As Victorian cemeteries prospered so did local monumental masons, their workshops often sited in the streets immediately around the cemetery gates. These workshops could be advertisements in their own right, conveniently positioned for a display of both skill and prosperity. One of the most exuberant is the house and workshop of John Cramb, built in 1886 plumb opposite the main entrance to Hampstead Cemetery and crusted with Egyptian and Byzantine motifs. The output of such local firms has been almost entirely neglected, but their work is as interesting as it is diverse. It is only necessary to recall the astonishing Casement monument at Kensal Green, with its full-size Indian caryatids bearing the canopy over the sarcophagus, executed in 1844 by a local mason, F. M. Lander, to realize the quality that such workshops could achieve.

Among the styles exploited for both monuments and buildings in early Victorian cemeteries was Egyptian, associated neither with popery, as was Gothic, nor with dissent, as classicism increasingly became, but – thanks to inevitable association with the pyramids – carrying with it appropriate funerary connotations. Among the earliest examples was the Bartholomew Street Cemetery in Exeter – opened in 1837 and essentially an extension of an earlier burial-ground – which was equipped with an Egyptian catacomb range built into the medieval town wall. With the scholarly advice of Joseph Bonomi, William Hosking provided Abney Park with impressive Egyptian gates and lodges. And Highgate, of course, offered the most theatrical example of the style in the Egyptian Avenue and

Kensal Green Cemetery, London; monument to Major General Sir William Casement, d.1844, sculpted by F. M. Lander, with detail of one of the Indian caryatids.

catacomb circle. Lotus bud and palmetto columns, inclined walls, Egyptian detailing generally, all made appearances on individual mausolea and tombstones as well, while the use of selected Egyptian motifs on an obelisk could mark it out from more orthodox classical versions: a splendid example is the obelisk to the architect William Mawson in Undercliffe Cemetery, Bradford. Although nobody used Egyptian for cemetery buildings after the 1840s, the style reappeared sporadically, most often to impressive effect, until the early twentieth century. In London, Putney Vale Cemetery, not founded until 1891, has a spectacular Egyptian mausoleum with paired palmetto columns and a great bronze door: intriguingly, and not inappropriately, there is no record of when it was built or of whose remains are enclosed by its glittering granite.

Just as Egyptian had been abandoned for cemetery buildings by 1850, so also, effectively, had Greek, through – again like Egyptian – it continued to be used for monuments and particularly mausolea, until the twentieth century. The style that was left in sole possession of cemetery architecture was, of course, Gothic. The establishment of Gothic, as was discussed earlier, resulted from a complex of factors that included the civic prestige of Barry's Palace of Westminster, Pugin's impassioned advocacy of Gothic as the only Christian architecture, and the Cambridge ecclesiologists' campaign for the adoption of a historically informed Gothic as the paradigmatic style for Anglican church-building. The measure of the Gothic victory was its general cultural acceptance as the style that connoted Christian belief. What other style could be possible for the funerary buildings of an avowedly Christian nation? By the time the Burial Boards were being established throughout the country, Gothic, or one of the medieval styles at least, was invariably used for cemetery chapels, and usually for gates and lodges as well. In memorials the classical repertoire was increasingly ousted by crosses, pointed headstones – often with an inset arch – Gothic tomb chests, and elaborately detailed pinnacles soaring upward towards a Christian heaven.

As the century progressed the demand for historically correct Gothic grew, a demand confidently and competently met both by national architects, like Gilbert Scott in his 1871 chapel at Ludlow Cemetery, and by local practitioners, like Edward Ashworth in the twinned chapels of 1866 in Exeter Higher Cemetery. The scale on which the Burial Acts were adopted, created in the Burial Boards a major source of publicly funded architectural patronage – a situation not unlike the one that was to be produced in the early 1870s, when Foster's Education Act led to the creation of the Board Schools. The new cemeteries of the 1850s called for a variety of skills, from the design of their buildings to the planning of their drainage systems. There emerged a number of architectural firms specializing in cemeteries, particularly in the first decade after the passing of the legislation. Locally based, these firms usually operated within a particular geographical area. In London, the partnership of John Barnett and W.C. Birch were the architects for St Pancras Cemetery and St Marylebone Cemetery in 1854, and Putney Lower Common Cemetery in 1855. The Liverpool

The City of Liverpool Cemetery, Anfield; the Egyptian mausoleum of Alexander MacLennan, d.1896.

Toxteth Park Cemetery, Liverpool, 1855-6; the Anglican chapel, designed by T. D. Barry.

Tottenham Cemetery, London, 1855-6; the chapels, designed by Pritchett and Sons.

Great Torrington Cemetery, Devon, 1854-5.

architect T.D.Barry designed the buildings of both Toxteth Park Cemetery and Liverpool Cemetery, in 1855 and 1860 respectively, as well as picking up the commissions for many of the Burial Board cemeteries in south Lancashire: Heywood, Warrington, and Atherton in 1855; St Helens in 1856; Runcorn in 1858. The firm of W.F.Poulton and W.H.Woodman, whose office was in Reading and who also specialized in nonconformist churches, was successful in competitions for several cemeteries in central southern England: Aylesbury, Basingstoke and Windsor in 1856; the little mortuary chapel at Box in 1858; Abingdon in 1859. Most remarkable, perhaps, was James Pigott Pritchett whose substantial late Georgian and early Victorian practice centred on York, where he designed the fine Ionic buildings for York Cemetery in 1836–7; he was also responsible for a significant number of churches throughout the north-east, both Anglican and nonconformist. With the passage of the Burial Acts he proved adept at meeting the new demand for cemeteries. As a cemetery designer, his geographical range was considerably greater than that of other specialists in the field, and his firm continued as successful cemetery architects well after the initial wave of Burial Board commissions. In 1855 and 1856 respectively, he won first place in the competitions for cemeteries at Sudbury and Darlington, and in partnership as Middleton and Pritchett designed the cemeteries of St Andrew's, Newcastle-upon-Tyne, and Saffron Walden, again in 1855. His major practice, however, was as Pritchett and Sons of Darlington and York, and it was this firm that established what must have been something like a national reputation as cemetery architects: Boston in 1854; Tottenham in north London in 1855; Mansfield and Scarborough in 1856; Colne in Lancashire in 1859, as well as having entered the competition for Runcorn in the previous year; Whitby in 1861; the Yorkshire town of Great Driffield in 1864; Perth in Scotland in 1870. Under his own name again – though probably the firm is indicated – Pritchett was placed first in the competitions for Bishop Auckland Cemetery in 1881, and for the chapel and mortuary at Armley Cemetery in Leeds in 1885. Continuing the family tradition, his son, H. D. Pritchett, was an entrant in the competition for Agecroft Cemetery in Salford in 1898.

The difficulty of catering for different denominations within the same cemetery – so tricky an issue for the legislators and reformers, as was discussed earlier – was an architectural problem as well. An initial solution was simply to pair the chapels, often placing them in the overall layout of the cemetery so that they acted as pendants to one another, with the Anglican chapel distinguished only by a bellcote over the gable end. Pairing seems to have been particularly popular in the small cemeteries that Burial Boards provided for country towns. Devon has a number of examples in a range of medievalizing styles: neo-Norman at Tiverton, designed by the town's principal architect, Gideon Boyce, in 1854-5; Early English at Axminster and Great Torrington, both consecrated in 1856; Decorated at Barnstaple, also of 1856, where the architect was the town surveyor R.D.Gould. On other occasions, two different phases of Gothic could be used to distinguish between Anglican and nonconformist chapels: again, a Devon example is Torquay Cemetery, established by a joint stock company in the 1850s, where the Church of England chapel is Decorated, with an asymmetrically placed bell tower, and the plainer dissenters' chapel is Perpendicular. From the 1850s, however, a new building type emerged – one unique to cemetery design – in which the two chapels, designed symmetrically and set either parallel to one another or end to end, are linked by a *porte-cochère*, frequently topped by a steeple. The result is a single composite structure that registers denominational distinction while simultaneously asserting the equality of the two chapels. There were many variations in design. Thomas Little's chapels at Paddington, an early example dating from 1855, are placed at either end of a long range which has two *portes-cochères* either side of a central tower and spire, while at Barnsley, designed in 1860 by Perkin and Backhouse, the two chapels are joined by a long open screen. Other solutions to the relationship between the two chapels included placing them side-by-side with a party wall between – as in St Thomas's Cemetery, Exeter, designed in 1877 by the Board Surveyor, Samuel Churchward – and arranging them in a T-plan, as in Edward Browning's design of 1859 for Oundle Cemetery, Northamptonshire, and as in the 1877 cemetery of St Austell in Cornwall.

The 1860s saw the introduction or revival of a variety of Gothic, medieval and Tudor devices in monumental design: recumbent effigies with canopies, of which there is a remarkably accurate – though anonymous – example in

Loughborough Cemetery, Leicestershire, 1857; the chapels and triple porte-cochère, designed by Pearson Bellamy and J. Spence Hardy.

Kensal Green Cemetery, London; Godfrey Sykes' memorial to William Mulready, d.1863.

Early English in St Cross Cemetery, Oxford, and of which Godfrey Sykes' more famous memorial to Mulready in Kensal Green is an early Renaissance version; ornate pinnacles freely based on the Eleanor crosses; tabernacles and ciboriums modelled on E. Meikle Kemp's Walter Scott Monument in Edinburgh and the Albert Memorials in London and Manchester. At the same time, monuments increased in size, especially those bordering on central avenues or raised terraces: Undercliffe in Bradford is an excellent example, as are the central avenues in Duke Street Cemetery, Southport, and in Kensal Green – this latter showing off a unique sequence of pinnacles and mausolea in polychromatic masonry. Mausolea, both classical and Gothic, become more common from this period. Not infrequently, the ambitious memorials of the mid-century were designed by major architects. Despite losses, Norwood Cemetery still has what is perhaps the most impressive collection: Edward Barry's intricate Gothic monument of 1858 to Alexander Berens; the John Ralli mausoleum of 1863 by George Edmund Street; the 1865 mausoleum of George Dodd, designed by Thomas Allom in the north Italian Gothic advocated by Ruskin; William Tite's Gothic spire of 1866 in memory of J. W. Gilbart; most impressive of all, perhaps, is the Greek Revival Ralli mortuary chapel of 1872, probably designed by John Oldrid Scott, and one of the finest Victorian essays in the style. The severity of the Ralli chapel is something of an exception, for the increasing size of High Victorian monuments was usually accompanied by an increase in decorative variety and richness. The use of different types of stone – the combination of grey and red granites being highly popular – was carried over into smaller memorials, and mosaic work began to make an appearance. William Burges' tomb for Charles Ricketts, placed in Kensal Green in 1867, is an early example of a trend towards complex plasticity and richly encrusted decoration. On memorial crosses bases became heavier, often elaborately curved and moulded, detailed stone carving proliferated, inset figural sculpture was incorporated into cemetery chapels, as at Wimborne Road Cemetery, Bournemouth, designed in 1877 by the town Surveyor Christopher Crabbe Creeke, and in Patrick Allen-Frazer's eclectic chapel of 1875 at Arbroath. Naturalistic foliage, the offspring of Victorian botanizing and Ruskinian Gothic theory, became a staple of the memorial repertoire, producing, at one end of the scale, a standard motif like the ivy-clad cross, and, at the other, an exotic like Burne-Jones's 1892 monument in Brompton Cemetery to Whistler's patron, Frederick Leyland, with trails of copper foliage swirling over the surfaces of the stone.

The use of imported stone in major metropolitan centres and areas where local quarries were poor led, by the 1870s, to the import of monuments as well, often carved by Italian masons, who were thought superior to their English contemporaries in their handling of the

Norwood Cemetery, London; tomb of Alexander Berens, d.1858, designed by Edward Barry.

Kensal Green Cemetery, London; monument to Captain Charles Ricketts, d.1867, designed by William Burges.

human figure. Wholesale import companies grew up, from whose catalogues local masons' firms could choose memorials. Meanwhile, in areas where local quarries were good – as in West Yorkshire and Lancashire – masons used the catalogues as pattern books and carved in the indigenous sandstone. The most popular of imported figures were angels. Guardian angels had been introduced into church monuments by Flaxman at the beginning of the century, but had seldom featured in cemeteries before the 1880s, and then usually as relief carvings rather than in full figure. From the 1880s they become far more common, assuming a wide variety of attitudes and depicted in a wide range of roles. The English reception of such monuments was not merely passive: designs could be drawn up by English masons and sent to Italy for carving, and many Italian firms – experienced in the memorial traditions of their own country – would provide portrait likenesses on request. There was, however, an evangelical and Low Church reaction against this influx of overseas angels, often expressing itself through the alternative memorial form of a female figure standing against or clinging to a cross: ironically, these were often carved in Italy as well. The popularity of these memorials, as of the Italianate angels, continued well into the 1920s. Although individual monuments could become routine, the quality of the carving was often high, and, when assembled *en masse*, the effect is impressive: good examples are the group clustered near the entrance of Chaddesdon Cemetery, Derby, the sequence along the main terrace in the Church Cemetery, Nottingham, and the angelic convention gathered in the Roman Catholic section of St Pancras and Islington.

The closing decades of the nineteenth century saw the evolution of existing styles and the arrival of new ones, making the cemetery more aesthetically eclectic than ever.

The Church Cemetery, Nottingham; Italian angels and figure sculpture on a group of Edwardian memorials.

Tiverton Cemetery, Devon; a commemorative angel of Italian make on the tomb of William Haydon, d.1897; this particular figure was one of the most popular of the Italian imports.

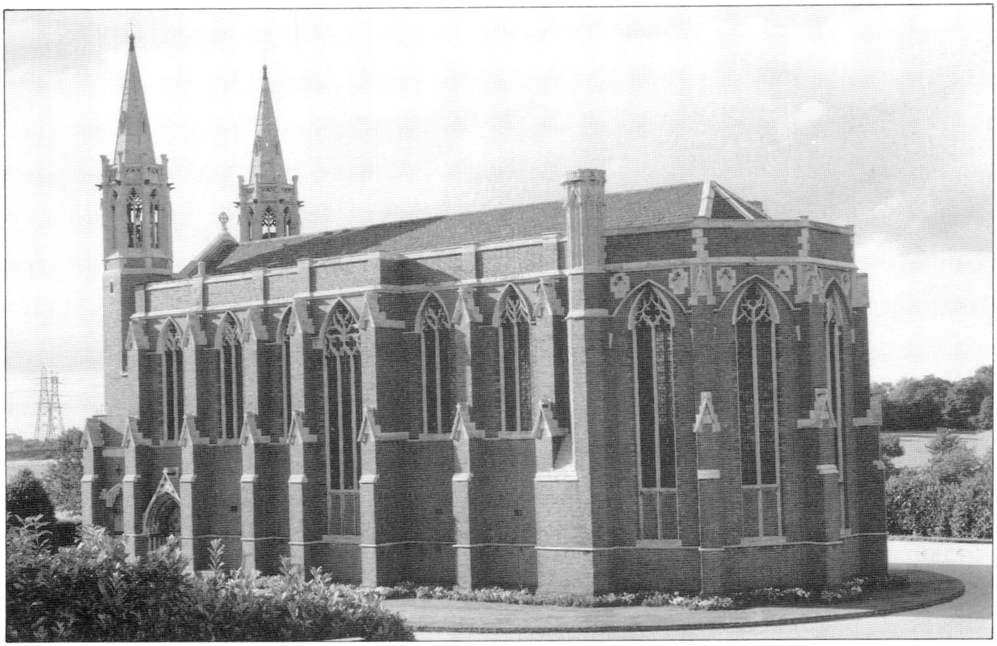

Handsworth Cemetery, Birmingham, 1909; the chapel, designed by W. H. Bidlake.

Developments in late Victorian ecclesiastical Gothic were followed in cemetery design with engagingly diverse results. At Tavistock in Devon, the chapel, built entirely in finely crafted granite, was designed in a compact free Perpendicular by E. H. Sedding, nephew of John Dando Sedding. The vast municipal cemetery of Handsworth in Birmingham, laid out in 1909, has a lofty red brick chapel, its single volume conceived something after the manner of Albi, by W. H. Bidlake, the designer of St Agatha's, Sparkbrook, and the leading Arts and Crafts practitioner in the Midlands. Even more the product of the Arts and Crafts movement is the chapel J. W. Cockrill designed for Caister Cemetery, Great Yarmouth, in 1904, long and low with eclectic detailing and brick-traceried windows set back under segmental arches. Non-medieval styles made their appearance as well, a significant break with the Christian connotations of Gothic. At Willesden Cemetery in 1891, the chapels and *porte-cochère* were built in an expansive and freely interpreted Renaissance style to the designs of C. Worley. At the same time, cemetery design began to incorporate elements from the Vernacular Revival. Lodges were particularly suited to the Vernacular manner, but at Chelmsford and Hendon Park Cemeteries the chapels were timber framed as well. New structural materials were also adopted: the twinned chapels and *porte-cochère* of Brandwood End, designed by J. Brewin Holmes in 1897–8, are clad completely in red terracotta, bright, permanent, rich in detail; the chapel of Newton Abbot Cemetery, designed by the Council Surveyor, Coleridge D.White, in 1911, is built entirely of moulded concrete blocks.

Paralleling architectural developments, eclecticism in style and material characterized late Victorian and Edwardian cemetery monuments. Alongside the shining marble angels, figure sculpture, much of it similarly commissioned from Italy, brought a new variety and expressive range to the cemetery: serenely refined in the 1896 relief of the Madonna and Child in Torquay Cemetery to the memory of Kitty, Baroness de Reede;

Hampstead Cemetery, London; monument of Jacob Arnhold, d.1903.

Hampstead Cemetery, London; William Goscombe John's bronze in memory of his wife, Marthe, d.1923.

Torquay Cemetery, Devon; memorial to Kitty, Baroness de Reede de Ter Aa, d.1896.

St Cross Cemetery, Oxford; terracotta memorial to Sir John Rhys, d.1915.

both elegant and tender in the full-length figure in Brompton Cemetery of Blanche Roosevelt Macchetta, who died in 1898; brooding and intense in the Rodinesque figure of 1903 that grieves over the monument of Jacob Arnhold in Hampstead. More eccentric is the life-size marble lion that dozes on top of the 1912 memorial to Frank Bostock in Abney Park. As well as sculpture, there was, from the opening years of the twentieth century, a marked increase in the use of bronze for monuments, perhaps as a reaction against the extent to which masons relied on imports for figural monuments. St Marylebone Cemetery has F. Lynn Jenkins' 1909 Tate memorial, with its naked bronze figure rising theatrically atop a Renaissance sarcophagus, and, directly opposite, a touchingly delicate bronze mourner for the 1914 Ripley monument by William Reid-Dick. At East Sheen, also in London, a powerfully dramatic Angel of Death spreads her wings across the 1920 tomb of George Lancaster. Similarly striking is the Wilson memorial of 1918 in Lawns Wood Cemetery, Leeds, executed by Caldwell Spruce in a Michaelangelesque style clearly influenced by Watts. Most moving, perhaps, is the 1923 bronze William Goscombe John erected in Hampstead to the memory of his own wife – heavily robed, she moves away from the spectator, her head turned for a final backward glance, her fingers on her lips to kiss goodbye.

New types arrived among non-figural memorials as well. The 1890s saw the beginning of the vogue for Celtic crosses, their popularity doubtless increased by the erection of one such cross on Ruskin's grave in Coniston churchyard. Terracotta was taken up for monuments as it was for buildings. St Cross Cemetery in Oxford has a delightful scallop shell moulded from the wings of two angels no more than 18 inches high, to the memory of the Professor of Celtic, Sir John Rhys, who died in 1915. At the other end of the scale, the late Gothic mausoleum of 1897 to Sir Henry Doulton in Norwood, is entirely of orange terracotta – appropriately enough for the head of the Doultonware firm. A few yards from the Doulton memorial at Norwood is another terracotta mausoleum, this time to the sugar king Sir Henry Tate, who died in 1899, and Nunhead has a fine example in the Romanesque style to the memory of the Stearne family. Other sorts of ceramic, often glazed and coloured, occur in monuments of the date, and in the immortelles which were introduced to British cemeteries in the last years of the nineteenth century. These were miniature grave decorations consisting of flowers and other ornaments in alabaster or ceramic, protected by a glass dome. Once common, these fragile monuments now survive only rarely, usually in rural cemeteries: remarkable in this respect is the little Cornish cemetery of Charlestown, laid out in 1901, where dozens of immortelles still remain, sometimes three to a grave.

Although monuments of major quality continued to be erected into the 1920s and even the 1930s, the Great War effectively ended the happy diversity of the late Victorian and Edwardian cemetery. Before 1914, eighteenth-century decorative motifs and lettering – influenced by the Queen Anne Revival – began to appear, and these fed directly into the vocabulary of Neo-Georgian, one of the two styles which came to dominate the design of twentieth-century cemetery monuments. The other, closely related, was a simplified classicism derived from the architecture of Lutyens and his contemporaries. It was, of course, Lutyens and the other architects of the Imperial War Graves Commission who gave architectural form to the First World War cemeteries, and thus to the bereavement of a whole generation. After the war, however, the same style in routine hands became mechanical and reductive: the process of decline towards the standardized anonymity of the modern cemetery had begun.

2

THE PRESENT STATE

The Decline of the Cemetery

THE GREAT URBAN CEMETERY OF the nineteenth century was designed for posterity. Just as its monuments, by and large, expressed optimism about the future life of the individual soul, so the cemetery itself was conceived and planned with a culturally and socially optimistic perspective upon the future. Trees would take years to grow; existing planting would need to be cultivated and further planting laid out; buildings and monuments would require long-term maintenance. Had the hopes of men like John Strang and J. C. Loudon been fulfilled and sustained, Victorian cemeteries by now would be great planned landscapes, their monuments expressions of both piety and art, their planting fully mature. Instead, they have been damaged and depleted, frequently neglected or treated with indifference, sometimes destroyed.

The origins of this decline are to be found in the fundamental processes of social, economic and cultural change that have shaped Britain in the twentieth century. Although the great Victorian cemeteries were inter-denominational, they have been crucially affected by the post-Victorian shift in the significance of institutional religion. As early as the 1840s – as Highgate and Kensal Green flourished – the historian J. A. Froude wrote of the Nemesis of Faith; as urbanization and industrialization grew, Thomas Arnold saw the emergence of a large working-class population neither High church nor Low Church but No Church. What was apparent of one class by the second half of the last century has had application across the broad social spectrum in this. It was George Orwell who identified loss of belief in personal immortality as the central problem of twentieth-century consciousness. The progressive secularization of education, social welfare, morality itself, has pushed organized religion far more on to the periphery of national life, and thus of everyday experience, than it was a century ago. This process, and its attendant shifts of priority within the churches themselves, has meant inevitably that cemeteries and the formalized commemoration of the dead no longer have the central imaginative and spiritual importance for us that they had for the Victorians.

The sharp decline in the quality of the design and landscaping of public cemeteries in Britain after the Great War has already been indicated. The same deterioration is evident in architecture and monuments. Part of the popularity of the Neo-Georgian manner that was emerging in the years before 1914 lay in the readiness with which it could be adapted to smaller scale monuments. This preference became increasingly marked after the First World War and has, of course, continued, strengthened by the steadily growing costs of labour and materials. Initially, however, it expressed a general rejection of the Victorian panoply of mourning and commemoration, a desire to avoid what was thought of as ostentation, a feeling that it was inappropriate to lavish money on memorials to the dead that could be spent on – or by – the living. Memorial inscriptions dwindled in length and came, more and more, to avoid any but the most platitudinous of religious statements. During the interwar years, birdbaths and standing sundials made their appearance in cemeteries, along with the so-called 'garden-job' – a sort of scale model of a patio garden: all, perhaps, generated by a benign if woolly pantheism, an urban desire to symbolize unity with the natural world that also found contemporary expression in naturism and the Ramblers' Association. Less comfortingly, uniformity of design derived from the pattern set by the military cemeteries of the Great War – who knows with what degree of self-awareness? – but with little of their dignity and none of their architectural distinction. Cemetery authorities imposed conformity: surrounded by level grass, small headstones without kerbs and with a minimum of individuality became the standard memorials for the ideal lawn cemetery: ideal partly, if not wholly, because it is cheap to maintain.

Cost of maintenance has been the most obvious of the economic factors determining the particular crisis with which cemetery authorities increasingly have been faced. Victorian cemeteries were not laid out with ease or economy of maintenance as priorities. Labour was cheap, materials plentiful, and the general public – particularly the middle and upper middle classes – were prepared and able to spend a substantial proportion of their income on funerals, memorials and mourning. We have seen how privately owned and managed cemeteries were profitable concerns, with investors enjoying dividends of up to 30%. Such profitability meant that adequate maintenance could be ensured; indeed, because a cemetery needed to attract potential customers, a high level of upkeep was obviously in the economic interest of the cemetery owners. Yet, by the end of the nineteenth century there were signs, in the older cemeteries at least, that things were changing for the worse. In *The London Burial Grounds*, published in 1896, Mrs Basil Holmes saw clear evidence of decline at Tower Hamlets Cemetery, which had become 'a regular ocean of tombstones, many of which are lying about apparently uncared for and unclaimed; in fact most of the graves, except those at the edges of the walks, look utterly neglected'. Two factors seem to have led to the situation at Tower Hamlets: sheer pressure of numbers had caused overcrowding, and many of the burials packed into the cemetery were of people who were poor. Consequently, money was a problem even as the need for management and control became more critical. The inevitable result was neglect. In this century the difficulty of financing maintenance has bcome increasingly widespread and acute; since the last war all the major cemeteries in the country have suffered. A primary cause has been the erosion of profitability by growing inflation. Up to the 1970s the effect of inflation was exacerbated by the fact that charges for burial, whether in private or local authority cemeteries, were fixed by the Department of the Environment and became increasingly unrepresentative of the actual cost of interment. From the point of view of the private cemeteries, the situation has been worsened further by competition with local authority cemeteries, which have always been subsidised out of the rates. In 1973–4 it was estimated that for every £1 paid by clients of local authority cemeteries a further 63p had to be found from the funds of the authority itself. Few private cemeteries could compete, and the consequent loss of income had an inevitable effect upon the availability of money for maintenance. Some cemeteries, indeed, have suffered a complete loss of income simply as a result of becoming full; with burials no longer possible, revenue stops and companies are faced with a situation in which their entire asset has become a liability. If bankruptcy does not follow immediately, the complex legal constraints on the re-use of burial grounds make it an eventual certainty.

The increasing frequency of cremation has also contributed to the decline of cemetery revenues, particularly apparent in the case of private cemeteries. From its first controversial beginnings at Woking in the 1880s, cremation has grown steadily: something between 60% and 70% of all funerals now involve the cremation rather than the burial of the dead. Rational, efficient, economical of both space and labour, cremations are also much cheaper than interments. Although the costs of maintaining the usually far less elaborate memorials and associated gardens of remembrance are correspondingly lower, the smaller income deriving from cremations means that less money is available for looking after the earlier monuments and landscaping of the cemetery as a whole. Public preference for cremation over interment has been particularly marked since the 1940s, leading to predictions that it would eventually account for 95% of all disposals of the dead. Although the evidence suggests that such predictions are unlikely to be fulfilled, in the 1950s and 1960s particularly they seemed to spell the end of the great Victorian cemetery – condemned as old-fashioned, too large and too expensive. Certainly, such forecasts have done nothing to encourage the sympathetic treatment of historic cemeteries in the post-war period.

In specific cases, economic decline can be attributed to the actual management – or rather mismanagement – of privately owned cemeteries. Provided the general requirements of the Burial and Public Health Acts are complied with, the operation of a privately owned burial ground, unlike that of a crematorium, is not subject to any special government licence or regulation. The terms within which cemetery companies have operated, and the restrictions governing them, are those of their original articles of association, contained, in the case of most private cemeteries, in an Act of Parliament. Without standard regulation and inspection, unscrupulous companies or their employees found exploitation easy. Nunhead Cemetery's long history of financial troubles began with its first superintendent who, between 1840 and 1865, the cemetery's most successful period, defrauded the company of thousands of pounds. Other frauds were more mundane: most familiarly, money paid for perpetual maintenance simply failed to arrive in the appropriate fund. The pressure to ignore inconvenient obligations increased as cemetery companies found themselves in financial straits. Faced with uneconomic operation, maintenance ceased and directors took all they could out of remaining funds, trusting that, when the gates closed, the local authority would take over responsibility for looking after the cemetery. Essentially, the rate-payer and the public sector were expected to pick up the tab for the failure of private enterprise.

In practice, local authorities have proved reluctant to do this. Legal difficulties certainly stand in the way of their assuming control: at both Nunhead and Tower Hamlets an Act of Parliament was required before ownership could be transferred. But the main deterrent is undoubtedly economic. Large sites containing substantial buildings, filled with thousands of monuments, and often partly overgrown, can be expensive merely to secure. Maintenance costs are high, particularly as both the layout of cemeteries and the condition into which many have fallen make the use of machinery impracticable. The costs of improvement, of converting a closed cemetery to a different sort of social amenity, can appear even higher. Given the many and diverse calls upon local authority funds, there are inherent difficulties in finding an alternative public use for cemeteries that will be seen to justify large-scale expenditure. In the past, money for such purposes has not been provided by central government. With the current strict controls upon local government spending, it is not surprising that councils are very wary of taking on new financial commitments.

The problems facing local authority cemeteries are of a different nature, and stem not so much from neglect as from inappropriate action and attitudes. Major policy changes in the management of cemeteries have resulted from a number of specifically twentieth-century factors: the model of the war cemetery, with its uniform monuments; the steady reduction in the size of monuments as a result both of increased costs and of the smaller area taken up by cremated ashes; the development of chemical and mechanized methods of horticultural control. Bureaucratic zeal for conformity has also had its effect. Many cemeteries now limit the size and shape of monuments and specify the words that are permitted upon them; some authorities have taken prescription to the length of enacting bye-laws that limit memorial inscriptions to name and date alone. The passion for standardization can have results that are almost as ridiculous as they are distressing. In November 1986, a Plymouth widower who had placed boxes of flowers on his wife's grave in Weston Mill Cemetery was ordered to remove them, and was threatened with a High Court injunction banning him from the cemetery if he refused to comply. His plea that his wife 'loved flowers and would have wanted her grave covered with them' met the City Council's mechanical response that 'only one vase per grave was allowed, to keep them tidy'. Bullying people into tidiness, no matter what their personal feelings, is one of the more unedifying consequences of adopting ease of maintenance as an almost exclusive priority in cemetery management. The major design characteristic of recent cemetery extensions has been the elimination of features that might get in the way of the lawnmower: the greater the degree of uniformity that can be imposed – on mourners as well as monuments, it would seem – the easier and cheaper will be the maintenance.

Given the prevalence of such attitudes, coupled with a failure to appreciate or understand nineteenth-century landscape and monumental design, it is not surprising that the management policies adopted in the newer areas of cemeteries have been applied to the older sections as well. The need to find economical means of maintenance must be recognized, but, all too often, historic cemeteries have been subjected to drastic schemes involving the clearance of the majority of the older memorials and the entire alteration of the layout. Such schemes have been pushed through without reference to the quality of the landscape or the historical and artistic importance of the monuments involved. Indeed, some cemetery authorities regard the older monuments as merely irrelevant, an attitude bolstered in the past by active hostility to Victorian memorial art. After an outbreak of vandalism at Batley Cemetery in Yorkshire in 1979, a local clergyman was quoted in the press as saying that, although the vandals were 'sick', they were 'no more sick than some of the monuments' in the cemetery they had wrecked – an aesthetic and historical judgement that is as crass as the social analysis that precedes it is platitudinous. Supported by such philistinism, indifference and neglect lead to inevitable decay, and the structural dereliction into which larger monuments are allowed to fall then provides a ready excuse for demolition.

In the last few years, of course, private enterprise has re-entered the field it largely left to the management of public authorities in the middle of the nineteenth century. The enthusiasm of Margaret Thatcher's government for privatization wherever possible led Westminster Borough Council, under the doctrinaire direction of its leader, Lady Porter, to sell off three Burial Board cemeteries in 1986: Paddington Cemetery at Mill Hill, St Marylebone Cemetery at East Finchley, and Westminster Cemetery at Hanwell. All three were still in use and had valuable adjacent land attached: the price asked was a token 15p. The object was to save maintenance and management costs, running at £406,000 annually. Westminster is the wealthiest borough in London, and the cost of running the cemeteries is negligible when seen against the council's total expenditure of £219.7 million in the financial year 1987-8. The result was a fiasco, subsequently condemned in reports by the district auditor and by the local ombudsman. Commenting on the ombudsman's findings in December 1988, the *Independent* summarized the woeful course of events.

> Prior to the sale in 1986, no serious attempt was made to value the cemeteries and other land; nor, the ombudsman concluded, was thought given to enforcement of the buyer's obligation to maintain the cemeteries properly, even though Commonwealth and Dutch war graves and memorials were involved. Not long after acquiring the cemeteries and land, the initial purchaser on-sold them for £1.25 million, retaining some buildings which had been included. The standard of maintenance slumped. Bones were found on paths, and a grave-digger was seen lining a water-logged grave with rubbish. Eventually, following complaints from deeply upset relatives, the council decided to draw up compulsory purchase orders to re-acquire the cemeteries. The present owner, a company based in Panama, wants £2.5 million for them, and £3 million for the vacant land.

By the second half of 1988, maintenance in the three cemeteries had improved. Even so, the ombudsman's report, as the *Independent* crisply puts it, 'is a withering indictment of insensitivity, incompetence and mismanagement on the part of the council', while the sale of the cemeteries by the original purchasers for a profit of £1.25 million minus 15p, was nothing but profiteering. To the reader of Walker's *Gatherings from Graveyards*, the catalogue of scattered bones, water-logged graves, and callous gravediggers is wholly familiar, for it echoes precisely the list of abuses he found in the London burial grounds in the 1830s, and particularly those commercial grounds run by private enterprise. Based on the evidence of Westminster, there is no reason to alter Chadwick's conclusion that public cemeteries should be provided by public authorities, not left to the commercial interests of private companies.

The curtailment or, not infrequently, abandonment of maintenance in a major nineteenth-century cemetery changes its identity. As the large staff of gardeners that was required for its upkeep dwindles, so the original balance in its design between the natural and the artificial shifts. If the cemetery is still in use for burials, maintenance is concentrated in the working area at the expense of areas which are full. If the whole cemetery is full – 'buried up' in the undertakers' phrase – maintenance can largely cease. Main drives are kept clear and may even be kept in repair, but subsidiary paths are left untouched. Verges may be tidied but the inner reaches of the cemetery become neglected. Shrubs and bushes remain unclipped; coppices and stands of trees are not thinned out; where no relatives visit, graves are left untended. Gradually the original outlines of the cemetery's planning and planting become blurred. New trees, self-seeded, spring up alongside the old; pathways vanish beneath wild grasses; graves and monuments disappear under brambles. The cemetery is submerged in a green sea of vegetation. The artificial is subsumed in the natural. In every major Victorian cemetery which retains its monuments and historic layout, there is a part of the grounds that is now growing wild. In several, including a number of the earliest, nature has taken over completely. Most of Highgate, and all of Nunhead where monuments remain, is now woodland; in large tracts of Brookwood Cemetery gravestones and memorials are all but invisible beneath ferns and brambles; substantial parts of Abney Park and Tower Hamlets are impenetrable. Overgrown, whether in whole or in part, the nineteenth-century cemetery becomes a new environment with its own history. The natural history of cemeteries, both that they have inherited by design and that they have acquired by neglect, is central to any account of their present state.

Natural History and the Historic Cemetery

In recent years, naturalists and environmentalists have given considerable attention to urban natural history and to the question of how best to make use of open space within the city. Research has ranged from appraisals of entire urban areas, to surveys of the royal parks, to studies of the suburban back garden. The results, at first surprising, are now familiar: foxes and badgers in suburban London, hawks and herons nesting in city centres, rare migratory birds on the reservoirs of the Thames Valley. The city, it is generally agreed, has much to offer the naturalist and could offer more. In all this, surprisingly little has been said about the urban cemetery, and little thought has been given to its potential as a resource for natural history and nature conservation within built-up areas.

Quite simply, nineteenth-century urban cemeteries, however much their untended condition may pose problems to those anxious for the tidy management of open space, are natural refuges for birds, insects and plants in a way that public parks could never be. The natural overgrowth that quickly occurs in cemeteries where maintenance has been reduced or abandoned, and the relative freedom from disturbance that is characteristic of disuse, are premier requirements for a nature conservation area, whether the focus of interest be fungi or insects, treecreepers or hedgehogs. Such areas can be a major resource for the local and, indeed, the wider community. At present, cemetery management policies that operate upon narrow definitions of economy and efficiency pay little heed to this potential: wholesale clearance, the burning off of vegetation, the unthinking use of herbicides, will ruin a natural refuge and can destroy wildlife habitats that have taken years to establish.

The sections that follow are based on the contributions of four naturalists concerned with different aspects of cemetery natural history: geology, by Eric Robinson; molluscs, by Michael P. Kearney; insects, by Eric Robinson and Mark Hanson; birds, by Tom Slack. The subjects discussed are representative, and must stand for many that could have been chosen. Each section has a different focus, but all emphasize the interdependence of setting, flora and fauna, and stress the sensitivity of that interdependence to change. All four offer some advice on conservation and management with regard to their particular subjects, and some indication of how a conservation programme can work is given in the outline case history that follows.

Geology

While there may be geological interest in the site of a cemetery, the principal focus of attention for the geologist-naturalist must be the monuments themselves: the rock type used, the stone carving and mason-work, and the weathering characteristics of the stone, all involve issues of fundamental geological importance.

All three principal classes of rock are found in monuments: sedimentary, which consists of consolidated sediments originally deposited by wind or water; igneous, which is formed from melts within the earth's crust; and metamorphic, which are rocks of any original form that have undergone change as a result of heat or pressure.

Before – and, indeed, during – the nineteenth century, the use of one type or another was often determined by local occurrence. In the case of London or other large city cemeteries, however, it is diversity rather than uniformity that is the rule. This diversity exemplifies the prodigious growth of the masonry trade in the nineteenth century, and is a direct consequence of the revolution in transport that is at the centre of Victorian social and cultural development. The memorial slabs and tablets of the earlier years of the century were usually of sandstone or white Portland Stone. Portland, quarried on the Dorset coast, was traditionally transported by sea, and large tonnages continued to be moved in this way throughout the mid nineteenth century. But the easier internal movement of materials that resulted firstly from the growth of canal transport and secondly from the spread of the railway network, ensured a steady expansion in the range of available stones. Mid-Victorian masons produced columns, pedestals and mausolea in marbles, gneiss, serpentine, and particularly, polished granites. From the 1850s, pink Petershead granite was used with increasing frequency, and the dark grey granite of Aberdeen more and more widely employed; less familiarly, the pink, large-crystalled Shap granite from Westmorland began to appear. A little later in the century foreign stones began to be imported for use in cemetery memorials: white marble from Carrara – often something of a disaster in the English climate – and the black or deep red granites of Scandinavia. This process continued into the early years of the twentieth century, when cheap sea freighting and the development of stone-working industries in other countries resulted in an almost bewildering increase in the range of rock types available for monumental masonry. All major cemeteries contain a number of 'exotics' which are likely to test the experience of any geologist.

Aside from its aesthetic qualities, carving and mason-work can be informative about the qualities of the stone itself. Not all rock types with a good or tolerable reputation as building stone are similarly successful for monuments. When dressed into thin slabs, or cut across natural bedding in order to exploit contrasts of colour or texture, some stones can fail dramatically. Strongly bedded sandstones, erected vertically, can, with weathering, open up like the pages of a book. In other stones, the physical impact of cutting an inscription can be enough to start destructive flaws. Such failures are relatively rare, however, the craft of the mason being largely judged by the durability of the memorials he made. Indeed, it was the quest for such durability that led to some of the geologically most interesting craft practices. High among these is the perfecting of polishing techniques in the 1860s, producing the mirror-smooth surfaces of granite memorials – surfaces which defy weathering and pollution. Such polished surfaces make the urban cemetery an open-air museum of practical geology, perfectly revealing mineralogy and textural characteristics. What can be seen only indifferently in specimens one might hammer from a natural outcrop, can be fully appreciated on the polished surfaces of a headstone or pedestal. The identification of constituent minerals and the gradations of texture in the stone, important to the petrologist in the classification of rocks, allows considerable refinement in taxonomy: thus, the stone used in a memorial may be recognized not just as 'granite' – the trade name for almost anything that will take a polish – but as types as specific as Larvikite, Adamellite or Gabbro.

Of the three aspects of the geology of cemeteries mentioned above, weathering is possibly the most important scientifically, because it is a process that is difficult to investigate purely on the basis of laboratory experiment. Faced with the question of how good or how durable a particular stone might be, it is not easy to set up laboratory tests which will fully simulate the different processes of natural weathering. Such processes in nature, though dynamic, are slow-acting. Cemeteries can provide what laboratories cannot: the test units are relatively large scale and give evidence of the weathering effects of micro-climate at different heights above ground level and on surfaces both exposed to and sheltered from prevailing wind and rain. Moreover, because memorials are precisely dated, comparative rates of decay can be accurately assessed. All in all, cemeteries can provide us with information about the durability of materials that is difficult to obtain elsewhere and that has direct relevance to our contemporary built environment.

If we are to get the most from the geology of cemeteries, some measure of conservation is necessary. The geologically most interesting of the stone memorials should be kept clear of excessive plant growth, particularly ivy, which has dangerously penetrative roots. It may be desirable to wash monuments from time to time in order to remove surface grime, but this is an operation that needs care and advice: intensive washing can destroy the surface of the stone itself. Elaborate tombs and composite structures inevitably will need repointing over the years: here again, care and advice is needed for the wrong mortar mix can adversely affect the stone. Most difficult of all, perhaps, are decisions about the treatment of decay, and the instinct to clear up what seems an unsightly mess may need to be consciously resisted. As was argued earlier, the processes of weathering are of considerable intrinsic interest, and the appearance of age is, after all, part of the identity of a monument. What is more, decaying stone may well provide the environmental niche vital to a particular plant or an insect community. As is often the case, good conservation practice may be a matter of balancing and reconciling different objectives.

Molluscs

The important needs of most land molluscs – snails and slugs – are lime, a moderate degree of moisture, shelter and relative freedom from human disturbance. Old graveyards and cemeteries can provide a combination of all these requirements and are thus among the most favourable habitats for molluscs. In many intensively farmed areas such as the Midlands or East Anglia, heavily cropped and sprayed to the detriment of molluscan life, churchyards – if not too obsessively tidied up in recent years – have become important refuges. When such regions were investigated for the recently completed national survey of molluscan species, churchyards were often the first places selected for study. There is no doubt that many nineteenth-century urban cemeteries provide similar refuges and are similarly rich, although, with the exception of Highgate – which was the subject of a molluscan survey after a visit by the Conchological Society in 1972 – little detailed information has yet been compiled. Broadly speaking, however, a neglected urban cemetery develops a characteristic mosaic of different habitats, each with its own population of slugs and snails: grassy banks, invasive woodland, ivy-covered walls, moist nooks and crannies of all kinds, and, of course, the weathered surfaces of the tombs and gravestones themselves. In addition, the weathering of monuments made from calcareous rocks – limestones and, to a lesser extent, marbles and calcareous sandstones – together with the old lime-based mortars and plasters, may help to enrich the molluscan fauna in places where the natural geology provides only neutral-to-acid soils.

This effect, as well as the range of species that can be expected in urban cemeteries, is well illustrated at Highgate Cemetery. There, despite the fact that the soil, based on the London Clay and Claygate Beds, is naturally poor in lime, a number of lime-loving species occur, such as the Kentish Snail, *Monachia cantiana*, and the tiny grass snails, *Vallonia costata* and *Vallonia pulchella*. Rather surprisingly, none of the species which habitually feed on vertical rock surfaces and which one might expect to find – like the so-called Door Snails of the family *Clausillidae* – occur at Highgate. This is probably the result of atmospheric pollution which causes grimy deposits on suitable surfaces in the cemetery and a consequent poverty of lichen and algae. Despite such absences, however, a total of some twenty-two species of molluscs are found at Highgate, comprising thirteen species of snails and nine of slugs – the latter including the local tree slug, *Limax marginatus*, and the rare *Arion owenii*, for which Highgate remains the only known site in the London area. There is no doubt that Highgate Cemetery, with its thick foliation and mixed vegetation, now supports a much richer molluscan fauna than one would expect to find on such a site, on the edge of Hampstead Heath, in its 'natural' state.

Highgate clearly has an excellent variety of ecological niches favourable to molluscs, and this must be characteristic of other urban cemeteries with a similar history. It is likely, however, that conditions at Highgate are now near their optimum and are in danger of deteriorating. Intrusive sycamore woodland, which produces heavy shading with a relatively impoverished flora and invertebrate fauna, threatens to cover much of the site. It must be stressed that a cemetery in such a state of growth should not be totally cleared and turned over to being trimly maintained like a municipal park. Ecologically, such a strategy would destroy it. On the other hand, merely abandoning a cemetery to enveloping growth is likely, in the end, to be just as biologically detrimental. In order to ensure conditions favourable to molluscs – and, indeed, to many other groups – management policy should aim to promote ecological diversity. In practice, this would mean combining a certain degree of clearance – the removal of sycamore saplings for example – with some measure of controlled neglect – allowing the field layer in some parts of the cemetery to grow wild, for instance. Such a policy should be integral to the management of an urban cemetery, and there is no reason why it should conflict with the controlled maintenance of cemetery landscape and the conservation of its monuments and buildings.

Insects

The idea that disused cemeteries could be used for the conservation of insects is, in all probability, a far less immediately attractive proposition than similar plans to encourage birds or wild flowers. So it is, perhaps, worth making the otherwise obvious point that the category of insects includes much of our most beautiful and most-loved fauna – the butterflies and moths, the different varieties of bees – as well as the ostensibly less appealing beetles, wasps and ants. Moreover, and regardless of personal preference, it has become increasingly apparent in recent years that the maintenance of the insect population is essential to the ecological balance of any environment. Without insects, the flowers and birds that are the most obvious candidates for conservation simply could not exist. Happily, an understanding of this interdependence is generally increasing. One example of this is the effort now made by many town gardeners to grow flowering plants expressly to encourage butterflies, a technique that has been dubbed 'butterfly gardening'.

Mature urban cemeteries can naturally provide the kinds of habitat that such individual efforts are directed towards promoting. The broken soil, enriched with lime-wash from headstones and mortar, supports many fragrant shrubs and scented flowers attractive to insects. Butterflies, for example, will be more strongly drawn by nettles, lilacs, and the spreading buddleias which regenerate so freely, than by any of the annuals which, at first, we might be inclined to plant on their behalf. Buddleia in particular – sometimes called the 'butterfly bush' – is a prime attraction to the Red Admiral, the Peacock and the Large and Small Tortoiseshell. Other equally colourful butterflies – the various Skippers, the Meadow Brown, the Small Heath, and, if there are copses of trees, the Speckled Wood – need only freely growing grasses to maintain them through the caterpillar stage to their adult form, when they too become dependent on nectar-providing flowers. Other plants are more specifically associated with individual species: thus, to take one example out of many, the birdsfoot trefoil is the food plant for the caterpillars both of the Common Blue Butterfly and of the Black and Red Burnet Moths. Like butterflies and moths, bees also are attracted by fragrantly scented flowers, by foxgloves and thistles, by herbs like thyme and lavender, by shrubs like the many varieties of cotoneaster: all of these are common in cemeteries, either growing there naturally or introduced as part of the planting. In addition, cemeteries can provide excellent nesting sites for honey-bees and bumble-bees in the crevices and cavities of walls and of the larger monuments. Many more examples of the endlessly varied insect life to be found in urban cemeteries could be given: from the different species of beetle scavenging through the organic debris of the soil to create the rich humus which will sustain further growth, to the ants and millipedes flourishing in the rotting wood of fallen branches. But, this introduction having been given, it is instructive to turn to a more detailed and more particular record, based upon Mark Hanson's work in the churchyard of St Mary Magdalene, East Ham, now managed as a local nature reserve by the Passmore Edwards Museum of Stratford, East London. The pattern of fauna and natural regeneration in this churchyard can be regarded as one which would occur in any urban burial ground or cemetery passing out of active use.

The churchyard, long established though now closed, consists mainly of rough grassland dominated by false oat-grass *Arrhenatherum elatius*, but including other plants such as fireweed *Epilobium angustifolium*, creeping thistle *Cirsium arvense*, and convolvulus *Calystegia* sp. There are small areas of secondary woodland which comprise mainly sycamore *Acer pseudoplantanus*, but with elder *Sambucas nigra*, hawthorn *Crataegus monogyna*, and suckering elm, *Ulmus* sp., also substantially present.

The main habitat is obviously rough grassland, and the majority of the insects recorded are those typical of this setting, among them the uncommon black-winged robber fly *Dioctria atricapilla*, the hover fly *Chrysoltoxum bicinictum*, the common yellow empid *Empis trigramma*, and the grass-stem mining flies *Opomyza germinationis* and *Geomyza balachowskyii*. Of special interest are two species of fly that have a predominantly coastal distribution in Essex, the hover-fly *Tropidia scita* and the distinctive banded-wing fly *Ceroxys urticae*. Both species would be found more normally in the grassland about the dykes and sea-walls of Essex; their presence in a marginal habitat like St Mary's probably indicates the local destruction of their true habitat, thus providing a further instance of the way urban cemeteries can act as refuges. Also interesting in this context is the presence, in some numbers, of Roesels bush-cricket *Merioptera roesellii* and the lesser marsh grasshopper *Chorthippus albomarginatus* – again, two species more usually found in coastal areas, the bush cricket being largely confined to the Thames Estuary. Although grassland predominates, other parts of St Mary's offer a variety of habitats: several species of picture-winged flies – particularly *Tephritidae Trypeta zoe* – are found in association with the ragworts and thistles, and soldier-flies breed in the decaying stumps of the churchyard elms; bees nest in the comparative safety of the secondary woodland, while wasps have been found nesting in a cavity in a brick wall. All in all, no less than 113 species of insect have been recorded in St Mary's churchyard – a striking testimony to its importance as a nature reserve and refuge.

Birds

One of the surprising facts about towns and cities is that a large variety of birds manage to adapt to living on close terms with people and their everyday activities. Urban cemeteries have a crucial part to play in this, a role more important than public parks and similar open spaces which offer less cover and protection. Cemeteries, as they pass out of use, meet most of the requirements of bird populations: they provide food and water; somewhere to roost and nest; access to shallow pools or dry soil for bathing; and, finally, freedom from undue disturbance. If these characteristics were fostered and developed, which could be done with little difficulty or expense, a major contribution would be made to the conservation of birds in the heart of the city.

The food needs of birds can be met by the wild grasses, nettles, and the wide range of weeds which grow naturally as cemeteries pass into disuse. Often, birds will prosper on the enriched insect life which, in its turn, has developed during the process. Feeding can be further extended by the planting of certain berry- or fruit-bearing shrubs. These include the various species of cotoneaster, rowan, holly, flowering currant, snowberry and honeysuckle. In any properly worked-out conservation programme, such planting would need to take account of the original character of the planting in the cemetery, but it is easy to see how the introduction of such shrubs could be a means of providing new colour and variety of texture, as well as directly benefiting the bird population. Water is especially important to birds: in an environment like a cemetery – part natural, part man made – the principal source would, of course, be rainfall. Without much difficulty, this could be supplemented by artificial means: few cemeteries have ornamental ponds or basins – though these are obviously worth preserving where they do occur – but shallow basins set into the ground, and even conventional pedestal bird-baths, help maintain the supply of water. More ambitiously, the introduction of small ponds is always worth considering: even the smallest pond benefits a wide range of wild life, attracting, in the case of birds, stream and riverbank species as well as interesting migrants.

Shelter, including nesting places, would be provided by the cemetery shrubs and trees, particularly if planting was designed to conserve copse thickets where they already existed, or to introduce them strategically if not. The ledges and crevices of the larger free-standing tombs also provide nest space. Although ivy and creepers will need to be carefully controlled in order to protect buildings and monuments, they offer good cover for nesting by smaller birds. Boundary walls or railings which have become ivy-clad could very well be left to fulfil this need where such cover is being cleared elsewhere in the cemetery. For a combination of shelter and food, pedunculate oak or the evergreen holm oak are excellent choices for new planting, free from the problems associated with the too vigorously spreading sycamores, birches or chestnuts. Finally, the provision of nesting boxes should be seriously considered, not only for the tits and robins, but also for the larger birds, like owls and kestrels, which have suffered from the loss of elms on town sites in recent years.

The bird population of Abney Park Cemetery in north London has been closely studied in recent years: the results that have emerged usefully indicate the range of species that might be expected in other large urban cemeteries that have become partly overgrown. Abney Park, famous for its Victorian arboretum, is now generally quite heavily wooded; as yet, no attempt has been made to introduce management techniques, such as those outlined above, specifically designed to benefit birds, so the species found there have been attracted simply by the cemetery as it is. In the *Guide to Abney Park Cemetery*, Dr Alan Hunt has summarized the current status of the bird population, and one cannot do better than quote from his account.

Abney Park contains very large populations throughout its length and breadth of the common woodland and garden species (Blackbird, Song Thrush, Dunnock, Wren and Robin). The varied areas and habitats within the cemetery also attract different groups of birds. The shrubs and leafy glades attract warblers; Willow Warblers, Blackcaps, Chiffchaff, Spotted Flycatchers and occasionally Whitethroats return each spring from Southern Europe and Africa. The dense tree canopy provides nesting sites for Mistle Thrush, Stock Dove, Woodpigeon, Jay, Magpie and Carrion Crow, while old mature trunks provide sites for hole-nesting species. Blue Tits and Great Tits are abundant; Coal Tits have bred and Starlings inhabit almost every Poplar tree. The presence of the Great Spotted Woodpecker is a truly woodland feature and the regular attendance of hooting Tawny Owls lends an aptly eerie quality to the cemetery's nocturnal aspect. The finches are represented by Greenfinch, Goldfinch and the striking but shy Bullfinch. In summer large numbers of Swifts and House Martins and, less frequently, Swallows hunt insects overhead and around the spire of the chapel. Kestrel also hunt for prey in and around the cemetery ... [which] ... also provides an important feeding area in winter, because being in such a built-up area it is warmer than the countryside outside London. In winter the resident birds are joined by Chaffinch, Linnet and Redpoll; the harder the weather the more important is the protected cemetery. In the hard winter of 1978–79 the uncommon Woodcock was recorded.

Abney Park is the most important centre for bird life in the Borough of Hackney, and, indeed, the surrounding boroughs. There is every reason to believe that similar wealth could be found in other urban cemeteries, and that the range of species could be increased by deliberate management. Bird watching and the recording of species has grown to be a national pastime in Britain, now sustained and promoted by a considerable organization of clubs and societies, all keenly interested in new ornithological ventures. In these circumstances, urban cemeteries in the process of being conserved or placed in trust can expect not only useful advice on management and on the potential of sites as nature reserves, but also practical assistance.

The Burial-Ground as Nature Reserve: a Case History

As will be gathered from the preceding sections, naturalists see the conservation of urban cemeteries as a way of establishing wildlife reserves in cities. Such reserves need not involve undue enclosure or restriction of public access. To see a flexible management approach in action and to learn what benefits can result from a well-designed scheme, we will return to St Mary Magdalene churchyard in east London, where the Passmore Edwards Museum operates an Educational Nature Reserve for the London Borough of Newnham. The work and aims of the reserve are here described by Colin Plant, Assistant Curator of the Museum.

The churchyard is situated in what at first glance must seem a most unsuitable spot for a nature reserve. Bounded as it is on the east by houses and on the west by the noisy and dirty North Circular Road, with the main A13 road to the south and yet another busy local road along the northern limit, the casual observer could be forgiven for dismissing the idea as simply impractical. The churchyard remains, however, a 9 acre oasis of green in an area of solid urban development, an area with a considerable list of flora and fauna, accessible to schools and the local community. Apart from the flowers and trees, there is a great variety of animal life. Several species of ants, woodlice, spiders, snails and hover-flies occur, together with reptiles, mammals and a tally of breeding birds that includes the spotted flycatcher. Recording and listing the flora and fauna has been a major task for a number of naturalists and it is a process which continues. Long term plans have been drawn up, including the building of an information and study centre. But any plans must be flexible: this was demonstrated when changes became necessary after breeding colonies of bush-crickets were discovered in an area which had been designated for tree-planting. An essential part of all plans, however, is the development of a pond for aquatic nature study classes. Ideally, it should be large enough to have at least one island, it should shelve from a shallow end with reed-beds to deeper waters where fish can safely develop, and should be big enough for school parties studying pond-life by collecting. An essential addition is a sound-proofed pond side observation hide – a vital part of natural history teaching too often neglected.

Paths planned about the reserve are carefully routed to cause minimum disturbance, particularly those leading to the hide. Helpful here is the planting of willows along the paths. These not only provide screening but, in the future, will be the material for coppicing and woodcraft activities planned for older children. At the same time, care will be taken in planting so as to enhance rather than diminish potential for research. This could include planting around a mercury vapour moth trap, arranged in such a way that light would penetrate all the available habitats, at the same time as the trees screened the reserve from the nearby glare of the street lights. Similarly, the planting of a mixed thorn hedge could create a barrier against litter, provide nesting cover for birds, and allow for the siting of mist nets for bird ringing. Both the moth trap and the bird nets would be important for educational activities and for research programmes. St Mary Magdalene continues to serve as a place of worship and it is interesting to note that there has been the fullest cooperation from the church authorities and from the congregation in setting up the reserve. Finally, with regard to the memorials, the Archaeology and Local History section of the Museum and the East London Family History Society have undertaken the systematic recording of all inscriptions.

A vital aspect of this east London scheme is its relationship to local community needs, in particular to those of local schools. The emphasis in natural history teaching today is such that opportunities to carry out practical field work exercises are important. It helps if such field work can be undertaken without needing to travel too great a distance from the school. Although not all plans for urban cemeteries need involve such a role, and it may be inappropriate for some sites, links with local education are of considerable importance and always worth exploring. After all, the great urban cemeteries of the nineteenth century should not be the sole province of the specialist historian or naturalist; they are a resource for the whole community. Indeed, only the concern and sympathetic interest of the community at large can ensure their long-term survival. That the survival of the Victorian cemetery is threatened cannot be doubted. Indeed, many major cemeteries, with all their historical value, all their aesthetic interest and variety, all their actual and potential importance for wildlife and the environment, have already been destroyed.

The Destruction of the Cemetery

The problems posed by historic cemeteries are a direct result of their economic decline and of the consequent financial difficulties facing the authorities responsible for their management. Dwindling resources have led to the neglect of those parts of cemeteries no longer used for interments – often, of course, those parts of the greatest historical and artistic interest. Reductions in cemetery staff and increasing costs generally have meant that any serious attempt to continue regular maintenance of the older sections of a cemetery have been abandoned. As we have just seen, the overgrown cemetery can become a major habitat for wildlife: but, as has also been stressed, mere abandonment of management leads ultimately to an impoverishment of the ecology of the cemetery. From the historical and architectural point of view, total neglect is disastrous. Memorials become overgrown; vaults, mausolea and the larger monuments become delapidated; historic landscaping and layout is lost, and original planting swamped by intrusive vegetation; cemetery buildings and boundary walls begin to crumble. With neglect, inevitably, comes vandalism and even downright pillage. Ordinary visitors to the cemetery, should they venture beyond those sections that are still in use, cannot penetrate areas that often look little more than an overgrown muddle. When all or part of a cemetery has been abandoned, where nobody seems to care, destruction can go on unchecked: monuments are smashed, tombs broken open, buildings burnt out. Hugh Meller's eloquent and distressing account of the devastation that befell Nunhead at the end of the 1960s may stand for similar, if less extreme, cases throughout the country.

> It was decided to close the cemetery. By then the nonconformist chapel had been demolished and the remaining buildings were in a shocking state. The Anglican chapel had been burnt out by vandals, the lodges were in ruins and the vaults and catacombs plundered for their lead and jewellery. Two exceptional monuments had been damaged, a bronze figure from the grave of a boy scout had been stolen and the Romanesque style Doulton terra cotta mausoleum of the Stearne family had been invaded. Wild stories of black magic rituals appeared in newspapers and a white robed ghost had been reported hovering among the graves.

Only the trees and undergrowth flourished, but in an unchecked rampage.

In varying forms, these are the components of the crisis that still confronts cemetery authorities. More usually, the problems, though deriving from the same complex of factors, are less dramatic and less widespread than those at Nunhead. Individual monuments may have seriously decayed, and even become dangerous; parts of the cemetery may be growing wild; ground may be required for new interments. Most pervasive of all is the seemingly intractable difficulty of financing maintenance. While acknowledging the extent of the difficulties, it is profoundly ironic that the most frequent response of the authorities has merely compounded the threat to historic cemeteries. Throughout the country, a supposed solution to neglect, lack of maintenance, and vandalized buildings and monuments, has been the clearance of cemeteries, with monuments removed wholesale, grave mounds levelled, and, eventually, the whole area put down to grass.

In the nineteenth century, the closure and subsequent clearance of urban burial grounds and churchyards was one consequence of the Burials Acts of the 1850s: in some places the headstones were used for flagstone paving; elsewhere – as at St Luke's, Chelsea, and the Naval Cemetery at Chatham – the gravestones were marshalled in uniform ranks around the perimeter walls. Most closed churchyards in London, however, were simply left. A few, seven in all by 1877, were cleared and laid out as public gardens, most notably the large churchyard of St George in the East. In 1877, the Metropolitan Open Spaces Act eased the way for turning the closed London burial grounds into places of public 'exercise and recreation'; further provision was made in an amending Act of 1881, and in the Disused Burial Grounds Act of 1884; in 1887 the terms of the Metropolitan Acts were extended to the rest of England and Wales. Meanwhile, in 1882, Lord Brabazon, later the Earl of Meath, founded the Metropolitan Public Gardens Association, committed to providing more public open space in London. The Association, along with the National Health Society, directed its efforts particularly towards the old burial grounds: between 1885 and 1895 it was responsible for clearing thirty London churchyards and converting them to public gardens. By what seemed a natural progression, the Association began to think about the London cemeteries as well, particularly with its success in clearing and laying out Victoria Park Cemetery in 1893. As was discussed earlier, Victoria Park was an exploitative enterprise, congested and unseemly; closed by the late 1880s, its chapel, such as it was, had been looted for building materials, its monuments smashed, and its grounds become the haunt of thieves and prostitutes. Its conversion into Meath Gardens was the renewal and reuse of what was otherwise an urban wasteland. But the Association, in its zeal, saw Victoria Park as little different from the other cemeteries of the metropolis. In *The London Burial Grounds*, published in 1896, Mrs Basil Holmes, the wife of the Secretary of the MPGA, described the Association's activities in terms of a moral crusade.

> There are many sad sights in London, but to me there are few so sad as one of these huge graveyards. Not that the idea of the numbers of dead beneath the soil produces any thought of melancholy, but I feel inclined to exclaim with the disciples, 'To what purpose is this waste?' Can there be any more profitless mode of throwing away money than by erecting costly tombstones? They are of no use to the departed, and they are grievous burdens laid on the shoulders of succeeding generations. The only people who profit by them are a few marble and granite merchants, and a few monumental masons – and they might be better employed. The whole funeral system is an extravagant imposition, and has been for years.

Such views reflect the changing attitudes of the turn of the century. Reaction against earlier funerary practices was setting in, partly under the influence of American planning which favoured spacious lawn cemeteries, and Mrs Holmes was a leading advocate for 'reformed funerals', cremation, and burial reform generally. Mrs Holmes' ideas are part of the social history of her time: unfortunately, they have come to dominate much subsequent thinking about the treatment of cemeteries. Underlying such views, then as now, is the conviction that Victorian and Edwardian cemetery art and design do not matter, a conviction expressing itself at best as indifference and at worst – witness the Batley clergyman quoted earlier – as downright hostility. Yet to adopt the arguments advanced by Mrs Holmes now is, to say the least, anachronistic. Her views, whatever their merits or demerits, belong to the historical context of the debate in which she took part: they are as irrelevant to the treatment of historic cemeteries *now* as are the pronouncements of sixteenth-century iconoclasts to the present-day conservation of medieval cathedrals. Yet crusading destructiveness in the manner of the MPGA, clearing cemeteries wholesale and turning them over to grass, continues apace.

The fate of the Northampton General Cemetery is representative. Opened by a private company in 1847, the grounds were laid out and planted by Robert Marnock, the distinguished horticulturalist and landscape gardener responsible, among much else, for Regent's Park Botanical Garden. A local architect designed a chapel in the Norman style and a little picturesque lodge. Now all this has largely gone. Northampton Borough Council has cleared a great number of the memorials, laying down open lawns instead. The lodge has been destroyed and its modern replacement, now disused, vandalized. The chapel was demolished in 1982 and the site levelled. Grass grows over the paths and roadways; surviving monuments stand isolated or in random groups; Marnock's planned layout, visually essential here as it is in any Victorian cemetery, is being rapidly lost. Even the cemetery gates have been carted off. Instead of a major example of Victorian cemetery landscaping and design, Northampton has acquired a bleakly uniform municipal park, devoid of character or visual distinction.

Since the Second World War, and more particularly over the last twenty five years, the kind of destruction wrought at Northampton has been meted out to cemeteries all over England. In London the treatment of the joint stock cemeteries has been particularly brutal: at Norwood, with the exception of the gateway, all Tite's buildings have gone, many monuments have been detroyed and large tracts of ground cleared of headstones; the lodges and chapels of Tower Hamlets, designed by Wyatt and Brandon, have been demolished and much of the cemetery cleared; the great octagonal chapel of Nunhead is a burnt-out shell, and all memorials have been removed from the larger part of the cemetery; Hosking's chapel at Abney Park has been gutted; many of the monuments at Brompton have been weeded-out. Many other London cemeteries have fared as badly: in 1966 the little cemetery of Barnes Common, established by the Church of England in 1854, was acquired by the Borough of Richmond who laid waste to it, razing chapel, lodge and boundary railings as if to set an example to the local vandals, who proceeded to smash most of what was left; the three chapels of Camberwell Cemetery, including two by Gilbert Scott, were demolished in the 1930s and 1940s, and substantial areas have been ruthlessly cleared of monuments more recently; Chingford Mount Cemetery, set up in 1884 by the Abney Park Cemetery Company, was abandoned by its owners in the early 1970s, after which the lodges and chapels were burnt out by vandals; at Fulham Cemetery, which dates from 1865, Hammersmith Council have progressively removed all monuments more than fifty years old and are turning the grounds over to open lawn; even the mighty City of London Cemetery, well-kept as it is, has been injured by selective, but extensive clearance.

In Birmingham, Charles Edge's fine Doric chapel in Key Hill Cemetery was demolished in 1966; it had managed to survive a few years longer than the chapel and cloister range of Warstone Lane Cemetery, which went in the 1950s and which had formed, soaring above the two-tier catacomb circle, one of the most astonishing landscape features in any English cemetery. In Witton Cemetery, north of the centre of Birmingham, the grand principal avenue, linking the two chapels and forming the core of the cemetery's layout, has been spoiled by the demolition of the nonconformist chapel. Further north again, Wolverhampton General Cemetery, opened in 1850, has had its chapels demolished and all but a handful of its older memorials destroyed. In Manchester's Harpurhey Cemetery, the important Greek Revival lodge and chapel of 1837 were knocked down by the City Council in the early 1960s, as was the cemetery's Gothic chapel of 1857. At Philips Park, in the same city, only one of the three original chapels now survives; this is better than has been managed at Weaste Cemetery, laid out on the west of the Manchester conurbation in 1857, where Salford Council has demolished all four of its chapels. In Liverpool Low Hill has disappeared beneath a ring road and a clearance programme, supposedly selective, has stripped St James's of much of its character. In Bradford's Undercliffe Cemetery, William Gay's pretty lodges of 1854 and the 1878 chapels by Lockwood and Mawson have all been demolished, thus permanently damaging one of England's most dramatic cemeteries. Beckett Street, or Burmantofts Cemetery, in nearby Leeds, has retained its lodges, built in 1880, but its two chapels, which dated from the

St James's Cemetery, Liverpool, in 1988, cleared of its monuments and historic planting in the 1960s.

Wellington Cemetery, Somerset, in 1988, the chapels overlooking the Blackdown Hills replaced by a municipal shelter in 1984.

establishment of the cemetery in 1845, were flattened in the 1960s. Up in Middlesbrough, that prodigy of Victorian urban growth, the city's principal cemetery, Linthorpe, lost the last of its chapels as recently as 1987. And so the catalogue continues.

Outside the cities and major towns the saga of destruction has been much the same. Some examples from the South West are representative. At Taunton, St Mary's Cemetery, its 14 acres laid out on the western edge of the town in 1854, now retains only some grand conifers, a lodge, and an imposingly scaled entrance arch: the chapels have been knocked down and the arch leads to an expanse of desolate grass swept clear of headstones and monuments, the remnants of which were awaiting removal in the last months of 1988. Equally recent has been the destruction of Wellington Cemetery, also in Somerset: almost all its nineteenth-century memorials have gone and its paired chapels, carefully sited on a viewing platform that looks over the whole sweep of the Blackdown Hills, were demolished in the mid-1980s, to be superseded by a kind of funerary bus shelter. In Devon, the Burial Board cemetery at Tiverton has lost one of its two neo-Norman chapels and, like both Barnstaple and Axminster, also of the 1850s, has suffered from partial clearance. At South Molton, the town cemetery still retains its pair of good Decorated chapels, dating from 1857, and its lodge of 1882, but they stand in a bleak rectangle of grass from which all but a few memorials have been erased. At Ilfracombe, the little cemetery founded south of the town in 1855 by members of the Church of England, 'in token of their love for their Christian brethren of all denominations and for their use for ever', is now totally overgrown, its gates smashed, its monuments sunk in woodland, its well managed Perpendicular chapel semi-derelict and doing service as a hen-house. Almost as desolate is the early 1840s nonconformist cemetery of Launceston, over the border in Cornwall: largely overgrown, with monuments subsided and smashed, it does occasional service as a rubbish tip. Further west, Camborne Cemetery of 1889, has been swept clear of its Victorian and Edwardian monuments and the eccentric little chapel – the cemetery's sole remaining visual pleasure – now looks out over a flat and treeless lawn gradually filling with regimented ranks of mean headstones. In Truro Cemetery, the earliest in Cornwall, superbly positioned on a steep site south of the town with views down over Pearson's cathedral, all memorials more than fifty years old have gone, and piles of uprooted headstones litter the margins of the cemetery.

Braunton Road Cemetery, Ilfracombe, Devon, in 1988, its derelict chapel in use as a hen-house.

The extent of the destruction that has overtaken Britain's historic cemeteries since the Second World War is a national disgrace, a testimony to the philistinism and indifference of our culture. Simple neglect has been damaging enough, but the processes of decay are gradual. By contrast, the strategies adopted to deal with neglected and overgrown cemeteries have been disastrous. Again and again, clearance, total or partial, has been opted for: it is a wholly unacceptable response to the problems of managing a historic cemetery. It is, indeed, precisely equivalent to the demolition of a historic building; like demolition, it can take place quickly and is equally irreversible. The overt reasons for adopting such a scheme are almost always financial – a desire to avoid the difficulties and expense of continuing upkeep and to ensure cheap and easy maintenance of the site in the future. Often such reasons are a plausible mask for ignorance or even hostility. Whatever the economic arguments, 'lawn conversion' is a management strategy that lays waste what it should be maintaining – a consummation that makes ironic nonsense of the whole idea of management. Buildings of considerable architectural value are destroyed and the products of a great and inventive tradition of monumental art are lost: even where lodges, chapels and the grander memorials are preserved they are robbed of their context and, with it, a major part of their significance. The qualities of original landscape and layout are obscured, or lost altogether to the gang mower and the open lawn. The indiscriminate clearance of vegetation not only depletes the rich variety of plants that can grow in a mature cemetery, but also destroys the habitat of many forms of wildlife that find refuge there. The nineteenth-century cemetery, whether on the scale of Kensal Green and the Glasgow Necropolis, or comprising a couple of quiet acres on the edge of a country town, is an irreplaceable part of our social history. A historic cemetery can only be understood in its entirety, and with all the evidence of its development over the years intact. To ensure this cemeteries need management: yet, as we have seen, the management policies currently pursued by cemetery authorities have produced, all too often, not the preservation of our common past but its destruction in the interests of financial expediency. Though much has gone, much still remains; but the problems of neglect, lack of maintenance and vandalism are growing. Unless there is a fundamental change of attitude and approach, and, it is to be hoped, a change in the law, the solution for the difficulties faced by many cemeteries inevitably will be clearance. If that happens on the kind of scale that the evidence of the last few decades suggests, then the loss will be irrecoverable.

Yet there are signs of a public reaction against the way in which historic cemeteries have come to be treated. The National Association of Master Masons, alarmed by the fact that the market for memorials has contracted by two-thirds since 1945, has supported the creation of the Memorials Advisory Bureau in an attempt to stimulate demand for monumental masonry. The Bureau, in its turn, has increasingly come to associate itself with cemetery conservation and to oppose wholesale clearance. The accelerated resurvey of historic buildings undertaken by the Department of the Environment between 1984 and 1987 has resulted in the statutory protection of significantly more cemetery buildings and structures. Most important, local voluntary groups have been set up in order to protect and conserve particular cemeteries – usually the now derelict cemeteries originally established by private companies, whether still in private hands or taken over by local authorities. Whatever their success in specific cases, the existence of such groups suggests a growing concern for historic cemeteries and for their amenity potential. The context for such concern has been created by the general spread of architectural conservation over the last fifteen years, the greater professionalism and efficiency of conservation groups, the emergence of a heritage lobby and the consequent increase in media coverage. Of major importance also has been the growth of environmental conservation and the recognition by naturalists that urban cemeteries can form nature reserves and refuges. There have been a number of significantly different attempts to manage historic cemeteries, and the case histories that follow have been chosen to illustrate these varying approaches: landscape reconstruction and 'restoration' at Norwood; conversion to varied amenity functions at Nunhead and Tower Hamlets; ecological management at Highgate and Spring Bank; historical conservation at The Rosary and, prospectively, at Kensal Green. They reveal very different perceptions of the difficulties and the opportunities historic cemeteries present; they also show how certain strategies – adopted with the best of motives – can create fresh problems and even work against the interests of long term conservation.

Landscape 'Restoration': Norwood

Norwood Cemetery was laid out in 1837 by the South Metropolitan Cemetery Company. Its Gothic chapels, lodge, gates and boundary wall were designed by Sir William Tite, and the cemetery included an extensive catacomb beneath the Church of England chapel.

Norwood attracted a wealthy clientele. In consequence, as was noticed earlier, it contains – or contained – many monuments of the highest aesthetic quality, including memorials designed by Victorian architects of the first rank, men such as George Edmund Street, John Loughborough Pearson and William Burges. A crematorium was added to the cemetery's complement of buildings in 1915.

Signs of neglect were evident at Norwood as early as the first years of the present century. Its history in the fifty years following the First World War makes a depressing catalogue. Tite's lodge was the first building to go, demolished in 1936. During the Second World War both chapels suffered bomb damage: nothing serious was done to repair them and the nonconformist chapel was knocked down in 1955, followed by the Anglican chapel in 1960. On the site of the latter and shutting off the catacombs, a new crematorium, replacing that of 1915, was built: 'a squat ill-proportioned architectural disaster', to quote Hugh Meller, 'in pink brick with some terrible ironwork decoration'. Norwood was taken over by the London Borough of Lambeth in 1966. It was crowded with monuments in various states of subsidence and decay, mostly unvisited and largely unmaintained; the grounds were becoming unkempt and were partly overgrown. Rather than try to maintain the cemetery as well as could be afforded, Lambeth decided to embark on an ambitious programme aimed at reconstruction. The Victorian Society was consulted and gave its general support to a scheme for returning Norwood to something like its condition in the 1840s, with concentrated groups of tombs set off against clumps of deciduous trees.

Such a strategy was an error and the Victorian Society was certainly mistaken in supporting it. In the first place, Norwood was set up in what was then countryside but has since become a built-up and densely populated area. The cemetery developed with its surrounding district. As one of the staff at the cemetery was reported as saying in the early part of this century: 'soon after the grounds were opened people were applying for land to build on quite close to our barrier. They wanted to be near their dead.' The historical change in surroundings since the 1840s had altered the whole character of the cemetery. Secondly, the demolition of the lodge, the chapels, and the cloisters over the catacombs meant that all the major original buildings – so essential to the appearance of Norwood in the 1840s – had gone for good. Most important of all, the problems of deciding which monuments to keep and which to replace with lawn were insoluble.

The majority of the largest and individually most interesting monuments date from the later nineteenth century, with some from the early twentieth century as well. It was inevitable that these were among the ones most likely to be kept. At the same time, however, large numbers of more minor memorials were certain to go. The consequence of such a policy was to produce a complete imbalance in the surviving monuments, with the exceptional and extraordinary remaining at the expense of innumerable, far more representative memorials. Such disproportion highlights the extreme difficulty, if not impossibility, of deciding upon appropriate criteria for selective clearance. A historic cemetery must be thought of as an integrated entity, the accretive product of many decades of development: the clearance of individual areas or of certain sorts of monument, for whatever reasons, not only destroys part of what was otherwise whole, but also necessarily devalues the significance of what remains. Indeed, the nature of the relationship between individual tombs, or groups of tombs, and Norwood Cemetery as a whole, was not thought through adequately. Obviously, the status of monuments dating from the late nineteenth and early twentieth centuries in a landscape purporting to be of the 1840s is anomalous. Nor is this merely a pedantic point. The gradual filling of a cemetery over the years is itself an important factor in determining the size, location and design of later monuments. A 'restored' landscape destroys their proper context, whilst they make nonsense of the 'restored' landscape. In fact, large areas of Norwood have been cleared and turned over to lawn – and all, initially at least, under the guise of 'restoration'. This has led the Borough authorities to reuse the historic cemetery, despite the fact that Lambeth possesses an extensive cemetery, already cleared, in Tooting. Tiny, ugly monuments have been erected, contextually quite inappropriate and ruining, ironically enough, those very areas of Norwood that supposedly have been restored to their original or 'intended' condition.

All the present indications are that any attempt at a coherent, historically conscious policy towards the management of Norwood has been abandoned. In the early days of its ownership of the cemetery, Lambeth Council stressed its intention of carrying out repairs, acknowledged as urgent, to major memorials. There are few signs

Nunhead Cemetery, London, in 1988; overgrown memorials away from the main paths, and a vandalized monument on the principal carriage drive.

of this happening, and now not even the most basic work is being done to ensure that monuments survive. Thus – to take just one example – the famous Berens monument, designed by the younger Barry in 1858, and recognized in Lambeth's own paper on the cemetery as 'one of the finest High Victorian monuments in the country', is becoming a ruin, with a substantial sapling now growing through its broken roof. Meanwhile, apparently indiscriminate clearance continues to devastate more and more of the historic cemetery.

Even worse has been the appalling damage that Norwood has suffered at the hands of presumably unsupervised cemetery employees. With scandalous unconcern, scores of monuments in areas of the greatest historical interest have been systematically smashed. This reached a peak during the winter of 1982–3. Visitors to the cemetery discovered that dozens of vaults had been broken open, the ledger-stones covering them having been smashed or prised off. Coffins were exposed to view and, in at least one case, it was evident that the vaults had been entered and the coffins tampered with. In many instances, graves had been filled with smashed masonry from other tombs. In others, open graves had filled with water. Many monuments in perfect condition had been destroyed – sometimes, incredibly enough, by having had lumps of masonry hurled at them. Others were simply heaved over and abandoned. Sledgehammers, crowbars and other wrecking tools were lying about nearby. Despite complaints, no explanation of substance was offered.

The initial management policy at Norwood was wrongly conceived. In itself unworkable, it has been abandoned without any coherent policy as a replacement. Although the crude destructiveness of a few years back has now ceased, the legacy of Lambeth's reconstruction scheme has been the laying waste of large sections of the cemetery which were, with all their varied, crowded, subsiding and weathered monuments, the irreplaceable creation of decades. A new scheme of management for Norwood is desperately needed: without an unambiguous conservation policy, the long-term survival of what remains of the historic cemetery must be in jeopardy.

Conversion: Nunhead and Tower Hamlets

Nunhead Cemetery, in south London, provides the major example to date of a management policy aimed at changing the use of a historic cemetery in order to provide for a number of different communal purposes.

Nunhead was the sister cemetery to Highgate, north of the river, and was established in 1840 by the London Cemetery Company. The cemetery was laid out by James Bunning, later to become architect to the City of London; Thomas Little designed the octagonally planned Anglican chapel in Decorated Gothic, including a fine *porte-cochère*, and the simpler nonconformist chapel. Catacombs were also constructed. As was described earlier, Nunhead had fallen into a deplorable condition by the 1960s – semi-derelict, overgrown, heavily vandalized. The London Borough of Southwark took over the cemetery in 1975, partly in order to remedy this situation, partly to satisfy the borough's need for burial land, as the municipally established Camberwell cemeteries were nearing capacity.

With the help of Southwark engineers, a plan of action was drawn up and its provisions embodied in the GLC (General Powers) Act of 1976. The cemetery boundaries – which had lost their iron railings during the Second World War – were made secure; the catacombs were blocked up; some paths and avenues were resurfaced; the remains of the burnt-out Anglican chapel were stabilized, and one of Bunning's entrance lodges by the main gates was restored and occupied by a council employee. A Manpower Services Commission scheme ran for two years, resulting in a certain amount of clearance of vegetation from the sides of the main avenues and the removal of many dead and diseased trees. The main feature of the management plan was the division of the cemetery into three sections: a nature reserve, an area of public open space, and a functioning burial ground. The conservation of exising monuments was not a primary consideration in any part of the scheme. Accordingly, in pursuance of the plan, large areas were cleared of memorials and the cleared ground either seeded with grass or treated in preparation for new burials. At this point, however, work temporarily stopped: partly as a result of the extraordinarily high cost of restoring the lodge, the whole project lost much of its attractiveness to the Borough. In 1982, however, a new initiative was taken with the establishment of the Nunhead Cemetery Working Party, composed of councillors, council officers, and members of the then recently formed Friends of Nunhead Cemetery.

The initial problems confronting the Working Party, however, were organizational. The first of these was the tripartite division of the land, which meant that different sections of the cemetery fell under the jurisdiction of the parks and of the cemeteries staff. Almost inevitably, this prevented a co-ordinated policy from being pursued successfully, even with regard to such elementary tasks as weed control in the cleared areas. This was a problem which could be eased by liaison through the Working Party. A more intractable difficulty was the lack of council staff on site, for the cemeteries staff was based at Camberwell. The absence of regular supervision meant that vandalism continued unabated, Nunhead's reputation among local residents and police remained bad, and the boundary walls and fences were repeatedly breached. Local government spending cuts affected more than staffing, and renewed incursions of undergrowth soon made it difficult to distinguish the areas that had been partly cleared during the MSC scheme of 1977–8. Nunhead had already lost many of its monuments in the process of clearance, and little was done with regard to existing structures within the cemetery, repairs to which remained a low priority. The cost of restoring the one entrance lodge so far tackled meant that proposals for the restoration of the other were shelved. Spot repairs were carried out on graves that had been broken open, but damage that did not result in the exposure of coffins was generally left unrepaired. Inefficient planning also caused needless expenditure, absorbing resources that were already scarce. After the roads and paths had been resurfaced, it became apparent that the cemetery's drainage system was in need of repair and that the heavy clay soil in the new burials area was waterlogged. New drains had to be put down, a process which often involved digging up recently laid road surfaces, which then had to be laid all over again. Moreover, in the course of these works, the roadways were unintentionally widened: as a result, gullies that originally lay at the edge of the roads were left outstanding and no longer functioned with the camber.

The history of Southwark's attempt to reuse part of Nunhead for new burials is monitory. The Borough hoped to secure an area of the cemetery as a reserve burial ground sufficient for the next forty years. The attempt to introduce a quantity of new graves on a pronounced sloping site has led to severe and unforeseen problems. Most seriously, inadequate drainage has resulted in waterlogging so great that the new burials area is always muddy. Ironically, mourners also complained about the lack of a standpipe for watering flowers. Shortage of staff meant that rubbish skips were never emptied. By 1983, Nunhead had become so unpopular as a place for new burials that Southwark was forced largely to abandon this part of its management scheme, turning instead to Camberwell Old Cemetery – flatter and already largely cleared – for new burial space. Nunhead remained open only for those few people who, usually for family reasons, specifically wished to use it.

Despite all these problems, public concern for Nunhead, and interest in its future, was considerable. After a public meeting in 1982, a group called The Friends of Nunhead Cemetery was formed, with much support from the local community and a determination to see adequate conservation measures adopted. When the Friends of the Earth put forward a scheme for managing part of the site as an ecological reserve – a scheme which would have involved destroying even more of the surviving monuments – the Friends replied with a management plan based on both natural and historical conservation. The Friends hoped to implement their programme under licence from the Borough, but met with a major obstacle in the refusal of the trades unions, whose members formed the cemeteries staff, to allow volunteers to carry out work. Unofficially, the Friends organized regular working parties to clear litter. Meanwhile, Southwark's scheme for the cemetery seemed increasingly unworkable: the attempt to introduce new burials had been costly and had largely failed; new vegetation had invaded areas cleared in the 1970s; the bureaucratic separation of authorities responsible for different areas of the cemetery continued to frustrate hopes of a coherent overall policy; the absence of full-time staff meant that work was carried out only sporadically, and then without much direction. Faced with this situation, Southwark withdrew from the attempt at community partnership which the Working Party had represented, and the Working Party ceased to meet. In the hope, presumably, of escaping the impasse into which affairs had fallen, the council embarked on a new policy. It approached the official ecologists who had recently been appointed by the Greater London Council and offered to lease them the cemetery as a nature reserve. Such a lease could, perhaps, have established a single unified authority responsible for all operations in the cemetery. The Friends of Nunhead also met with the GLC ecologists to make a bid for the lease themselves. Negotiations were inconclusive and the abolition of the GLC put an end to the matter.

In the meantime, Nunhead Cemetery had been declared a conservation area, and the Friends persisted in their pressure for a licence. By the autumn of 1985, the principle of voluntary work had been accepted by all parties concerned – councillors, officers, and trades unions. The Nunhead Cemetery Steering Group was set up in place of the old Working Party and met for the first time in September. The Friends were recognized as representative of the broad spread of conservation interests at Nunhead and as the only group who could effectively organize voluntary labour in the cemetery. Negotiations on the granting of a licence began in earnest. In April 1986, presumably responding to the progress that was being made, Southwark undertook to appoint six full-time staff to work at the cemetery. Finally, in July 1986, the Borough Council granted a licence to the Friends to undertake voluntary work at weekends throughout the year in a specified area at the northern end of the cemetery. The schedule that was agreed upon sought to balance wildlife conservation with care for monuments and the historic landscape. No monuments were to be removed or destroyed; intrusive sycamore saplings were to be selectively cleared; although some new planting was to be introduced, the major concern was to encourage species that were already present in the cemetery; an informal boundary hedge was to be planted, path verges cleared, and shrubs thinned to allow woodland fringe grasses and plants to establish themselves; nesting boxes were also to be provided. Where possible, small repairs to damaged monuments were to be carried out, fallen stones re-erected, vegetation causing injury to monuments removed, and ferns used to hide irreparable damage or defacement. The whole scheme will take many years and those aspects of it concerned with maintenance and control will need to be continuous. Over the last couple of years a substantial start has been made, and the future of Nunhead begins to look brighter.

The programme worked out by the Friends is admirable. Nevertheless, it took Southwark an unconscionably long time to recognize the need for a proper conservation policy. This recognition came too late, of course, for a large part of the cemetery and nothing can repair the losses that have been sustained over the last fifteen years. Even so, much survives that is of interest and value, and Nunhead is already a major site for London wildlife. Although the area in which the Friends will work is a relatively small proportion of the whole cemetery, it is sufficient to prove the worth of their programme, and it is clearly sensible to restrict initial operations so as to avoid over-stretching resources that are necessarily limited. If the Friends succeed, then they will have set a precedent for Southwark to follow in the management of the rest of Nunhead.

A marked contrast to the administrative confusion that has characterized the management of Nunhead is provided by the recent history of Tower Hamlets Cemetery. Opened in 1841 by the City of London and Tower Hamlets Cemetery Company, the cemetery's custom, as we saw earlier, came from the working-class districts of East London, its inhabitants destined to be as closely packed together in death as they had been in life. Maintenance was inadequate and the cemetery was already overgrown by the 1890s. Space was running out and room for new burials was created by building new hillocks over existing graves. By the 1960s, Tower Hamlets was certainly the most overcrowded, and probably the most overgrown cemetery in London. In 1966 the Greater London Council took a hand. The GLC (General Powers) Act of that year allowed the Council to purchase the site, recognizing that the cemetery posed too great a problem for the local borough. The GLC decided to turn the cemetery into a public park: sports facilities were already provided nearby at Mile End Park, but it was felt that the locality lacked space for gentler recreation. The lodge and chapels at Tower Hamlets had suffered severe bomb damage and were derelict. They were declared dangerous structures in 1968–9 and demolished. When work began on the cemetery proper, the approach was equally drastic – and without the apparent excuse of public safety. The first stage of the scheme was the complete clearance of some 4 acres in the south west of the cemetery. Such extensive destruction of monuments and trees aroused considerable public protest. The strength of the opposition seems to have been recognized by the GLC: large-scale clearance ceased and, as a future strategy for managing Tower Hamlets, was abandoned. Little further work was carried out during the 1970s, but a deliberately low-key maintenance and development scheme evolved, culminating in 1979 with the publication, by the GLC's Department of Recreation and Arts, of a phased plan of works. The guiding principle of the plan was retention rather than clearance, and the programme of works was intended to cause as little disruption as possible. One of the most important points which the plan accepted and sought to embody was that Tower Hamlet's historical identity as a nineteenth-century landscaped cemetery was not to be changed.

Phase I was completed in the spring of 1982. This involved a general tidying-up of litter, selective tree felling, and a programme of repair sensibly confined to the major roads and paths. The perimeter paths were resurfaced, undergrowth cleared for 10 feet to either side, and the verges reseeded with grass and wild flower mixtures. In Phase II similar repairs were carried out on the paths crossing the cemetery; this involved the removal of some monuments, particularly where these had been erected in paths and avenues that had fallen into disuse. The planting proposals, and many of the notions of general effect, were based on the published schemes of the Friends of Highgate Cemetery. However, the management strategy at Tower Hamlets differed in one important respect from that at Highgate: the decision to concentrate on paths and verges, and only gradually to extend work back into the large areas beyond, meant that it was possible to control areas where work had already been done, thus

Tower Hamlets Cemetery, London, in 1988, its tightly packed tombstones entirely overgrown.

avoiding the problems of continuing maintenance that, as we shall see in the next section, have dogged the Highgate programme. Phase III involved substantial advances into the overgrown tracts of ground between the paths. Perimeter graves have been left intact; in areas that have subsided badly, however, many memorials have been removed and a large number of trees felled, followed by reseeding and new planting. Regrettable as the clearances are, they were necessitated by the GLC's requirement that strict standards of public safety should be met.

Despite the considerable merits of the Tower Hamlets scheme as a whole, especially as remedial action to an area that essentially had been neglected for over forty years, funding for the project was uncertain. In April 1981, the programme received financial support only by default, because it was ready to start when other schemes with a higher priority were not. During the first three years of the plan some £160,000 were spent, almost a third of it on tree planting. All this, however, has been capital expenditure. At the time of the abolition of the GLC in 1986, no money had been provided to recruit staff to manage the site, and maintenance depended on one employee who, quite obviously, could manage to keep only the most public areas of the cemetery tidy. Since then, few advances have been made. Substantial tracts of the cemetery are virtually impenetrable; monuments have been vandalized; the main paths are deteriorating and the subsidiary paths becoming more and more overgrown. Tower Hamlets Cemetery is currently in limbo. A coherent policy for managing the cemetery and conserving its historic identity is now badly needed.

Ecological Management: Highgate and Spring Bank

Highgate Cemetery in north London is probably the most famous historic cemetery in England – if only because the tomb of Karl Marx in its eastern half, sternly frowning out across the graves of lesser mortals, continues to be a place of pilgrimage. The original cemetery, on the west side of Swains Lane, has also been the subject of the most ambitious and widely publicized scheme of ecological management yet attempted in a British cemetery. Highgate was established in 1839 by the London Cemetery Company, with Stephen Geary as principal 'projector'. Throughout the nineteenth century its *haut bourgeois* attractions were rivalled only by Kensal Green and Norwood. The financial position of the London Cemetery Company began to deteriorate sharply after the Second World War. In 1956 the chapels, either side of the entrance arch, were closed and were badly vandalized subsequently. General neglect set in and continued even after the original company had been subsumed within the United Cemeteries Company in 1960. The older west cemetery was closed in 1975. The same year saw the establishment of the Friends of Highgate Cemetery, who, along with the Highgate Cemetery Trust, took over responsibility for the management of the west cemetery.

From 1976 to 1983 the strategy adopted by the Friends was based upon a report by the landscape architect Jenny Cox, who recommended managing the cemetery as woodland. The aims of the Friends, as set out in their 1978 publication *Highgate Cemetery* were admirably inclusive: 'to promote for the benefit of the public as an environmental amenity the conservation of the cemetery, its monuments, buildings, wild life, and the natural beauty of its setting, and to secure the repair, restoration and preservation of the cemetery by aiding the carrying out of works.' As events turned out, the somewhat narrower aims of woodland management soon came to dominate the programme of work. At the same time, the general objectives of the Friends' activities, particularly those relating to the historic identity of the cemetery, tended to become lost in a diffuse and unexamined desire to maintain what was thought of as the 'magical' atmosphere of Highgate.

By the time the Friends took over, the west cemetery had largely degenerated into a woodland of self-sown sycamore seedlings, with ash as the second most frequent species. Some root damage to tombs was obvious, but it was otherwise assumed that the overgrowth, and in particular the ubiquitous ivy, was not harmful to the monuments. In fact, it was not until 1980 that Highgate was properly examined by an architect. The initial plan was to replace the sycamore with a mixed oak woodland which, it was argued, was ecologically appropriate to the area. Except where historical continuity demanded the replacement of certain exotic trees, only native species would be used in the new planting. Species were chosen for their associated insects, or because they provided food for birds; indeed, for this latter reason, ivy was to be encouraged until it reached fruiting stage, regardless of whether it engulfed monuments in the process. Removal of the sycamore canopy was expected to admit sufficient light to the ground to encourage the growth of introduced wild flowers. In order that changes would not be too abrupt, the thinning of the sycamores was planned to take place in stages, allowing newly planted trees to grow up and replace felled ones. Ivy was regarded as a visually unifying feature. From 1976 to 1980, the principal work undertaken was the felling of sycamores followed by replanting; by 1980 this had been completed over the whole 16 acre site. By then, however, it was apparent that the management scheme was, in some respects, failing to achieve the desired results: in particular, the unforeseen problem of continuing maintenance was becoming critical. The year after an area had been partially cleared of sycamore, unsuspected bulbs flowered in the now sunlit ground and wild flowers were planted. But bramble was also responsive to the increase in light and gradually began to choke the very areas of the cemetery that had only recently, and with such effort, been cleared.

A number of factors underlay the failures of the management programme. Principal among these was the sheer scale of the operation. As sections of the cemetery were cleared they were replanted: by 1980 the entire 16 acre site had received new planting in some form, the whole of which required continuing maintenance. With other types of work competing for volunteers, however, there were not enough people to meet this requirement, and only a few selected areas were given the degree of upkeep that was needed. It had been hoped that the planting scheme would be self-maintaining. So in time, doubtless, it would have been, but inadequate provision had been made for the early years of intensive maintenance necessary for the scheme to establish itself. In addition, the particular ecological position espoused by the Friends led to a prohibition on the use of chemical herbicides, which would have been the most efficient means of large-scale control. The thinking behind such a ban is well-rehearsed and deserving of respect, but the situation that resulted at Highgate was ironical indeed. On the one hand, the ambitiousness of the overall ecological scheme meant that maintenance over the whole site became essential; on the other hand, the ecological principles upon which the scheme was based ruled out the only practicable means by which such maintenance could be ensured. In 1982 the first attempts to use defoliants to control bramble were made. In general, the programme adopted by the Friends had insufficiently realistic short-term goals and lacked adequately objective criteria by means of which to judge the advances made. Indeed, the pervasive but unfocused concern with the atmospheric qualities of Highgate was not conducive to any such hard, and perhaps self-critical, analysis.

In 1980, the major structures in the cemetery were surveyed by the architect Martin Caroë: he drew attention, for the first time, to the extent to which the terrace, the catacomb avenues, and other major buildings had been damaged by root action and the encroachment of vegetation. The architectural and historical character of Highgate re-emerged as a central issue in the question of how best to manage the cemetery. Caroë's findings clearly pointed to a potentially serious divergence between the aspirations of ecological management and the interests of architectural conservation and restoration. The debate that ensued tended to concentrate on immediate issues; but there were also theoretical differences, more difficult perhaps to discuss. What was really in question was the historical appropriateness of the landscape model the Friends had chosen. The woodland scheme adopted by the Friends in the mid 1970s was essentially a Romantic reaction – not in itself inappropriate – to the visual character of the west cemetery as it then was. Pleasure in seeing nature triumph over the works of man is a response diagnostic of the picturesque, and would have been recognized as such by the early nineteenth-century founders of Highgate. But Highgate was originally much more than an exercise in picturesque ruralism, important as that element in its make-up undoubtedly was. Its design, as we have seen, countered natural effects with high artifice – the formal terrace with its view of the modern Babylon, the Egyptian avenue, the catacomb range and circle. Once the historical character of Highgate is considered as a whole, once buildings and layout are considered as well as planting, Jenny Cox's scheme can be seen as fundamentally discrepant from the original conception of the cemetery: by so strongly favouring nature, ecological management at Highgate undervalued, and even ignored, art.

Such discrepancy was due to a lack of historical perspective. Its practical consequence at Highgate was that the built fabric of the west cemetery – buildings, monuments, roadways – was, in the long term, almost as threatened by the new management strategy as previously it had been by simple neglect. Thus, the Friends wished to remove the self-seeded sycamore woodland only in order to replace it with a different sort of woodland. Plans for eventual thinning were left vague and, although the scheme assigned different mixes of trees and shrubs to different areas, the positioning of individual trees – and thus their relationship to existing monuments and structures – was usually left to the *ad hoc* decisions of the volunteers planting them. Other aspects of the scheme were equally unsatisfactory. When the Friends took over, many of the asphalted road surfaces in the cemetery had already been disrupted by vegetation; other roads had been covered by soil creep. The landscape plan, in pursuit of picturesque effect, recommended the planting of verges so as to create a country lane appearance, and actually encouraged the invasion of paths and roadways by vegetation. None of this took account of the cemetery's drainage system: road surfaces began to disintegrate and vehicles using the roads subsequently churned many of them into mud. Further problems were caused by ivy, the unifying visual element of the woodland programme. Advocates of ruralism argued, variously, that ivy covering monuments protected them from vandals, softened outlines, and provided food for birds. Whatever weight one gives to such considerations, it was also unfortunately evident that ivy was causing substantial structural damage to both monuments and buildings.

In 1983 the Friends formed a subcommittee to assess criticisms of their ecological programme. The result was a modification of approach: priorities shifted towards the conservation and restoration of memorials and buildings. In fact, some work on structures within the cemetery had already begun. Proposals to seal the terrace catacombs, largely as a response to vandalism, had been defeated in 1981, and a small group of volunteers had started repairs. Damaged coffin niches were resealed; inscribed slabs were fixed in their proper places again; piers were rebuilt. The work was successful enough to attract a GLC grant of £20,000 towards the repair of the catacombs in 1983. In the same year, an application to the Manpower Services Commission secured a funded scheme of works for the cemetery. Earlier repairs to monuments undertaken by the Friends had been inconsiderable, and very much subordinate to the overall programme of woodland management: their stated object had been to make repairs that would blend unnoticed with the general appearance of age and decay. The MSC programme was one of renovation: vegetation was removed from buildings and monuments; a start was made on clearing and repairing the cemetery drainage system; ironwork was treated against rust and repainted.

Highgate Cemetery, London, in 1988; ivy surrounding the vandalized monument of John Acheler.

Clearly, goals quite different from those of the original management scheme were being pursued and some conflict of interest was inevitable. One focus of contention was the Highgate terrace, a major element not only in terms of design, but also, as we have seen, in the cemetery's cultural significance. Additionally, the debate about its treatment raised the issue of authenticity of materials – a problem that any restoration scheme needs to confront. Originally, the terrace had been laid with asphalt by Claridge, who, a little earlier, had treated the catacomb roof area at Norwood similarly. Since wartime bombing and subsequent redevelopment, the Norwood example has been lost, leaving the Highgate terrace as probably the earliest surviving asphalted building in the country – even though, with many repairs in the interim, little of the original asphalt remained. In pursuit of the Friends' programme of ecological management, it was proposed that the asphalt be removed from the terrace, polythene sheeting put down as a waterproofing layer, and turf laid over it. Such a scheme would have destroyed the identity of the terrace and fundamentally altered the architectural character of the catacombs. Those concerned with the repair of the cemetery's buildings objected. The dispute was resolved only when trial excavations on the terrace roof showed that the central depth was too shallow for the proposed turfing. Although the theoretical issue at the centre of the disagreement was not formally settled, the arguments about the terrace marked a decisive shift in the policy being pursued by the Friends. The terrace has been newly asphalted and the conservation of the Gothic catacomb range below completed. Further MSC schemes were initiated, the last of which was finished in 1988, and these schemes included brickwork repairs and rerendering as well as clearance and the maintenance of planting. One of the Egyptian catacombs has been fully repaired and restored, with striking success. Over the last year or two, the gatehouse with its flanking chapels has been the subject of a major programme of renovation. The brickwork has been repaired and repointed, the Anglican chapel restored with the intention of reusing it as a book shop and information centre, and the nonconformist chapel converted to offices. Behind the gatehouse, the entrance courtyard has been resurfaced. In the cemetery itself, work is continuing to keep a central area, known as the Meadow, largely free of trees, thus recreating something of Highgate's original balance between openness and enclosure.

Clearly, experience has shown the need for fundamental modifications to the programme adopted by the Friends when they first took over Highgate. The central and solid achievement of the ecological management scheme has been the clearance of the sycamore woodland. The new problems that this produced were largely the result of inherent weaknesses in the scheme itself and in how it was operated. It was initially over-ambitious and insufficiently tailored to the labour resources available. As a consequence it proved impossible to sustain the necessary levels of maintenance, and much of the ground cleared and replanted with so much effort in the 1970s is now once more overgrown. Generally, the objectives of the woodland management scheme had not been defined with sufficient precision. As a result, progress was difficult to measure and voluntary labour was inadequately directed. Most important of all was the failure to see in advance that the interests of ecological management could conflict with the interests of architectural and historical preservation. As we have seen, the work undertaken by the Friends in the last few years has recognized, implicitly at least, the shortcomings of the original programme. New problems have also emerged, the ironic result of the Friends' success in attracting public interest in their work and in the cemetery generally. Throughout the 1970s Highgate was only open to the public on a couple of days in the year. This was expanded to Sunday opening in the early 1980s. From 1984 to 1988, the Friends opened the cemetery every day, but restricted public access to guided tours. In 1987 Highgate had an astonishing 100,000 visitors: gratifying as this was, it meant that a significant part of the Friends' volunteer labour force had to be committed to guiding and supervising the visitors. With the ending of the last MSC scheme in 1988, the Friends are again reliant upon volunteers for the primary task of maintenance and repair. In 1989, Highgate has returned to opening for the public only on Sundays.

When Spring Bank Cemetery in Hull was acquired by Hull City Council, ecological management was proposed as an alternative to clearance. The cemetery had been opened by the Hull General Cemetery Company in 1847, and for a long period was considered one of the city's principal visual attractions – as indeed its Victorian founders had intended it to be. By the time the cemetery company went into liquidation in 1974, however, Spring Bank, overgrown and vandalized, was accounted an eyesore. The plan announced by the Council was drastic – as was so much that was done to the historic city of Hull during the 1960s and 1970s. With the exception of memorials claimed by relatives and a few monuments picked out as being of historical importance, it was proposed to clear the cemetery, with the chapel being preserved as a ruin. The cemetery paths were to be resurfaced, part of the cleared area was to be turned into parkland, the rest was to be allowed to revert to a wild state. Objections to the scheme came from the Friends of Spring Bank, who were supported by the Victorian Society in their objection to the clearance of monuments. The Friends put forward alternative proposals for ecological management, based on suggestions by Jenny Cox, author of the Highgate scheme, but with more overt provision for the preservation of the cemetery's historic fabric. The Council, however, went ahead with their original programme: after some consultation with local history groups to decide which memorials to retain, and a survey of inscriptions, largely carried out during the process of clearance, most of the gravestones and memorials were destroyed. To complete the devastation, the boundary walls were demolished, along with the cemetery offices.

The historical identity and visual character of Spring Bank has been obliterated, as well as a vast amount of historical evidence. What was the original cemetery now opens directly into the contiguous municipal cemetery, the boundary marked by the point at which woodland gives way to neatly mown lawn. The cleared area of the old cemetery is well used by pedestrians and, despite being open to the street, there has been little vandalism – doubtless because there is not much left to vandalize. The chapel has fallen further into decay, but the perimeter paths have been asphalted. The planting of ornamental shrubs, in an attempt to create the standard municipal park out of the eastern end of the cemetery, has largely failed. But in the main area, cleared of monuments, a form of ecological management is evident. A type of meadow gardening has been adopted, the grass being allowed to grow long, with access paths mown through at intervals. Given the destruction of Spring Bank's historical significance, an ecological approach could well be the most rewarding way of managing the cemetery for the future. One problem that needs to be confronted is the tendency of the public to regard an area that looks overgrown as merely neglected and uncared for: indeed, such an attitude has been fostered by the relentless tidy-mindedness that characterizes most public parks. As simple a measure as the mowing of paths at Spring Bank gives evidence of deliberate maintenance. More, however, should be done: an ecological programme, like any other, needs positive management if it is not to become a mere pretext for abandoning maintenance. Building a nature study centre on site and encouraging its use by local schools and interest groups would make a major contribution to Spring Bank's amenity value, and would be a direct way of altering popular perceptions of the cemetery.

It is naive to assume that conservation interests are uniform, that different objectives can be simply reconciled merely because they all carry the conservation label. The concerns of the cultural historian and the student of art and architecture do not automatically coincide with those of the ecologist. At Spring Bank, it is ironic that what looks like becoming an interesting ecological scheme should have been implemented only after the cemetery had been stripped of its historical and cultural significance. Equally, it is a pity that an all out ecological policy should have been adopted at a cemetery like Highgate, where the interests of natural history and those of architectural conservation were bound to diverge. Nevertheless, it is clear that many towns and cities have small disused cemeteries in which the monuments are of secondary importance and where ecological management could be of great value. A ready example from Hull is provided by Sculcoates Cemetery: it is situated in a run-down industrial area, the boundary walls have been demolished, the grounds are overgrown, gravestones are fairly scattered and are not generally of major interest. The whole cemetery offers an excellent opportunity for positive ecological management, and particularly for meadow treatment. Many of the kinds of proposals put forward by Jenny Cox could be tried out at cemeteries like Sculcoates with far greater chance of success than they have at the great historic cemeteries like Highgate.

Conservation: The Rosary and Kensal Green

The management policy currently being pursued at The Rosary Cemetery in Norwich is the one example to date of a scheme committed to the preservation of a historic cemetery in its entirety. Opened in 1821, the Rosary was the first non-denominational burial ground in England. It was run by a Trust until 1954, when it was handed over to Norwich City Council. Decline set in and, during the 1960s, the cemetery became overgrown. Some clearance took place in the early 1970s but there was local opposition and, in 1974, the then superintendent of The Rosary gave an assurance that 'no monuments would be taken from the cemetery as this would be destroying valuable history'. Nevertheless, by the beginning of the 1980s, a scheme had been drawn up by the Council that, in the name of rationalization, would have entailed clearing a number of headstones, removing kerbs, and levelling terraces.

In October 1981 the Norwich Society, anxious for the future of the cemetery, called a public meeting at which a representative of the Victorian Society spoke on The Rosary's historical importance. Subsequently, the Norwich Society compiled a report which opposed any clearance of monuments and made suggestions for ways of maintaining the cemetery economically. In 1982 Norwich Council accepted this report, and with it the principle that the historic cemetery should be retained and preserved intact. At the same time, events at The Rosary itself served to focus attention on the need to change the priorities of its management. A mature beech was scheduled for felling; partly for economy and partly because emphasis was put upon getting rid of a dangerous tree rather than upon preserving monuments, the contractor was asked to minimize damage rather than to remove the tree in such a way as to cause no damage at all. In the event nearly twenty monuments were injured, more or less seriously, by its fall. As a result the Council redefined the job of the cemetery superintendent: to the responsibility for keeping The Rosary safe and tidy was added that of preserving its historic character. Shortly afterwards, the Council set up The Rosary Working Group. From the Council the Group included officers from the Planning, Conservation, Estate Surveyors, and Public Health Departments, and the Arboricultural Officer; from amenity and conservation bodies there were representatives of the Norwich Society and the Victorian Society. The Friends of The Rosary Cemetery group has since been formed to help the work of preservation.

Norwich Council allocated some £2000 towards a rolling fund for conserving and renovating monuments, and a schedule of urgent repairs was drawn up. Some of the work – for example, replacing kerbs – was to be done by the regular cemetery staff, but, for the technically more specialized work, a professional mason was employed. A series of excellent repairs has been carried out: broken stonework has been refixed, plinths reset, and new foundations have been provided for monuments that had subsided badly. The fact that there are no mausolea at The Rosary, and that relatively few memorials are architecturally complex, has meant that one man has been able comfortably to do the necessary repairs. Other, more general conservation work was done by a Manpower Services Commission scheme. The major landscape features of The Rosary are stepped terraces and a network of cobbled rainwater gullies. Work on these began in 1983: gravel paths were resurfaced, blocked drainage gullies cleared, and loose cobbles reset. The removal of grave kerbs has been stopped and, where mowing within the kerb is not feasible, ground cover will be planted. Some headstones had fallen and some had been laid flat, ostensibly to avoid damage during tree-felling and pruning: where possible, these have been re-erected. Many of the trees in the cemetery are now nearing the end of their lives, and thought has had to be given to removing and replacing them. In preparation for this a record of existing trees has been compiled; when replanting becomes necessary, only species in keeping with the date of the cemetery are to be used. The density of graves in The Rosary makes new planting difficult, but it is intended to introduce some new species to create an arboretum in the City Cemetery, established in the 1850s when such planting was popular. Permanent bedding for the entrance drive, based on a Victorian winter bedding scheme, was laid out in 1984.

Since the City Council adopted the Norwich Society's report and recommendations in 1982, the management of The Rosary has been exemplary. Although money has been inevitably limited, monuments and cemetery structures, as far as possible, have been repaired and maintained. Alterations inappropriate to the cemetery's historic character have been proscribed. The major planting and the larger landscape features have been preserved; where new trees or shrubs are needed, these are to be in keeping with the historical record. The cost of continuing upkeep remains a problem, but methods of relatively low-level maintenance have been adopted successfully in some parts of the cemetery. While formal features such as the flower beds continue to be carefully tended, controlled overgrowth has been encouraged at the higher end of the cemetery, and a nature trail is planned. The success of The Rosary stems from Norwich City Council's recognition of the cemetery as a historic site and their acceptance of a responsibility to manage it as such.

The resultant management programme is the product of collaboration between the Council, as the cemetery authority, and amenity groups at both local and national levels: between them they have evolved a conservation strategy that, at relatively low cost, goes a long way towards securing the long-term preservation of The Rosary.

Although the case history of The Rosary offers the only example to date of cemetery management that is fully committed to historical and architectural conservation, proposals announced in 1988 for the future management of Kensal Green show the same enlightened approach. Kensal Green, the first great metropolitan cemetery, is still owned and administered by the General Cemetery Company; interments continue, but available space is now very limited and the cemetery will be full within a few years. In February 1988 the company stated that it wished to support the formation of a voluntary group to be called the Friends of Kensal Green Cemetery. In April, Julian Litten of the Victoria and Albert Museum brought together representatives of English Heritage, the Council for the Care of Churches, the National Trust, the Royal Horticultural Society, the Courtauld Institute, the Victorian Society, and SAVE Britain's Heritage, to hear the General Cemetery Company's chairman, Michael Nodes, outline plans for the long-term management of the cemetery and for its preservation, once full, as a Memorial Park, as stipulated in the company's original Act of Incorporation. The proposals are comprehensive: the Anglican chapel is to be conserved and repaired, and the derelict nonconformist chapel restored; the original planting scheme of the 1830s, which remains substantially intact, will be preserved and, where it is possible, reinstated; there will be a long-term programme of memorial conservation, supplemented by photographic recording. The whole scheme, planned to an agreed schedule, will take twenty years to complete and will be administered by the Friends, who will take over the management of Kensal Green from the company once the cemetery has been 'buried up'. In addition to running the conservation programme the Friends will hope to provide wardens and guides for the cemetery; a substantial list of publications is also planned. Funding for all this work in its various phases will come from a number of different sources: financial help can be expected from central government through English Heritage, and from local authorities; there are a number of trust foundations from whom grants can be sought; the Friends themselves will raise money both through membership subscriptions and through special events.

It is entirely appropriate that The Rosary, first of all English cemeteries, should also have been the first in which a management scheme committed to historical conservation should have been adopted. It is also appropriate that at Kensal Green, biggest, best known and most influential of the early-nineteenth-century cemeteries, conservation strategy on a grand scale should be planned. Both schemes are cause for optimism, as also is the work now being carried out by the Friends of Highgate and the Friends of Nunhead. Elsewhere, organizations of Friends have been formed to work for the preservation of Abney Park, where a start has been made on repairing the burnt-out chapel, Undercliffe Cemetery in Bradford, Beckett Street Cemetery, also known as Burmantofts, in Leeds, and the fine 1830s cemetery of York. In 1986, the National Federation of Cemetery Friends was established to exchange information and ideas. If the cultural legacy of our great nineteenth-century cemeteries is not to be lost, such examples need to be followed by those responsible for their management and maintenance throughout the country.

3

MANAGEMENT FOR CONSERVATION

Approaches

THE RECOMMENDATIONS AND SUGGESTIONS THAT follow are aimed at those who have responsibility for the management of historic cemeteries: usually this will be a local authority. But the advice is also directed at amenity groups and voluntary organizations that may be involved in the process of conservation and management, possibly in partnership with the local council. In no sense is this section intended as a complete guide to the conservation and restoration of historic cemeteries. Rather, it seeks to recommend some overall approaches and to identify some of the major practical problems that such work involves.

Many of these problems can only be solved with the help of experts – architects, surveyors, craftsmen and women, landscape gardeners, horticulturalists. Such specialists may be employed already by the local authority concerned, or may need to be commissioned to deal with particular aspects of management and conservation. But specialists will not be needed all the time, and financial constraints may severely limit the availability of full-time cemetery staff. Volunteers can play a vital role in saving our historic cemeteries, and, with care and guidance, can do a great deal of essential work. Voluntary groups may also contain experts of their own. The advice given here, then, is general. Specific problems need specific remedies, though this does not necessarily mean that they can only be tackled by professionals. Much detailed advice is available in printed sources, some of which are mentioned in the course of the text, more of which will be found in the Bibliography.

Any nineteenth- or early-twentieth-century cemetery is potentially, and probably, a site of substantial cultural, architectural and historical importance. This should be given priority in the management strategy adopted, which should have as its objective, therefore, the preservation and maintenance of the cemetery as a historic site. Cemeteries that have remained in private ownership are frequently overgrown by the time new management begins. Such a site will probably have become a refuge for wildlife, and its conservation as such should also be an objective of any management plan. The goals of historical conservation and wildlife conservation are not the same, though they can be complementary – as they are in the scheme adopted by the Friends of Nunhead. Management strategy will need to reconcile what may be competing claims, but policies designed to foster the natural history of a cemetery should always be contextualized by the need to safeguard the historical integrity of the site. In a functioning cemetery, maintenance for wildlife purposes can only ever be partially successful. In a cemetery that has been closed for burials, provision must be made for the maintenance and protection of buildings, monuments and historical landscape, for security, and for access. Specifically ecological principles of management, in particular, can jeopardize such provision, as happened at Highgate. Indeed, in circumstances where an important cemetery retains its main architectural and landscape features intact, an unqualified ecological programme may be inappropriate and even damaging to the cemetery's historic identity.

In confronting a cemetery that has been closed for burials, that is, in all likelihood, overgrown and neglected, the first essential is to find out what it contains. A survey should be organized, not only of the cemetery itself, but also of documentary sources relating to buildings, its original layout and planting, its historical development, and its burial plan. Some information may be available from published sources such as *The Victoria County Histories* or the relevant volume of Nikolaus Pevsner's *Buildings of England*. For a full picture, however, it will be necessary to consult primary sources: these could include the Act of Parliament by which the cemetery was incorporated, original plans and designs, correspondence, accounts in contemporary newspapers or journals; for the period when the cemetery was in use there should be a register of burials and a grid plan of the site. The most likely place to find all this documentation, or information as to where it is held, is the city or county Record Office. The local planning authority may also have relevant material.

Documentary research should proceed side by side with the survey of the cemetery itself. This latter needs to be organized methodically, area by area, so as to prevent muddle and duplication of effort. If the cemetery is badly overgrown such a survey can present real physical problems: monuments may be lost under vegetation, paths blocked and obscured, planting patterns difficult to recognize. Nevertheless, it should be possible to reach an overview that, even if incomplete, should inform and help direct the work that is to follow. The survey should compile information about: the cemetery's architectural structures, including boundary walls and gates; the principal monuments, including those to people of historical interest, local or national, as well as memorials of artistic and architectural quality; major landscape features; the remains of original planting, with details of subsequent planned planting; paths and roadways; the cemetery drainage system; the present botanical make-up of the site, including intrusive and self-seeded vegetation; those areas of the cemetery that are of importance from the point of view of natural history and wildlife conservation.

Specialist advice may be necessary, particularly with reference to surviving historic landscape and planting, and to the cemetery's present ecology and natural history. Help can be sought from any of the organizations given in the section of the Bibliography dealing with natural history, and may be available from the local museums service. Historical advice may also be obtained from this latter source or from the Victorian Society. The survey of the cemetery will also need to establish whether any of its structures have been included on the list of statutorily protected buildings of historical or architectural interest, and whether any of the trees have Tree Preservation Orders on them. The local planning authority will have details of this. Once all the information has been assembled a phased programme of work can be decided upon. This will need to be tailored not only to the particular characteristics and problems of the cemetery itself, but also to the available levels of funding and to the available work-force.

Practical Conservation

Landscape

The most likely starting point for a programme of work on an overgrown cemetery will be the removal of intrusive trees, particularly where they are causing damage to tombs. Trees should be felled with an eye to the safety of monuments as well as people: lack of control over the direction of fall, and failure to remove large branches in advance, can easily result in memorials being smashed. If wood is to be burned, bonfires should not be lit close to monuments, for both heat and smoke damage marbles and limestones. Burning should never be used as a method of weed control, or as a substitute for stripping ivy by hand. Stumps of felled trees should be killed by drilling and pouring in an acid or other chemical preparation: advice on stump-killers can be obtained from the Arboricultural Association. Once a stump is dead, it is often possible to winch it out of the ground; this needs to be done with caution, however, as carelessness can result in irreparable damage to brick foundations and vaults. Tree clearance will also need to be regulated by considerations of natural history. There are substantial ecological advantages to be gained from removing sycamores, for example. On the other hand, the ecosystem of a large urban cemetery is sensitive and complex, and uninformed clearance can disturb or destroy important habitats. The initial survey of the cemetery should include details of areas of particular wildlife interest, and this should be used to guide tree-clearance and felling.

It is advisable to concentrate the early phases of work on areas close to paths and roads, where the effects of tree clearance will be most readily apparent, and maintenance will be easiest. The example of Highgate shows that the attempt to clear large areas in sequence can result in a maintenance burden that is too great for the available manpower. In many Victorian cemeteries, the siting of important monuments along roadsides was encouraged, so work focused on these areas will bring about an immediate and obvious improvement. It is important to keep roadway and footpath verges clear of intrusive vegetation, especially if the road surface is decaying or has lost its camber. Ensuring that drainage gullies and roadside gutters are clear will help prevent the further erosion of roads and pathways. More generally, the facilities for land drainage and rainwater disposal, and the supply of mains water, need to be checked and, as far as possible, put into repair. At both Nunhead and Highgate, failure to give proper attention to the cemetery drainage system led to major problems.

Once the initial stages of work – clearing intrusive trees, unblocking gutters, repairing drainage – are completed, or well underway, the question of new planting arises. The decision to introduce new planting into a cemetery is subject to several considerations: the existing state of the site; the survival of the historical layout and planting; the ecological desirability of protecting or establishing wildlife habitats; relative priorities within the overall scheme of management; not least, the availability of manpower. Once the decision has been made, the first requirement of any new planting is that it should not endanger what is already there. Trees and shrubs must be sited so as to avoid any likelihood of root damage to structures: roots can affect features both above and below ground, disturbing foundations, vaults and underground pipes, disrupting roads and surface guttering. Some types of tree or shrub are more likely to cause such problems than are others, so the decision about where to plant is directly related to the choice of what to plant. In a historic cemetery, this choice should be principally determined by historical continuity, the necessary preliminary to which is a survey of existing trees, related, if possible, to documentary evidence. In interpreting such a survey, particularly where documentation is lacking, it should be remembered that the original planting scheme would have included many shorter-lived varieties no longer apparent

As we saw in earlier chapters, fashions in nineteenth- and early-twentieth-century horticulture changed; the general pattern of that change is, however, clear and can be a useful guide to any new planting. Few exotic trees were used in the very early cemeteries, except for those, like cedars, which had specific funerary and religious connotations. In cemeteries of this date, native British trees would form an entirely suitable basis for replanting. By mid-century, after Loudon's recommendations, conifers became the staple component of cemetery planting, and the use of imported and exotic trees had also greatly increased. In these cemeteries, new planting ought to be in keeping with the original choice of species. From the mid-century, and increasingly as the century progressed, varieties of non-native species were combined to create arboreta: where these survive, they could be further varied by introducing new exotics. Edwardian cemeteries saw the increasing use of flowering trees and shrubs, still a common element in modern horticultural practice. As well as seeking historical continuity, new planting, as was stressed earlier, must be located so as to avoid putting monuments and other structural features at risk. The danger of root damage can be further obviated by ensuring that the right sort of tree is chosen. Here, Loudon's preference for conifers has much to recommend it, since the average rootspread of conifers is smaller in proportion to their height than that of broadleaves, and observation confirms that monuments in their vicinity are far less likely to suffer injury. Species chosen for areas in which damage from roots is possible should be those with restricted rootspread, especially if trees are to be planted amidst already established graves. The Royal Botanic Gardens at Kew have been conducting a survey of reported cases of root damage to buildings; so far, however, only the literature on golf courses offers much relevant advice, and this is largely concerned with those trees whose roots cause upheaval or disturbance of the ground surface. Nevertheless, some general points are clear. Poplars and willows can cause major disruption to drainage systems and should be avoided where such damage is at all likely. Because of their wide rootspread, oaks can cause considerable disturbance and should not be planted among established graves. In terms of cultivation, regular pruning can be used to restrict root growth. Obviously, if trees are planted in isolated positions – in forecourts, for example, or on islands at the junctions of cemetery roads – these considerations are less important.

A further factor that legitimately could affect the choice of new planting is the desirability of adopting ecological principles of management. In cemeteries of major historical or artistic interest, ecology will need to be reconciled with – and probably subordinate to – those principles of continuity and safety already discussed. There will be occasions, however, when important habitats need to be safeguarded, when areas of particular naturalist interest need to be preserved, or, indeed, when it will be appropriate actually to establish such resources. Ecological management, as we have seen, brings problems of its own. Most ecological schemes are premised on the desirability of establishing a mixed plant community, sometimes by encouraging existing flora, sometimes by introducing new species through such techniques as planting woodland turfs. The principal threat to succesful ecological management comes from a lack of maintenance during the critical first years of a scheme. Once the tree cover has been removed and daylight can reach the ground, it is very easy for one plant to dominate the field layer. Bramble, in particular, needs to be rigorously checked: once firmly established it is difficult to eradicate, even with the use of chemicals. The best way to guard against vigorous and monopolistic plants like bramble is to remove them before they get any kind of firm hold. This means careful maintenance of ecologically managed areas, particularly during the early stages of a scheme when other, less vigorous species are still establishing themselves. Once the early stages are past, and a varied plant community has been established, then such areas can be virtually self-maintaining.

Walls and Buildings

Those structures in a cemetery which are not meant to house coffins – boundary walls, offices, chapels – pose repair and maintenance problems precisely similar to those of historic structures generally. A large and increasing literature giving information on repair and conservation techniques is available, and useful advice may be sought from organizations as diverse as the Society for the Protection of Ancient Buildings and the Building Research Establishment. Before work on specific structures begins, however, it is most important to establish what sort of approach is to be adopted towards the conservation of the cemetery as a whole: whether, for example, a vandalized chapel is to be conserved in its derelict state, restored in some way, or converted to new use – as a study centre, for instance. Such decisions can only sensibly be made as part of an overall management strategy, and that will be determined by the initial survey of the cemetery in question, and by the levels of funding and labour that are available. Large-scale architectural projects, such as the restoration of the lodges at Nunhead, obviously need professional direction, but there are basic points about repair and routine maintenance that can be made.

Perimeter walls and gates should be kept secure and serviceable. Repairs that are crudely makeshift or out of character with the existing structure suggest neglect or indifference and can help to invite vandalism. A major problem affecting walls is the growth of ivy or other creepers: thick ivy roots can seriously disrupt foundations, as can root action from trees growing too close to the boundary wall. When ivy roots in the wall itself it can draw moisture from the mortar and, by drying it out, render it likely to crumble. Where it is not severe, the growth of ivy and other creepers can be controlled by cutting back: not infrequently, however, such growth will need to be removed altogether. This must be done with care: simply pulling off the climbing shoots of ivy will almost certainly damage the surface of the wall, particularly if it is rendered. The best method of removal is to cut the main stem of the plant near the ground and clip away all the leaves; severed from the main root, the attached stems die off and can subsequently be pulled away without injury to the fabric of the wall. The main root can be destroyed with a stump-killer or other chemical preparation.

Victorian architects, reacting against the perceived weakening of earlier mortars, tended to use overly hard mixes for their mortars and renderings. The buildings of Highgate Cemetery are a case in point: all the catacomb range has decayed badly because both the mortar and the render, Portland Cement, were harder – that is, less porous – than the structural brickwork. As a result the bricks themselves have decayed and frost action has split off the external render. In such circumstances it would clearly be foolish to repair using the original materials, which would lead merely to a recurrence of the same problems. Mortars and renders need to be soft, and the first essential is to get the constituents and proportions of the mix right: almost certainly, this will involve using a lime-based mix, though commercial preparations that claim an effective level of porosity are available. The best source for information about mortars and renders is the technical pamphlets published by the SPAB. When stucco or render is renewed care needs to be taken to match it in colour and, where possible, finish, to the original work; similarly, repointing needs to follow the character of the original pointing. It may be necessary to use brickwork or blockwork to seal gateways in the perimeter wall when entrance gates are missing or irreparably damaged. When the original walls are of brick, then brick, bonded to match the existing work, should be used for any infill; if the walls are masonry or stuccoed, then the new work should be rendered and the colour of the rendering matched to that of the original fabric. The same applies to similar sorts of repair undertaken on other structures.

When chapels or cemetery offices become redundant their decay is often accelerated by the neglect of quite simple maintenance. Even on unused buildings, gutters and downpipes should be regularly cleared, the roof kept weatherproof and watertight, lead flashings and valleys renewed or patched, doors and iron fixtures kept free of rust, invading vegetation removed, and tree growth in the vicinity controlled to prevent damage from roots and branches. As with all historic buildings, it is, in the long run, far less costly to continue regular basic maintenance than to incur, sooner or later, heavy bills for extensive repairs. Redundant buildings are also likely to become mantled in ivy, a picturesque effect that is sometimes thought of as particularly Victorian. But when the Victorians trained ivy on buildings, they kept it trimmed annually: unregulated ivy growth will damage buildings just as surely as it will damage walls.

Finally, although a building may have fallen out of use, work undertaken to ensure its security should not draw attention to its redundancy. The boarding-up of doorways and windows advertises a building's dereliction and invites vandalism. Metal grilles to protect existing glass should be used, or polycarbonate sheeting to replace glass that has been smashed; empty doorways, quite simply, need new doors. Above all, regular maintenance, even at a low level, clearly indicates that a building, even though unused, is still being cared for.

Mausolea, Catacombs and Vaults

Mausolea and catacomb ranges pose a special problem because of the accessibility of coffins. Many cemeteries have suffered from the desecration of such structures and from the breaking open of the coffins they contain; many cemetery workers have had to face the task of replacing bodies when coffins have been vandalized. The legal procedures involved in obtaining permission to move a body are both complex and costly, so practical means need to be found to protect coffins *in situ* and, without too much expense, to prevent their being damaged. Apart from any other considerations, public health legislation requires that coffins kept above ground should be secured from vandalism. For this reason alone, catacombs and mausolea, once damaged or decayed, should always be repaired or carefully restored, never simply conserved as picturesque ruins.

Because mausolea are privately owned there are legal constraints on cemetery authorities seeking to take specific preventive measures against vandalism directed at vaults. Where such structures are undamaged, the best safeguards are those of normal security and regular maintenance. Once a mausoleum has been broken into, however, the authorities can secure it against future entry as a matter of course. Wiring or replacement of windows has been mentioned already in connection with cemetery buildings. Vault doors are often of considerable aesthetic interest and present a more difficult problem. If the hinges remain intact doors can be rehung and secured with clamps, rather than the doorways being bricked up. Sometimes, however, bricking will be necessary: in such cases, bricking up behind the doors – the practice followed by the Friends of Highgate – is far preferable to exterior brickwork and is equally effective in preventing intrusion. In the vault range at Highgate, where the iron gates had frequently rusted so badly that the hinges were unusable, visual character has been preserved by the simple, but effective, expedient of propping the doors against the new brick walls. An additional advantage of interior brickwork is that it could be removed in the future with minimum damage to the mausoleum. Certainly, brickwork should never be laid directly against doors, as has been done at Kensal Green, since any attempt to remove it in the future will result in injury to the fabric. When sealing a structure containing coffins, care should be taken to ensure that it remains ventilated lest damage from dry rot should result. Similarly, any provision for drainage and water run-off should be kept in good repair.

Because of the difficulties inherent in the maintenance and security of catacombs, cemetery authorities have often closed them to public access. This is a pity, for, perhaps rather surprisingly, they have much general appeal. Restricted or controlled access should be possible at least, and guided tours may be a way of raising public interest and, indeed, funds. A major element in the popularity of Highgate has been the fame of the Egyptian Avenue and the catacomb circle, while occasional tours of the Kensal Green and Norwood catacombs have attracted considerable public interest, all of which suggests that catacombs are a potential asset for any authority seeking to stimulate a wider concern for the preservation and maintenance of a historic cemetery.

Monuments

Most stones are subject to fracture, which can come about by an accidental blow, by deliberate vandalism, or by the action of frost. Monumental masons and, indeed, masons trained in conservation techniques, have a repertoire of ways in which to repair such damage. Where the stone has been cleanly fractured and the broken pieces of masonry survive, repair should present little difficulty to an experienced craftsman. A wide range of adhesives for mending stone is now available, especially for marbles and limestones, and these can be matched for colour, or mixed with the appropriate ground stone. In most historic cemeteries, a conservation programme will need to include provision for such basic work to be carried out, as has been done at The Rosary in Norwich.

The more elaborate the memorial, however, the more complex are likely to be the difficulties of effecting satisfactory repairs. A central problem, particularly with grander monuments, is that, in order to give future access to the vault, they were often designed to be disassembled. Over the years, such structures can become unsteady. As a result, some cemetery authorities have ordered the removal of large memorials on the grounds that they constituted a danger to public safety. This is unnecessarily drastic, and, indeed, can be a mere excuse for clearance. If a grave has been filled or is no longer required for burials, there should be no objection to firmly mortaring or pinning together the component parts of the monument. After repairs have been carried out it may be advisable to lay some types of memorial, like crosses, flat on the grave, thereby reducing the risk of further damage. However, this should not be done with stones carrying inscriptions: the water that collects in the incised letters causes damage to the surface of the stone which, eventually, will lead to the loss of the inscription altogether. A particularly public example of this process in action can be found at the Barbican Centre in London, where gravestones from the old churchyard of St Giles have been set flat on raised brick plinths.

Victorian builders and statuaries, unaware of the ability of water to move through stone, frequently used iron dowels and cramps to fix masonry: when such cramps rust they expand, often forcing joints apart, sometimes splitting the stone itself. Although some cemetery authorities were conscious of the problem – as early as the 1830s Kensal Green allowed only copper cramps to be used in fixing wall monuments – most were not, with consequences only too evident today. In repairing monuments that have suffered in this way, iron cramps and dowels should be replaced in non-ferrous materials before joints are made good and any cracked or broken stone mended. The combination of incompatible types of stone in some polychromatic tombs has also created problems, particularly where sandstone and limestone have been used together. In such cases there is often little that can be done. Techniques for reconstituting the stone are very expensive, aesthetically unsatisfactory, and by no means permanent: in particular, partial reconstitution can lead in time to the stone splitting where the reconstitutive process stopped.

Air pollution has taken as hard a toll of cemetery monuments as it has of so many urban historic structures: its effects include the discolouration of stone, the powdering of marble surfaces, the loss of carved detail, and the corrosion of sculpture. As with historic buildings, cleaner air and anti-pollution legislation have, between them, greatly improved the situation, and simple cleaning using a fine water spray is now viable. Certainly, the adoption of such a cleaning policy could restore the wide range of stone colours and masonry textures characteristic of Victorian cemeteries. But water cleaning is not without its difficulties, particularly when monuments and headstones are heavily crusted in grime, as in so many cemeteries in the industrial cities of the north of England. Because of chemical reaction between aerial pollution and stone , the deposited coating may combine with the stone itself: in washing off the crust, the surface of the stone can be removed as well, destroying detail and leaving the softer underlying stone critically exposed to the processes of erosion. In such circumstances, restricted cleaning with limited amounts of water and a soft brush may be the answer; in any case, advice should be obtained from an experienced stone conservator. There is a further consideration as well, for the issues involved are historical and aesthetic as well as practical. The blackening of monuments in a northern urban cemetery is testimony to the nature of the industrial past that produced the surrounding city and, with it, the necessity for the cemetery itself. Thought of in this way, the coating of black is part of the historical identity of the site: as such, there is certainly an argument for allowing it to remain.

Damage from air pollution is aggravated when the surface of the stone is kept continually damp, most frequently by covering vegetation. Under a mantle of ivy, aerial pollutants may combine with water to form corrosive acids; salts can be gradually leached from the stone which, on crystallizing, will damage the surface and render inscriptions illegible. Sandstones, limestones and marbles are worst affected by this process. In the past, regular maintenance kept unwanted vegetation in check; in cemeteries where such maintenance is no longer feasible measures to control vegetation need to be taken if damage to monuments is to be forestalled. It is possible to prevent growth by using consolidating agents to increase the surface density of the stone, but such techniques are expensive and, in their long-term effects on the stone itself, uncertain. A more practical solution is the selective use of biocides painted on the stone. If ivy is being used as a ground cover, for instance, biocide treatment to the joints of large memorials will stop the ivy rooting in them. The removal of ivy that is already growing on a monument should be done in the way described earlier in the section dealing with walls and buildings. The extent to which the memorials in a historic cemetery are to be cleared of overgrowth is a decision that needs to be taken early in any management scheme, and is likely to be the result of the priorities that emerge after the initial survey.

The growth of lichens on memorials can pose something of a conservation dilemma. Cemeteries provide one of the few urban locations where lichens can grow, and recording their presence should be one aspect of the initial management survey; where they do occur, naturalists are rightly anxious for their conservation. On the other hand, lichens can injure masonry surfaces – particularly polished stone – and they can certainly obscure and will eventually impair inscriptions: these are areas of legitimate concern for those whose primary interest is the preservation of monuments, and more so when those monuments are of particular historical or aesthetic importance. Because of this divergence of interest hard-and-fast rules are undesirable: individual cases need to be decided upon their merits. Fortunately, the scale of damage associated with lichens is usually small, and their growth is a by no means unattractive aspect of the process of ageing.

Ironwork

The use of iron, whether in fittings or railings, or for entire monuments, presents special problems of conservation and repair. Cast-iron memorials are always a comparative rarity and should be preserved in good condition whenever possible. Railings on individual graves are far more common, but their survival today is patchy: in some cemeteries the removal of railings has long been a matter of policy, in others they were removed on a large scale during the Second World War. In cemeteries where a good collection of tomb railings survives intact, their preservation and maintenance should be a priority, for they are an essential part of the cemetery's historical and artistic identity. Even where they are not a major component in a cemetery's overall make-up, decorative railings ought to be kept wherever possible, and their retention should be an argument for retaining kerbstones that might otherwise be removed.

The obvious enemy of ironwork is rust, and this may well be concealed under several layers of paint. Simple repainting is not an answer: ironwork needs to be examined for rust and treated. As far as possible, all rust should be removed: depending on how robust the metalwork is, and how finely detailed, this can be done with a blow torch, a wire brush and wire wool. Before repainting, the surface should be treated with a fixative agent such as Jenolite, followed by an anti-oxidizing primer. Technical advice is available from a variety of sources, some of which are given in the Bibliography. In some cases corrosion will be so advanced that the surviving ironwork is too brittle to allow these operations to be carried out: in such circumstances it should simply be retained *in situ* for as long as it survives.

The choice of colour for top coats needs care. A wide range of colours was used for cemetery ironwork at different times during the nineteenth and early twentieth centuries, from sky-blue, white, gold and green, to elaborate polychromy for the railings of the more sumptuous Gothic monuments. In the present century, the Neo-Georgian revival brought a rejection of colours other than black for ironwork; more recently, shades of blue have been popular among a number of local authorities. In a historic cemetery, the adoption of any such uniform colour for painted ironwork is not only monotonous, it is historically inaccurate. Where original polychrome schemes survive the paintwork should be cleaned and conserved. This involves specialized skills and the advice of an experienced paint conservator should be sought. Where paint has largely disappeared, but evidence of original colour or colours remains, this should be followed in repainting: the finish should be matt. Care needs to be taken in colour-matching and expert advice may again be needed, for oxidization and air pollution may well have changed the colour of any paint that survives. Finally, where reliable information does not exist as to the colour used on a particular monument, green is a safe choice for most Victorian work, and blue or white for Edwardian.

Horticulture

Nineteenth- and early twentieth-century cemeteries were scenes of extensive, even lavish, floral display. Remarkably, some cemetery authorities manage to continue the intensive horticulture necessary to retain such high standards: flower-beds are regularly maintained, annuals planted out each year, trees and shrubs pruned, bushes clipped and shaped. So long as funds are available, such management deserves every encouragement.

But this is exceptional. Most cemeteries today face tight financial limits and the need to cut costs: inevitably, high-maintenance horticultural display is one of the first things to suffer. However, there are alternatives to the traditional forms of cemetery horticulture which are both practical and historically appropriate. One example is Victorian winter bedding: this consists of formal patterns of dwarf conifers, hollies, heathers and evergreen creeping plants, with ivy planted as an edging. Entirely fitting for a nineteenth-century cemetery, such planting could be the basis of permanent beds which would need minimal maintenance after the initial labour and outlay: a scheme of this sort has been adopted at The Rosary. What applies to the public horticulture of a cemetery can also apply to private graves. Sometimes, when a contract for perpetual maintenance exists, cemetery authorities continue the annual planting of flowers on individual graves. Here too financial factors must be a consideration, and, where cemetery resources are limited, it is legitimate to ask whether such expenditure could not be better directed. Often, for example, it would be more sensible for the money spent on this sort of annual planting to be put into a fund for repairing the monument itself. This would not mean abandoning the planting of the grave. As with the cemetery beds generally, alternatives to the customary flowers could be adopted: dwarf conifers or ferns would be appropriate, as would ornamental ground covers such as the hardy perennial varieties of Sedum.

This type of low-maintenance horticulture could be extended to form the basis of planting schemes that are both historically sensitive and economically viable. What is needed is the will and imagination to implement such schemes, for the usual result of a cutback in cemetery horticulture is the large-scale introduction of lawn. Lawns need regular mowing and this necessity, as was emphasized earlier, can come to determine a cemetery's future – or lack of it. In the joint cause of rationalization and the gang-mower, kerbs are taken away, mounds levelled, inconvenient landscape features eliminated and, eventually, gravestones and memorials removed. In the end the problem of cemetery maintenance has solved itself because the cemetery has ceased to exist. Such a pattern is only too familiar. It is essential, therefore, that low-maintenance alternatives to grass should be found, and that these should be capable of being adapted for use throughout a cemetery. Alternatives there certainly are, and their adoption could contribute substantially to a long-term answer to the problems of cemetery maintenance. Among the possibilities are: substitute lawn components like mosses, which do not require mowing and are particularly suitable for areas which, if grassed, would need maintenance by hand; herbaceous plants such as lavender or any of the mat-forming species of thyme; heathers, which are easy to walk through and which can be chosen to create a year-round flowering sequence; naturalized bulbs which, similarly, can be selected to form a continuous flowering cycle. There are also many varieties of ivy that can be useful as ground-cover, though their frequently vigorous growth needs checking in order to prevent potential damage to monuments and structures. Such alternatives offer scope for considerable variation: they can be combined with each other, with areas of grass that are easily mown, and with the planting of individual graves. Most important, perhaps, they can all be combined with a programme for managing a cemetery, or part of it, as meadowland.

Meadow gardening, as it has become known, sets out to encourage the growth of wild grasses, flowers and shrubs so as to create an ecosystem like that of the traditional meadow. It has obvious attractions for the naturalist and can form the basis for successful ecological management. Although, as was stressed earlier, tree planting needs to be determined on other than primarily ecological principles, the planting of shrub and field layers can be decided in this way without jeopardizing other cemetery features. Maintenance can be reduced to the mowing of principal paths and a periodic check against brambles and saplings. The meadow area itself will need to be mown occasionally, but this need only be a seasonal operation. It should be carried out with a nylon-cord strimmer, which can be taken directly up against stonework without causing damage. Cemeteries offer a great opportunity for the development of meadow planting and advice can be found in a range of current horticultural literature. Particularly useful is the Nature Conservancy Council's pamphlet *Creating attractive grasslands* which gives information on seed mixtures and principles of establishment. In the case both of lawn substitutes and of meadow gardening, cemetery paths and roads will continue to require special attention, not only to ensure drainage and prevent damage to surfaces, but also to ensure the preservation of the cemetery's historic layout. Road and pathside verges, particularly those without kerbs, require careful attention and should be kept clear of intrusive vegetation.

As will be clear from even such a brief review as this, the range of possibilities for the horticultural management of a historic cemetery is considerable. Success is dependent upon the commitment and imagination of those responsible for the cemetery – upon their willingness, that is, to do something other than rely upon lawn as a way of ensuring cheap maintenance. Obviously, the extent to which low-maintenance alternatives to traditional horticulture are adopted, and the particular combination of those alternatives, should be responsive to the character of the cemetery itself. The more historically and aesthetically important the cemetery, and the more intact its preservation, the more desirable it is that an attempt be made to continue high-level horticultural maintenance, and to keep planting historically accurate. In practice, however, different areas within the same cemetery will vary in their historical and aesthetic interest, and this should be recognized and reflected in any approach to horticultural management. For example, a section of the cemetery containing major monuments could merit continuing intensive maintenance; the areas beside the principal paths and roadways could be planted with heathers and ground-cover; an area in which memorials were of slighter individual interest, or of relatively low density, could be managed as meadowland; formal beds could be laid out with Victorian winter bedding schemes, banks and slopes planted with naturalized bulbs; and all within the setting of a fully mature landscape. With imaginative planning, the horticulture of historic cemeteries could make a major contribution to the visual and environmental quality of our lives – as indeed it was always intended to.

Legislation and Public Policy

Cemeteries, as opposed to parish churchyards and nonconformist burial grounds, are provided and maintained either by private companies or by local authorities. When founded, private cemeteries and Burial Board cemeteries alike offered four ways of disposing of the dead: burial in a grave that was purchased either leasehold or freehold; burial in a common grave; interment in a private vault; interment in a catacomb. To these were added three methods of disposing of cremated ashes, increasingly frequent as cremation became more commonplace: burial of cremated remains; scattering of cremated remains; placing ashes in some kind of a casket within a columbarium. Although not entirely outside the jurisdiction of ecclesiastical law, cemeteries managed by local authorities are subject to The Local Authorities' Cemetery Order 1977; where a privately owned cemetery was established by means of an Act of Parliament, the owners are bound by the provisions of that Act; where there was no Act of Parliament, the owners may be bound by the terms on which the founding company was incorporated, but this may not be so if the original company has ceased to trade and the cemetery has changed hands. The discussion of legislation in this section will be concerned largely with the provisions of the 1977 Order which relate to the removal of monuments and the clearance of cemeteries.

As we have seen, responsibility for cemeteries established by Burial Boards under the terms of the Burial Acts passed to the local authorities at the end of the nineteenth century. Those authorities were also empowered to establish new cemeteries as necessary. Space in municipally owned cemeteries is now at a premium – a state of affairs that doubtless would have occurred earlier had it not been for the widespread adoption of cremation. The need for space is a principal motive behind the clearance of headstones and monuments by local authorities, and it is evident that, in some circumstances, the selective removal of memorials may be a practical necessity. A similar course of action may also be determined by other pressures, most significantly, as was discussed at length earlier, those of cost. With the reduction of the revenue derived from burials, the cost of looking after local authority cemeteries has increasingly tended to devolve upon the rates. In the attempt to reduce ancillary expenditure, cemeteries have been an obvious target for local government spending cuts. Without the introduction of low-level maintenance policies the cost of the continuing upkeep of a cemetery filled with memorials can be high: a simple, if destructive, solution has been to remove the monuments altogether. Total clearance, either of whole cemeteries or of large parts of them, has also resulted from closure and the decision either to reuse or to sell the site.

Under the 1977 Local Authorities' Cemeteries Order provision is made for both partial and wholesale clearance of cemeteries, the latter in the case of landscaping for recreational use or sale for development. Essentially, in the case of partial clearance, only graves which are more than thirty years old are subject to removal. Objections must be considered by the cemetery authority, but only those lodged by the freeholders of the grave or the relatives of the person buried in the grave carry any legal weight; for the purposes of the Order 'relatives' are defined as: a husband or wife; a child or grandchild; a parent or step-parent; a grandparent; a brother or sister, or half-brother or half-sister; an uncle or aunt or child thereof. Under the procedure laid down by the Order, a local authority intending to remove a memorial must write to the last recorded address of the freeholders of the grave, or the people who erected the monument, informing them of the decision to remove it. If no reply is received within six months of the date of the letter, then the plot number is advertised outside the cemetery entrance, and published for two consecutive weeks in those newspapers which, in the opinion of the local authority, cover the area served by the cemetery. Objections from freeholders or relatives ensure the preservation of the monument for a further hundred years. If no objections are lodged within six months then the monument may be removed. This procedure should be followed whether one memorial is involved or hundreds. In the event of removal, the Order requires the cemetery authorities to make and keep a photographic or other record of any inscription on the memorial in question. The authorities are also required to keep a record of any memorial that they have moved and re-erected.

From the historical and conservationist point of view, the 1977 Local Authorities' Cemeteries Order is woefully inadequate. Cemetery authorities may remove any monument they consider to be delapidated or on which the inscription is illegible. In the case of monuments in good condition, however, the only criterion for whether they should or should not be considered for clearance is that of age – and the criterion is such as to work directly against the preservation of older monuments. Fairly obviously, the older the monument the less likely it is that its removal will be opposed by any relatives of the deceased. The furthest descendant whose objection to the destruction of a memorial carries legal weight is a grandchild. How many grandchildren of people buried as recently even as 1914 are still alive? How many of those that do survive would be likely to be resident in the same area as their grandparents, and so be liable to receive the required notification? It is at once apparent that, after a certain lapse of time, letters and public notices relating to clearance will not – indeed cannot – reach anybody whose objections would have legal force.

Apart from the possible objections of freeholders or family, no other reasons for preserving monuments are envisaged by the Order. At no point does it even suggest that architectural qualities, artistic or sculptural merit, historical importance, even general relationship to the landscape or environment, might be relevant criteria when considering the removal of monuments or the clearance of cemeteries. Cemetery authorities are not obliged to take account of any representations they may receive relating to such issues. The provision for transcribing inscriptions is a concession towards the historical record, though there is no mention of penalties for non-compliance. Architectural significance is recognized only in relationship to buildings or structures on the site that have been afforded the statutory protection of listing, in which case local authorities must obtain listed building consent to demolish. Because criteria such as those outlined above are ignored by the Order, no provision is made for consultation other than the attempted notification of relatives or freeholders. Cemetery authorities are not specifically required to seek the views of local people or of local amenity groups, nor to consult national conservation bodies such as the Victorian Society, who could give expert advice on matters relating to art and architecture, or such as the Nature Conservancy Council, who could similarly advise on environmental and ecological issues. Indeed, on this last point, the legislation nowhere takes account of the importance of urban cemeteries in terms of natural history, or of their role as natural refuges. Nor does the Order pay any attention to the fact that historic cemeteries are major landscaped areas where planting is as much a matter for concern as architecture and memorials. Finally – and almost necessarily given the absence of adequate consultation or discussion – the Order does not distinguish between types of memorial: in the terms laid down, a monument is a monument, whether it be a simple gravestone, a family vault, or an elaborate mausoleum. Such an indiscriminate approach almost encourages lack of discrimination in any proposals for dealing with older cemeteries.

If our historic cemeteries are to be saved, future legislation must recognize that present guidelines are far too limited. The legitimacy of objections on a broader basis than those allowed at present must be acknowledged. Procedures for consultation and discussion should be established and cemetery authorities given positive encouragement to seek guidance on the amenity and historical significance of the cemeteries for which they are responsible. The great urban cemeteries of the nineteenth century offer an unparalleled combination of landscape, art, architecture and natural history. They could and should become major resources for the community at large: nothing in the present legislation helps that to happen.

If changes need to be made in the legislation governing public cemeteries, so also do they in the administrative structure of the local authorities that run them. Invariably, the reponsibilty for the maintenance of a local authority cemetery rests with the Parks and Recreation Department, or its equivalent. In many ways, this is appropriate and necessary, for it is in such departments that horticultural and landscaping skills are to be found. But those skills are not sufficient by themselves for the adequate management of a historic cemetery. Only rarely do such departments have the expertise to recognize the historical significance of particular sorts of landscape, planting and layout: as a result, well-intentioned but ill-informed alterations to a cemetery can destroy important features. Cemetery buildings are even more frequently threatened: the care and conservation of historic architecture is not, after all, part of the brief of Parks Departments. In consequence, basic structural maintenance is often ignored, lodges and chapels brutally altered or, at best, insensitively repaired. Up and down the country, the numerous cemetery chapels with boarded-up windows, breeze-blocked doorways, broken gutters and leaking roofs, are a sufficiently eloquent testimony to the low priority that has been afforded to the buildings of historic cemeteries. By the same token, monuments can be equally at risk, particularly those that are structurally elaborate. Essential as the skills of a Parks Department may be to the upkeep of a historic cemetery, it cannot be expected to deal with the often complex architectural, historical and conservation issues such a site will present. If such matters are dealt with at all at present they are the business of other departments within local government. Overall responsibility for the care of a historic cemetery in the ownership of a local authority needs to be unitary and it needs to be far more broadly based than is currently the case. This responsiblity should be vested in the Planning Department, with an internal procedure established within the authority that ensures that all proposed alterations to buildings, monuments and landscape are first scrutinized by the Conservation Section, or, where this does not exist, by the County Conservation Section. Within local government it is only the Planning Department that has access to the range and variety of expertise necessary for the formulation of an appropriate management strategy – that is, a strategy that provides an integrated approach to all those issues of maintenance, conservation and repair that a historic cemetery will present.

Given legislative and administrative changes that permit and encourage the conservation management of a historic cemetery, what is to be conserved? What protected? It would not be sensible or even feasible to seek to preserve all nineteenth-century cemeteries intact – though there are cases in which this would be the right policy to adopt, particularly in the case of cemeteries that have been closed for burial. Certainly, this is the policy that is emerging at Highgate and that will be adopted at Kensal Green. In cemeteries that are still functioning as places of burial – as is the case with most that are owned by local authorities – total preservation is not possible; nor, in the majority of cases, is it necessary. If ground is to be reused for interments, then headstones will need to be removed; where chapels are no longer needed for their original purpose decisions will need to be made about their retention, or their conversion to new uses; where high-level upkeep is no longer possible, new maintenance policies will have to be adopted, and these will inevitably change the cemetery's character. What is required is: firstly, authoritative guidance as to which cemeteries – or which parts of cemeteries, which buildings, which monuments – are of historical or aesthetic importance; and secondly, a system of legal protection that adopts an integrated approach to the assessment of cemeteries, that considers them in their totality as historic sites. In practice, the two requirements could be combined within a single operation. At present the protection that exists for historic cemeteries is uneven and unsystematic. Individual structures – lodges, chapels, walls and gates – may be statutorily listed as being of historical or architectural importance by the Secretary of State on the advice of English Heritage, in which case they enjoy the protection extended to all listed buildings. Monuments may be similarly protected, and can be listed either singly or in groups, as has been the practice in major churchyards. As was remarked earlier, the Department of the Environment's accelerated resurvey, now in its final stages, has increased the number of protected cemetery buildings and monuments, though it is difficult to know to what extent. However, the resurvey did not encompass major urban areas, where, of course, many historic cemeteries are situated. Although listed building legislation takes some account of setting, and partly extends to it, there is no statutory protection for landscape. Recently, English Heritage has compiled an initial list of historic gardens as a preliminary step – or so, at least, one hopes – to legislation for their protection. There are possibilities that this might be extended to include the planned landscapes of historic cemeteries. All this is well and good, but none of the existing mechanisms is adequate to the protection of cemeteries as a whole; none, therefore, is sufficient fully to protect individual features either, for these – whether buildings, monuments or landscape – are only comprehensible in terms of the cemetery as a whole. A historic cemetery is a uniquely integrated environment. Nominating a cemetery as a conservation area will not suffice: recent redefinitions of the terms of conservation area legislation means that only structures above a certain cubic capacity are protected – and this is too large to include even the grandest monuments. To ensure that cemeteries are properly protected, whether as a whole or in part, they must be thought of in their totality, and the criteria upon which their protection rests must be national. English Heritage, perhaps in association with the Royal Commission on the Historical Monuments of England, should commission a survey of all Victorian and Edwardian cemeteries in England. The survey should be premised on the fact that the historic cemetery is a unique building type, comprising architecture, monuments, planting and landscape. Its task should be to gather basic documentary information about each cemetery, to compile a record of its history and its present condition, and to assess its historical and aesthetic significance; the importance of cemeteries as nature reserves should also be recognized and relevant details included in the survey. When complete, the survey would allow every Victorian and Edwardian cemetery, its design, its buildings, its monuments, to be placed in its national context: it would therefore be a wholly authoritative basis upon which to determine the nature and extent of the statutory protection which England's cemeteries need. As it would also be the definitive scholarly account of English cemeteries, the survey should be made available in published form: not only for academic reasons, but also because it would give those responsible for cemeteries - whether public authorities or private companies – the information and the criteria on which to base management policies.

Changes in legislation, improvements in administration, greater and more coherent statutory protection, will all safeguard the cemetery. But in the end, the historic cemetery will be saved only if people want it to be. As was noticed earlier, there are indications that public attitudes towards the Victorian cemetery are changing. The number of voluntary groups that have been set up to protect individual cemeteries is encouraging, sufficiently so to merit the establishment of the National Federation of Cemetery Friends. The use of cemeteries as study centres for local schools; the creation of nature reserves and nature trails within cemeteries; their inclusion in town trails and local heritage walks; the slowly growing number of cemetery guide-books and histories: all are encouraging signs. Above all, perhaps, Highgate's 100,000 visitors in 1987 showed unarguably that public interest exists on a large scale. Historic cemeteries are major cultural and environmental assets: they are assets that should be realized. Although built to meet dire necessity, nineteenth-century cemeteries were designed to be places of beauty, instruction, and reflection, as well as utility. Many still are; many more could be. All this, and more, was recognized by John Claudius Loudon as long ago as 1843:

> . . . a general cemetery in the neighbourhood of a town, properly designed, laid out, ornamented with tombs, planted with trees, shrubs, and herbaceous plants, all named, and the whole properly kept, might become a school of instruction in architecture, sculpture, landscape-gardening, arboriculture, botany . . . [for] . . . cemeteries . . . [are] . . . not only calculated to improve the morals and the taste, and by their botanical riches to cultivate the intellect, but [to] serve as historical records.

Loudon's Victorian values and their objectives are ones we could profitably adopt. And, remembering the neglect and destruction that has overtaken so many of our cemeteries in the last thirty years, we should also reflect on the words of one of Loudon's predecessors, John Strang, writing in 1831.

> A garden cemetery and monumental decoration afford the most convincing tokens of a nation's progress in civilization and in the arts which are its result.

4.

GAZETTEER

THE GAZETTEER THAT FOLLOWS IS restricted to cemeteries in England. Quite deliberately, it is not definitive and in no sense comprehensive. At the present level of research, nobody could assemble a catalogue of cemeteries that could claim either definitiveness or comprehensiveness. Rather, this gazetteer is intended to provide a cross-section of nineteenth- and early twentieth-century cemeteries in order to demonstrate their range, variety and quality. It includes a choice – and no more than that – of the great urban cemeteries provided for the rapidly expanding populations of London, the industrial cities, and their conurbations. As well as these, a number of cemeteries have been chosen as representatives of the smaller industrial towns.

Moving down the demographic scale, the gazetteer also includes a selection of cemeteries established to serve the older centres of population – county towns and cathedral cities. Finally, it tries to represent the large number of cemeteries in rural England, often of only a few acres attached to market towns, by examples drawn principally from two areas – the South West and the East Midlands. In short, this gazetteer is an introduction, and only that, to the riches that Victorian and Edwardian cemeteries have to offer.

BARNSTAPLE, Devon
Goodleigh Road Cemetery

Founded by the Barnstaple Burial Board in 1856 on a valley site, the land sloping down from the main entrance on Goodleigh Road then up again on the north side of the cemetery. The pair of identical chapels, neatly managed in early Decorated with slatestone rubble walls, are near the lodge, a substantial building of two storeys with stone-mullioned windows, double gables to the road, and a Bath stone bellcote over the door; massive gatepiers, largely in granite and good cast iron gates with Gothic detailing. Despite a crude red brick wall recently built, the whole ensemble of chapels, lodge and gates mass very well together: the architect was Richard Davie Gould, the town surveyor who, with his son John Ford Gould, formed the most important north Devon architectural practice in the 1860s and 1870s. Partial clearance of monuments has damaged the cemetery visually, but a number of interesting memorials remain, including: an octagonal Gothic canopy with freestone columns, dating from the 1860s, to members of the Britton family, designed by the local firm of monumental masons, William Youings and Sons; a fine freestone chest tomb with black and red tiles, to William and Ann Davis who died within a few days of each other in 1860, as the inscription emphasizes.

BATH, Avon
Abbey Cemetery

An Anglican cemetery designed to serve the wealthy and genteel, it was financed by the Rector of Bath Abbey, W.J.Brodrick, who, as the Archbishop of Cashel's son and, later, seventh viscount Midleton, was both wealthy and genteel himself. South-east of the town, with fine views over the Bath Valley, the cemetery occupies a triangular site of 5 acres, sloping steeply up to the apex. It was laid out to designs by J.C. Loudon in 1843–4, and the plan has the strong formality he liked. The carriage drive climbs up one side of the site; the principal path, still grassed, runs axially straight uphill from the base of the triangle to the single chapel, splendidly placed at the apex; the drive curves round to meet the axial path in front of the chapel, continuing round in a large oval and returning across the path further down the slope. There is a subsidiary path inside the oval, and others run parallel to the main axis. The planting is mixed, with evergreens predominating, and does not follow the formality of the lay-out, though trees are concentrated at some key points, as at the intersection of the oval and the axial path. The chapel, in the Norman style, was designed by the leading Bath architect G.P. Manners: its three stage tower, with pyramidal spire, looks down the long axial path, its bottom stage open on three sides through Norman arches and vaulted internally; the main vessel is of three bays, the windows framed by strip pilasters. As one might expect, the Abbey has numerous high quality and expensive monuments, most of them at the head of the cemetery. In prime position, in front of the chapel, is a two-stage pedestal tomb in white marble with sharply carved acroteria and laurel sprays, commemorating Anne Partis d.1846, who endowed a college for gentlewomen 'reduced by widowhood or orphanage from affluence to privation and distress'. Among the surrounding monuments: to Jane Williams d.1848, a classical plinth with canopy containing a draped urn attended by an angel and a female mourner; to Samuel Hinds d.1847, a draped urn within an elegantly managed peristyle set on a large base; medievalism makes an appearance in the chest tomb with floriated cross to Lady Joanne Habgood d.1849, and in the contemporaneous neo-Norman tomb nearby, its inscription now illegible. On one side of the drive as it curves up to the chapel, an obelisk with draped flags commemorates

Abbey Cemetery, Bath, 1843-4; the chapel, designed by G. P. Manners.

Captain Peter Capper d.1866; on the other side is a large, four-poster classical canopy over a rotunda topped with a coronet, all on a plinth carved with military trophies, in memory of Charles Pratt who served in Flanders, the Cape and the Peninsula and d.1844 – one of the earliest memorials in the cemetery. They are two of the best of a large number of monuments to military men, evidence of Bath's mid-nineteenth-century popularity with the soldiers of empire. So too, further down the drive, is the large obelisk built by public subscription to commemorate inhabitants of the town who died during the Crimean War.

Lansdown Cemetery

Opened in 1848, situated on Lansdown Hill to the north east of the town and, even now, well outside it; an exposed site with panoramic views of Bath and the surrounding countryside. The land for the cemetery was originally a pleasure ground belonging to William Beckford, in his youth perhaps the richest man in England, and builder of that definitive Gothic *folie de grandeur*, Fonthill; from the 1820s he lived in Bath, where he died in 1844, having passed most of his later years as a recluse. He was buried in the Abbey Cemetery. However, up on Lansdown Hill in 1825-7 he had built a great Italianate tower – as if to compensate himself for that at Fonthill – to the designs of Henry Edmund Goodridge, the architect of many buildings in late Georgian Bath. Beckford wanted to be buried near his tower, and his daughter, the Duchess of Hamilton, gave the land around it to the town as a public cemetery. The tower is 130 feet high, rising from a two-storey Italianate house; its square shaft is sheer, surmounted by a Tuscan belvedere and topped off by a lantern loosely based on the Choragic Monument of Lysicrates with, interestingly enough, cast iron columns. For the entrance to the cemetery Goodridge designed a grand gatehouse in an Italianate Romanesque style not dissimilar to Wyatt and Brandon's near-contemporary church at Wilton, just down the road from Fonthill: the deep, semi-circular central arch has richly carved detail, with Byzantine capitals to the shafts and a ribbed barrel vault internally, the ribs of the vault carrying finely lettered inscriptions; flanking the arch are pedestrian passageways, with blind arcading internally, and square-headed entrances, over one of which is carved 'Resurgat', over the other, less encouragingly, 'The Gates of Death'. To either side of the gatehouse, Goodridge's perimeter wall has inventive Romanesque piers. Relatively narrow and long, with the gatehouse and tower at its north end, the cemetery has a sunken central area with a terraced walk along one side, next to the perimeter wall; the central area has been largely cleared of monuments. Mixed planting – in which laurel bushes, yews and cypresses

Lansdown Cemetery, Bath, opened in 1848; Beckford's tower of 1825-7, designed by H. E. Goodridge, and, in the foreground, Beckford's tomb.

predominate – is concentrated around the tower, where the major monuments are also sited: a good, representative collection, both classical and Gothic. Somewhat unusual is the tomb of Annie Perugini d.1857 – a tapering Grecian pedestal with palm branches strewn liberally all over the top. And, of course, there is Beckford, re-interred, according to his wish, in 1848: his tomb, which he designed himself in association with Goodridge, is a long chest of polished pink granite, severely plain, with simplified Egyptian columns at the corners and applied bronze armorials at the ends. With characteristic exhibitionism the monument is surrounded by its own ditch; apparently, and disarmingly, it is also close to the grave of Beckford's favourite dog, Tiny.

Lyncombe and Widcombe Cemetery

An 8 acre Burial Board cemetery, opened in 1862 on the Lower Bristol Road. The grounds were laid out by a Mr Butler of Widcombe. The architect was the successful local practitioner C.E. Davis. The asymmetrically massed lodge is of two storeys, with a tall, hipped, red-tiled roof, and robust Gothic detailing. The lodge connects with the triple-arched entrance, the central carriage-arch gabled and springing from free-standing octagonal piers. The rectangular site slopes uphill from the entrance, its upper boundary formed by a railway cutting. The identical Decorated chapels are cruciform and polygonally apsed, each face of the apse separately gabled, all the window tracery reticulated; they are placed end-to-end and linked via short lobbies to a double *porte-cochère*, each arch separately gabled; rising over the centre is a bell-tower, its belfry stage now missing, its tall base heavily buttressed and pinnacled. With its varied outline, good detailing, warm Bath stone and red-tiled roofs, the chapel group makes a most attractive ensemble: unfortunately, it is fenced off and apparently in a parlous structural state. Planting is informal and mixed, with Cedar of Lebanon and yew near the chapels, single cypresses, and some fine mature beeches. Most of the early monuments have been cleared, though there are some good, if modest, individual headstones.

Perrymead Cemetery

A small Roman Catholic cemetery of 1860-61 immediately beyond the Abbey Cemetery and sharing one boundary wall with it. The small, steeply gabled Decorated chapel has a wheel window and door at its west end, the latter with crisply carved foliated capitals and dripstone heads, separate nave and chancel with a large bellcote over the division between them, and a separately roofed vestry south of the chancel; internally there is good quality Bath stone ashlar, boldly handled arches between nave and chancel, and chancel and vestry, with rich naturalistic foliage capitals, and a complete set of stained-glass windows. But the chapel is outdone by Perrymead's oustanding feature, the Eyre family chantry of 1861 by Charles Francis Hansom. The style is again Decorated Gothic, but more refined in both design and detail; of three bays with an apsidal east end, a north porch approached up a flight of steps from the cemetery

Perrymead Roman Catholic Cemetery, Bath; the Eyre family mortuary chapel of 1861, designed by C. F. Hansom.

entrance, and, again on the north side, a hexagonal belltower, sheer to the arcaded belfry stage, with a hexagonal stone spire above ornamented by a single circle of gableted trefoils; all the windows of two lights set high, with geometrical tracery, apart from the three-light west window, which has reticulated tracery of great linear clarity; the floor tiling of the porch incorporates the Eyre armorials. The cemetery's third building is a lodge, of rock faced masonry, very small, with uncusped lancets below square hoodmoulds and a miniaturized staircase wing under a separate gable. Domestic and workaday against the aristocratic sophistication of the chantry on the other side of the entrance, the lodge provides less room for a family to live in than the Eyres have to lie in.

BEDFORD

Bedford Cemetery

Established by the Bedford Joint Burial Board and opened in 1855 when all churchyards in the town were closed. Originally of 18 acres, doubled in size in 1885; the site slopes down to the south with views over Bedford and the Great Ouse Valley. Picturesque layout with winding paths and a wide variety of trees, informally planted. Buildings by Thomas Jobson Jackson of Bedford, who also laid out the cemetery following a survey by another local architect, John Usher, who established the partnership of Usher and Anthony, the most important architectural practice in the county in the second half of the century. Red brick gatehouse with a central carriage arch, all in an eclectic Gothic that picks up motifs from the thirteenth to the sixteenth centuries. The chapels are of local limestone and have lancet windows; they are set end to end with a central entrance tower, chunky in design, with a pyramidal roof. There is a tactfully designed crematorium, north of the chapels, similarly in local stone, similarly with lancets; it dates from the cemetery's centenary in 1955, when the chapels were also revamped internally. North-east of the chapels is the Wyatt family enclosure, railed and gated, with a good range of Victorian memorial types, and including the tomb of James Wyatt d.1878, the founder of the *Bedford Times* and the man who secured the land for the cemetery. John Usher d.1904 was also buried in the cemetery but his memorial seems to have been destroyed. Parts of the cemetery have been cleared of monuments, and it is now closed for burial.

BIRMINGHAM

Brandwood End Cemetery, Broad Lane

A large suburban cemetery on the south east edge of the city, opened 1898, and immaculately maintained. It has a strong formal layout with the straight main drive striking obliquely across the flat site from the lodge at the north to the Broad Lane entrance at the south, taking in the chapels and the Great War memorial. The main drive is bordered with clipped bushes of yew, privet and box, behind which cypresses screen the burial areas so no monuments are actually apparent from the drive itself: subsidiary paths cross it at right angles, several with fine avenues, including two of Wellingtonia that mark the war memorial. The buildings are by J.Brewin Holmes: Jacobethan lodge in red brick and terracotta, dated 1897; the chapels, joined by a *porte-cochère*, which has a fine pinnacled tower surmounted by an octagonal spire, date from 1898. The style is free Perpendicular and the whole group is clad in bright red terracotta, with plenty of pinnacles and lively detailing: its contrast with the dark foliage of the cedars and monkey-puzzles around the carriage turn is particularly striking. The best monuments are grouped near the chapels, and include a lot of Edwardian angels.

Handsworth Cemetery

Opened 1909, an extensive municipal cemetery, the most distinguished feature of which is the majestic chapel by the Birmingham Arts and Crafts architect W.H. Bidlake. Of red brick with dressings in smart white stone, it is very tall and forms a single vessel, apsed at both ends: flanking the west apse are a pair of towers each with an octagonal pierced-tracery belfry stage and a short spirelet. The doors, with excellent ironwork, are to north and south. The body of the chapel is of six bays, with a shallow transept, high parapets and, at clerestory level, slender two-light windows with free tracery: in the relationship between wall surface, windows and buttressing, the whole design recalls Albi. The chapel stands on a platform reached at its north east corner by a broad flight of steps from the principal carriage drive, which is bordered with alternate horse-chestnuts and junipers. Near the chapel is a single storey cemetery office, presumably also by Bidlake.

Warstone Lane Cemetery, Birmingham, 1846-8; the gatehouse and lodge, designed by J. R. Hamilton.

Key Hill Cemetery

Birmingham's first cemetery, in the Jewellery Quarter, 8 acres in extent, opened in 1835 and intended for all denominations though in practice it was used almost exclusively by nonconformists; the total cost was £12,000. For description see pp.16-17. The Doric chapel, designed by Charles Edge, had a tetrastyle portico: it was demolished in 1966. Something of the quality of his work can be gathered from the fine Greek gatepiers that survive at both the Key Hill and Icknield Street entrances. The earliest monuments are around the site of the chapel and in the catacomb hollow, above which was an observatory, the platform of which still survives. Greek-inspired designs predominate, with many obelisks and draped urns: Gothic pinnacles infiltrate amidst the nonconformist classicism later in the century. Among monuments of particular aesthetic interest: near the catacombs, the small Ashford sarcophagus of 1846 with carved wreaths and inverted torches, and the wholly severe monument to the manufacturer John Henderson d.1856, a great granite block on a stepped plinth; near the chapel, the badly weathered memorial to the Smith family, a tapering pedestal with large figures in relief around the plinth, its date now illegible. Joseph Chamberlain (1836-1914), who called Key Hill 'the most interesting place in the world to a Birmingham man', is buried here under a very modest headstone among many other leading figures of Birmingham nonconformity in the nineteenth century: they include Robert Dale, George Dawson, Harriet Martineau and Charles Vince.

Warstone Lane Cemetery

Established by the Birmingham Church of England Cemetery Company and opened in 1848 to provide an Anglican alternative to Key Hill, a few hundred yards away. Laid out on a 9 acre site that drops steeply downhill towards Icknield Street, its buildings, the designs for which are dated 1846, were by J.R. Hamilton of the Gloucester firm of Hamilton and Medland. His lodge at the Warstone Lane entrance survives, though abandoned: picturesquely handled Tudor Gothic in brick, stone dressings, a central carriage arch under an oriel. From there the main drive winds to the site of the chapel, which stood on a broad terrace above the two tier catacomb circle. The chapel, demolished in the 1950s, was Perpendicular with a diagonally buttressed west tower and octagonal spire rising to a height of 116 feet. Immediately behind the steeple, stretching north and south along the terrace, were transeptal cloisters, also Perpendicular, five bays to either side with vaults below. The catacombs, with individual entrances through paired Tudor arches, are on two castellated terraces of rock-faced masonry, arranged around a quadrated circle: all the archways are now blocked. Superbly positioned at the highest point in the cemetery, the whole ensemble of chapel, cloisters and catacombs was one of the most impressive conceptions in Victorian cemetery architecture – an authentic exercise in the sublime. The demolition of chapel and cloisters was a major aesthetic loss. The grounds have been selectively but extensively cleared; there are no outstanding monuments, though a pleasant scatter of headstones survives beneath the trees on the hillside west of the catacombs.

Witton Cemetery, Moor Lane

The City of Birmingham Cemetery, and the first provided for the city under the provisions of the Burial Acts. First proposed in 1853, the extensive 105 acre site north of the centre was not purchased until 1859; the first burial took place in 1861, the formal opening in 1864. The grounds were laid out by Ashwell of Coventry, his design focused on a grand central avenue, lined with lime trees, running between the Anglican and nonconformist chapels up the spine of the rectangular site see p.53. The buildings were designed by R.Clarke of Nottingham, who won a national competition for them in 1860. The cemetery office at the main entrance on Moor Lane, is consciously imposing: freely managed Decorated Gothic in rock-faced stone, L-shaped in plan, two-storeyed, and boasting a square clock tower with an open arcaded belfry stage below a tall, tapering pyramidal roof crested with ironwork and a weather-vane. Opposite the office is the more modest cemetery keeper's lodge. Of Clarke's chapels, only the Anglican one survives, on a terrace reached by a broad flight of steps from the south end of the central avenue: Decorated and emphatically asymmetrical, with a high, steeply gabled nave, and a slender tower and broach spire. At the north end of the main avenue the terrace and steps for the dissenters' chapel remains, but alas no chapel. Some Victorian and Edwardian monuments remain around the Church of England chapel: none are of particular distinction, though the view from here over the high-rise centre of the city is eloquent. Elsewhere, twentieth-century memorials fill the ground. In the north east corner of the site is the separate Jewish cemetery, with a little octagonal chapel in Decorated, presumably also by Clarke.

BOLTON, Lancashire

Tonge Cemetery

The earliest of the Bolton cemeteries, 35 acres in extent, opened by the Burial Board in 1857 with buildings by Charles Holt, who won the competition for their design. Symmetrical lodge and offices; the chapels in Early English with rock-faced masonry, the Anglican one equipped with a bell turret, the nonconformist one far simpler in detail; the Roman Catholic chapel that Holt also designed has been demolished. As on might expect, the cemetery has a good collection of monuments to Bolton's mid-Victorian industrialists and manufacturers, but there are also memorials to other, almost equally characteristic figures from the town's nineteenth-century culture, among them Thomas Yates, the radical reformer, who d.1857, and John Francet d.1867, composer of oratorios with such resonant evangelical titles as 'Paradise' and 'The Harp of Zion'.

Witton Cemetery, Birmingham, 1860-64; the cemetery offices and registry, designed by R. Clarke.

Box Cemetery, Wiltshire, 1858; the chapel, designed by W. F. Poulton and W. H. Woodman.

BOX, Wiltshire
Box Cemetery

A small rural cemetery, beautifully maintained, and of surprising architectural quality. The buildings, of 1858, were designed by a firm of cemetery specialists, Poulton and Woodman of Reading. The chapel is inventively Gothic, in Cotswold Stone, the crazed rubble masonry alternating with bands of ashlar, and with a graded slatestone roof. The main vessel, steeply gabled, is of three bays, the side windows paired with demi-angels carved between them; the east window has tight geometrical tracery, the west window, of five lights, has a trellis of trefoils and fleur de lys framing the central panel of tracery. At the north-west corner, grouped with the porch, is a slender octagonal spirelet propped by a flying buttress. The Gothic lodge and boundary wall have the same masonry treatment as the chapel. The only monument of aesthetic note is the oval chest tomb in local stone to Ann Elliott d.1861.

BRADFORD, West Yorkshire
Undercliffe Cemetery

Laid out on a 25 acre hilltop site north-east of the centre of Bradford, with panoramic views over the town, Undercliffe was established in 1854 by the Bradford Cemetery Company. The landscape architect was William Gay, the cemetery's first registrar, whose design brilliantly exploited the site with a great promenade running the width of the cemetery, approached by steep winding paths, culminating in a viewing platform and the 30 feet obelisk to Joseph Smith d.1858, the land agent who plotted the cemetery and had first choice of position for his own monument. In the centre of the promenade were the two chapels: these were designed by Mallinson and Healey in 1853, but replaced with two by Lockwood and Mawson in 1878, which were themselves demolished in the 1980s; also demolished at the same time were the sexton's lodge and the registrar's house, designed by Gay, either side of the main entrance from Undercliffe Lane. Although the loss of its buildings is profoundly regrettable, Undercliffe's glory remains in its outstanding collection of monuments, many to the magnates of the Bradford woollen industry. The perspective of obelisks, pinnacles and pedestals along the central promenade is one of the most striking achievements of Victorian funerary design. Of the memorials there is room here to mention only a few: the life-sized Grecian figure of a female mourner, carved by John Throp of Leeds, to the memory of Miles Moulson d.1856, himself a monumental mason; the memorial of Swithen Anderton d.1860, an elaborate, pinnacled canopy in Decorated Gothic to one of the city's first wool barons; Robert Milligan's tall and slender pillar of grey granite, dating from 1862; the massive Baroque tablet to Sir Jacob Behrens d.1889; similarly of 1889 is the Egyptian obelisk to the architect William Mawson, with a bronze portrait medallion. Also Egyptian is the mausoleum of the Illingworth family, of grey granite, its entrance flanked by guardian sphinxes. Another mausoleum of quality is that of the Holden family, this time Renaissance in inspiration, with Ionic corner shafts and a quadripartite barrel-vaulted roof, with good relief carving externally. The cemetery is now owned by Bradford City Council – who saved it from the destructiveness of a property developer in the early 1980s – and administered by the Bradford Undercliffe Cemetery Company; it is still used for burials.

BRISTOL
Arno's Vale Cemetery

Founded by the Bristol General Cemetery Company and opened in 1840, its buildings designed by Charles Underwood. The pair of tetrastyle Doric lodges face each other across the entrance, which is on the eastern margin of the cemetery's grounds. Inside, the drive divides to encircle a level area which is embraced by high ground, curving round to the south and west – a remarkable landscape setting that the cemetery's lay-out fully exploits. Both chapels have the rising ground as their backdrop: to the south is the Anglican chapel, in a Renaissance style with Corinthian pilasters and pedimented bellcote; to the west, the nonconformist chapel, with a tall Ionic tetrastyle, its immediate setting spoilt by a squat crematorium that nudges up alongside. From the chapels, paths run up into the higher ground amidst luxuriant mixed planting, which includes a number of flowering trees. See also pp.19-20. Ugly swathes have been cut through the monuments to make Gardens of Rest for the cremations that now form most of Arno's Vale's business, and sporadic clearances have made further inroads into the cemetery's historic fabric. But much remains, and only a selection of monuments from the area in front of the chapels and on the higher ground to the west is offered here: most exotic is the tomb of Raja Rammohun Roy d.1833, Indian scholar and social reformer, which has a cross-plan podium canopied with a conical dome based on a Hindu sikhara, the canopy supported on twelve columns, again based on Hindu forms, and decorated with blue ceramic insets; it was designed by William Prinsep and erected in 1844; opposite is a complicated little tower, made up of multiple stages of columns like a wedding cake, commemorating members of the Challenger family and apparently dating from 1907; near the Anglican chapel, Gothic pinnacles in memory of Jane King d.1876 and Walter Gardner d.1880, and a crisply ornamented Gothic pedestal tomb commemorating John Cornish d.1861; near the nonconformist chapel is the busily eclectic memorial to Lady Mary Wathen d.1881, its obelisk, decorated with foliage trails, rising from a gabled plinth with delicately carved angels standing at the corners; higher up the slope are monuments to the Wills family, the Bristol tobacco magnates, including the coped tomb chest of Henry Overton Wills d.1871, and the more than usually elegant draped urn on plinth in memory of his wife, Alice, who died ten years later.

Arno's Vale Cemetery, Bristol; tomb of Raja Rammohun Roy, d.1833, erected 1844 to the designs of William Prinsep.

BURTON-ON-TRENT, Staffordshire
Stapenhill Cemetery

Established 1865-6 by the Burton Burial Board at the very considerable cost of £20,500, Stapenhill had an original area of 12 acres, extended by a further 22 in 1883. All the buildings were designed by the Liverpool partnership of Lucy and Littler, who designed Birkenhead Cemetery in 1862. Set above the River Trent, the site slopes upward from the main entrance, which is managed with considerable originality: it is a detached wall in coursed millstone rubble with three pointed arched gateways, each gabled, and divided by bulky pinnacles containing statue niches under nodding ogees. The lodge, firmly asymmetrical, is detached and stands to one side of the main drive, which rises to a junction with the terraced promenade connecting the two chapels: beyond the junction, a formal circle is cut into the hillside. The chapels, in a vigorously handled Decorated, are identical, though one has lost its steeple: constituent masses are clearly demarcated, window tracery nicely varied; on the chapel that retains it, the asymmetrically placed steeple exhibits that inventiveness in form and profile of which the High Victorian Goths were masters. Away from the regularity of the avenue and circle, the cemetery's layout relaxes into informality, with mixed evergreen and broadleaf planting. The best monuments, as one would expect, are along the main promenade. Near the nonconformist chapel are two chunky High Victorian crosses to members of the Wayte family, both dating from the 1860s and signed W. Clarke; nearby the Gothic octagon to William Lowe d.1877, a Burton builder 'who was accidentally killed while driving to business'; in front of the Anglican chapel is a pink and grey granite obelisk to Charlotte Ratcliff d.1869.

CAMBRIDGE
Histon Road Cemetery

Now rather bleak, but historically important as the only cemetery that was fully carried out to Loudon's designs. it was established in 1843 by the Cambridge General Cemetery company. For history and description see pp. 38-9. The layout of Loudon's paths remains, as does the avenue of yews to the axial drive and the cedars around the site of the chapel. The Gothic chapel itself, designed by Edward Buckton Lamb, has gone, but his lodge remains: a characteristically robust Tudor design in yellow brick with red brick decoration, square-headed mullioned windows, a lean-to porch, and a prominent canted staircase bay between two chimney breasts, each with two square stacks. The lodge is centrally placed in the perimeter wall and railings to Histon Road, with gateways to either side, their unusually profiled piers in red and yellow brick heavily buttressed on all four sides. Some early monuments remain near the lodge, lining the main path as Loudon intended: but the rest of the cemetery has been cleared and now exhibits a mean scatter of twentieth-century memorials.

CARLISLE, Cumbria
Dalston Road Cemetery

A Burial Board cemetery of 1854, built a mile south west of the city at a cost of £14,000. The sanitary condition of Carlisle in the 1840s was appalling, and its six churchyards full: the cemetery was one of a sequence of measures designed to remedy the situation. It was originally of 43 acres, extended by a further 20 acres in 1885-7. the 1850s buildings were by J.W.H. and J.M. Hay of Liverpool: two red-brick chapels with white-stone dressings, in the Early English style, both with bell turrets; the entrance lodge and gate are in the same materials and style. Well maintained planting, with yew tree avenues bordered by flower beds. As well as a number of good representative monuments to Carlisle worthies, the cemetery contains a triangular obelisk to the memory of the Scottish architect Peter Nicholson d.1844, whose extensive publications included *The Architectural Dictionary* of 1812-19.

CHARD, Somerset
Chard Cemetery

Founded in 1857 by the Chard Burial Board at a cost of £3500, the cemetery occupies a rectangular 5½ acre site, the ground falling away to the east. The layout shows the direct influence of Loudon: an axial drive runs west-east the length of the cemetery, through the *porte-cochère* that links the two chapels, and a perimeter path runs round the whole site. Boundary hedges are composed of yew and holly; a fine pair of cedars stands at the rear of the chapels, either side of the axial drive, which, like the chapels, is bordered by clipped yew bushes. Apart from this, there is

Chard Cemetery, Somerset, 1857; the chapels.

no planting within the cemetery – everything is lucid and formal, as Loudon liked it. The chapels are linked to an ogivally arched *porte-cochère* by short corridors, lit by segmental headed windows; the chapels are identical, Decorated in style, with geometrical tracery. All the masonry is Ham Hill stone, beautifully textured, and the detailing is refined and delicate – see, for example, the shallow relief foliage carving in the spandrels of the *porte-cochère*. The most ambitious monument is the mausoleum of William Moore d.1901 and family: a white marble box with a heavenward pointing angel sitting on the roof, decoratively pierced iron doors, attractively patterned slate and marble floors, and a lancet end window with a Nativity in stained glass by A.L. and C.E. Moore of London, – presumably related to the deceased; the whole thing is in perfect condition. There are a number of good representative monuments; the most interesting is a railed grey granite obelisk to John Stringfellow d.1883, the inventor who designed the first engine driven aeroplane which actually flew.

CHELTENHAM, Gloucestershire
Lower High Street Cemetery

One of the earliest of English cemeteries, established to relieve the parish churchyard of St Mary's. It was 10 acres in area, laid out in 1830–31 with a Greek chapel designed by Charles Paul of the Cheltenham firm, Rowland Paul and Sons: Doric, with two columns in antis to the entrance front and funerary wreaths carved above; it cost £600. To judge from contemporary engravings the original planting included weeping willows around the chapel. The cemetery largely fell out of use in the 1860s, when the Bouncers Lane cemetery was built, and was neglected for a century. In 1966 the grounds were cleared and converted to a public park: the chapel, externally intact, is now used for a variety of community purposes.

Bouncers Lane Cemetery

Opened in 1864, and attractively sited below the Cotswold Hills; the buildings were designed by W.H. Knight of Cheltenham who was placed first in the 1862 competition for the commission; they cost some £4300. The Decorated Gothic lodge, T-shape on plan and robustly detailed, stands by the straight drive that runs from the entrance on to the street to the entrance into the cemetery proper – both with excellent wrought-iron gates. From the inner entrance the main carriage-drive, lined with mature conifers, curves to the chapel group. Geometrical Decorated in style, with rock-faced masonry and pattern tile roofs, the chapel group is expansively scaled, and rich in detail and plasticity. The chapels, differentiated by tracery detail, are set parallel to one another, the two-light side windows under tall separate gables pierced by traceried roundels at parapet level, the four-light end windows with individual shafts to the mullions; glazed, traceried corridors of five bays, the middle bay canted out, link the chapels to a central *porte-cochère* in a big, three-stage bell tower, the paired belfry windows deeply recessed; above the belfry stage a fine broach spire, with lucarnes and statue niches, rises to a height of 105 feet. Near the chapel group, and fetchingly domestic beside its grandeur, is an octagonal wooden shelter for visitors to the cemetery. Most of the monuments are relatively modest. The most signal exception is the powerful French Gothic canopy tomb of Thomas Champion d.1872, in polychromatic masonry with statues at the corners; also robustly High Victorian is the memorial to Annie Herbert d.1887, a thick-set spirelet crowded round with stubby pinnacles; more conventionally Gothic, and well-sited at the end of the principal pathway to the *porte-cochère*, is the pinnacle in memory of Andrew Brown, a local Congregationalist minister who died in 1879.

CHESTERFIELD, Derbyshire
Spital Cemetery

The earliest and most interesting of the three nineteenth-century cemeteries in the town, established on a hillside site originally of 6 acres by the Chesterfield and Tapton Burial Board, and opened in 1857. The competition for the buildings was held in 1856 and won by Bidlake and Lovatt of Wolverhampton; at the same time, a competition for landscaping the grounds was won by F. C. Gillett of Chesterfield. The lodge and paired chapels are Early English, built at a cost of £2,600. The layout is informal, with paths and carriage-drive following the contours of the hill. Among the monuments is an oddity: a sandstone Greek temple about four feet high, the date and epitaph no longer legible.

CREWKERNE, Somerset
Crewkerne Cemetery

A Burial Board Cemetery on a 4 acre hillside site north-east of the town, opened in 1874. The lodge, with a fine monkey puzzle in the garden, is unusually ambitious: big, entirely in Ham Hill stone, with a strongly irregular main elevation and blind tracery panels below the voussoirs of some of the windows. The layout is still picturesque, with paths meandering gently through and round the sloping, oblong site. The chapels, set end-to-end and linked by a *porte-cochère*, stand in the centre of the cemetery; they form a strong group, Early French in a robust High Victorian mood: over the *porte-cochère* a tower rises to a belfry with large lancets and tightly grouped corner pinnacles, then to an octagonal stone spire; the unbuttressed chapels are apsidally ended, each face of the apses separately gabled. Almost all the monuments are twentieth-century and dull, but the planting is impressive: around the chapels, majestic cedars, pines and monkey puzzles; shaped yew trees to the main path; around the perimeter, a mixture of mature evergreens above laurel hedges, including some shingle oaks.

DERBY
Chaddesdon Cemetery

Derby's first municipal cemetery, of 43 acres, opened in 1855 by the city's Joint Burial Board at a cost of £23,500.

Chaddesdon Cemetery, Derby, 1854-5; panoramic view from the main drive.

The buildings form a single group aligned along Nottingham Road; all in pale yellow-grey ashlar with dark grey slate roofs; all in a muscular Gothic, with big geometrical masses predominant, strongly handled and impressive. The central entrance is under a three-stage clock tower, surmounted by a pyramidal roof; the tower is linked by short single-storey ranges to the lodges, which in turn connect by curtain walls to the two chapels. The tower has paired corner buttresses, a semi-circular stair turret and plate tracery windows; more plate tracery to the street in the connecting ranges, which have waiting areas under pentices on the cemetery sides; the lodges have prominent external chimney stacks which balance the mass of the clock tower; the chapels are cruciform, their low pyramidal spires over the crossings bracketting the composition of the whole group. The grounds are flat, the main and perimeter drives curving, with a grid pattern of paths between. Planting is concentrated on the drives and around the boundary, including avenues of limes, with the burial areas kept clear of trees. The major Victorian monuments are sited along the principal drive and include: an obelisk with military trophies to Captain Charles Thorold d.1855, one of the first burials in the cemetery; three identical crosses with Early French detailing and memorial dates of the 1860s and 1870s, to employees of the Midland Railway Company, by J.B. Robinson of Derby; also by Robinson and again muscularly Early French, a gabled cross to John Mould d.1867; a heavyweight Celtic cross to George Holme d.1893. Away from the main drives are many late Victorian headstones of considerable inventiveness and iconographical variety. Near the entrance, Edwardian and interwar monuments predominate, sometimes concentrated into visually intriguing collections of pointed headstones, ivy-clad crosses, urns, open bibles, and heavenward-pointing angels – all in white marble.

EXETER, Devon
Bartholomew Street Cemetery

Essentially an extension of the seventeenth-century city burial ground, the inadequacy of which was scandalously evident in the cholera epidemic of 1832, but intended from the beginning to be interdenominational. It was laid

out in 1836-7 by the Improvement Commissioners to the designs of their surveyor, Thomas Whitaker, on a steep slope 5 acres in extent, immediately below the old burial ground. The consecrated and unconsecrated sections were divided by a wall, now demolished; there were no chapels, but catacombs were built in the medieval city wall with a terrace walk on top, all to designs in the Egyptian style by Whitaker: linked with tiers of underground chambers, they allowed for an astonishing total of 22,000 bodies. In fact, there were only ever a few interments in them. The cemetery itself was full by 1874, most burials having been in common graves, and it was closed and landscaped for public recreation, retaining some monuments near the entrance to the catacombs. Atmospheric, and dramatically positioned below the city walls, the cemetery was one of the earliest to be funded by public money.

Higher Cemetery

Laid out in 1866 on a hilltop east of the city, originally of 10 acres, increased to 38 by the First World War and now larger still. The openness of the site is reflected in the openness of the layout. The buildings all by Edward Ashworth of Exeter: good domestic Gothic lodge and paired Decorated chapels on the crest of the hill, approached by a short curving carriage drive. The buildings are in dark red local stone varied with restrained polychromatic masonry, the chapels carefully distinguished from each other by the detailing of stonework and ironwork. Behind the chapels the burial areas are laid out on a grid plan, with planting informally distributed by way of counterpoint: varieties of cypress and cedar dominate, with yews and monkey puzzles round the chapels, and bushes of rhododendrons, variegated holly and laurel; more bushes for the perimeter planting; flower beds near the lodge and along the main drive. The more recent areas of the cemetery are planted with deciduous and flowering trees. The most impressive monument is that designed and executed by Harry Hems to the 160 victims of the Exeter Theatre Royal Fire of 1887 – a monolithic Purbeck marble Celtic cross, almost abstract in the severity of its geometry. No major architectural monuments but many good headstones, crosses and pinnacles near the chapels: large gravestone to Harry Hems d.1916 and members of his family, with a delicately carved crucifixion by Hems himself for his son Archie d.1884; polychromatic cross to the cemetery architect, Edward Ashworth d.1896. Some areas of the cemetery have been cleared of monuments.

Bartholomew Street Cemetery, Exeter, 1836-7; general view from the catacomb terrace built to the designs of Thomas Whitaker.

FALMOUTH, Cornwall
Falmouth Cemetery

A Burial Board cemetery opened in 1857 immediately south of the town on an 8 acre site between the sea on the east and the landlocked Swan Pool on the west, towards which the ground drops steeply. The lodge to the main entrance on Pennance Road is of 1882 and dull, but immediately behind it are delightful twin chapels of 1856-7 in a miniaturized and very unarchaeological Neo-Norman, rendered white. Luxuriant planting, particularly dense in the higher part of the cemetery, with bushes of rhododendrons, laurels, azaleas and hydrangeas, all spreading informally beneath big conifers. The paths meander picturesquely down to a flight of steps leading to Madeira Walk, which marks the original western edge of the cemetery but now looks down into the twentieth-century extension. The Walk was conceived, very successfully, as a major formal feature, with a carriage turn and viewing terrace commanding the prospect over Swan Pool. There are no monuments of particular distinction.

GREAT MALVERN, Worcestershire
Wilton Road Cemetery

Opened in 1861 by the local Burial Board and quite large, a reflection of Great Malvern's popularity as an upper middle-class health resort in the mid-Victorian period. The buildings were designed by W.H. Knight of Cheltenham, the architect of the Bouncers Lane Cemetery there in 1862-3. Here there is a well-managed Gothic lodge which masses with the canted walls that flank the main gate to create an impressive entrance. The two chapels, in dark rubble masonry, are linked by a *porte-cochère* with tower and spire, all in a lighter coloured ashlar. As one might expect, there are a number of worthwhile monuments: most famous, and visually one of the most distinctive, is that to Jenny Lind, 'the Swedish nightingale', heart throb of early Victorian opera-goers; she died in 1887.

GREAT TORRINGTON, Devon
Bideford Road Cemetery

A delightful and very complete little cemetery of 6 acres, laid out by the Great Torrington Burial Board in 1854 at a cost of £1600 on land enclosed from the town common. The substantially buttressed wall to the main road curves in to the entrance, which retains its original cast-iron gates and has the two-storeyed barge-boarded lodge to one side. The cemetery's layout is formal, and managed to dramatic effect: below a dark avenue of mature pines, the straight carriage-drive runs between raised terraces to the two chapels, Early English, identical, and symmetrically placed end to end, both with gable bellcotes; between them the First World War memorial cross emphasizes the visual balance. Beyond them the cemetery opens out into a rectangular space, the ground drops away with fine views over the valley of the Torridge, and planting is kept to the perimeter with the exception of some formally placed clipped yews. It all seems to have been designed by the Burial Board's surveyor: who was he? Many small monuments, with quite a lot of variety and character: in front of the nonconformist chapel, a Greek chest tomb with thick acroteria, to Rev.James Buckpitt d.1866, next to the stumpy obelisk of Rev. Richmond Noble d.1877: near the Anglican chapel, a circular pedestal and urn to Richard Passmore d.1875; of 1880, a big headstone topped by an urn, with excellent armorial and foliage carving, to members of the Hole family.

GREAT YARMOUTH, Norfolk
Caister Municipal Cemetery

Founded in 1904 by Great Yarmouth Borough Council, originally of 8 acres, extended by a further 6 in 1914. Plans drawn up by the Borough surveyor, J.W.Cockrill in 1899 envisaged two chapels, along with other buildings, but only

Caister Municipal Cemetery, Great Yarmouth, Norfolk, opened 1904; the chapel, designed in 1899, by J. W. Cockrill.

one chapel built, and remarkably distinctive it is. Entirely of brick, T-shape in plan, so that the entrance and lobby is set across the west end of the main vessel of the chapel and has a separate hipped gable roof; pilaster buttresses, capped-off with curved weatherings, rise above the tall parapet, the entire width of the bays between the buttresses taken by broad windows set back below segmental arches and traceried in moulded brick; dense, free Perpendicular tracery to the east window. Both in its forms and its textures, the whole design is strongly influenced by Arts and Crafts. The two storey lodge of 1914, with tile hung upper floor, is also by Cockrill.

Gorleston Cemetery

Established in 1879 on a rectangular 13 acre site; the main gateway, at the north-east corner, is attached at an angle to the lodge: excellently detailed in moulded brick and terracotta, it has a central carriage arch flanked by narrow arches, that to the right providing pedestrian access to the cemetery, that to the left forming the door to the lodge. The single chapel of 1889 is of knapped flint, with lancet windows and an apsidal west end, and has a terracotta string course and cornice, with terracotta columns and mouldings to the outer door of the south porch. All the buildings are by the Borough surveyor J.W. Cockrill. The grounds are laid out on a grid plan, with mixed tree planting. The most distinctive monuments are to members of Cockrill's family, and presumably designed by him: a square-based pyramid to his first wife, next to a rough-hewn block in memory of his parents. Also several 1930s memorials above the common run, including one to C.V.Drumee d.1933, which has the seated figure of a young woman in contemporary dress, her head propped gloomily on her hand – an interwar redaction of the traditional female mourner.

HEREFORD
Brinton Road Cemetery

Established in 1858 by the Hereford United Parishes Burial Board: from the late eighteenth century each of the Hereford parish churches had a burial ground on the edge of the town, prior to which all burials had been in the cathedral close. The architect was W.H.Knight of Cheltenham. The lodge, in domestic Gothic, is of brick with limestone dressings: it cost £150. There is only a single chapel – where were Hereford's dissenters ? – which is Decorated in style, built of red sandstone, with separate nave and chancel, and a steeple with ballflower ornament to the belfry stage. Inside there are encaustic tiles by the firm of W. Godwin, of the Ludwardine Works, Hereford, manufacturers with a substantial mid-Victorian reputation for quality and historical know-how. The grounds were laid out by the Hereford city engineer, T.Curley, whose tree-planting includes a number of exotics. Amidst some good and representative monuments, two can be singled out: the tall obelisk to John Lye M.D. d.1864, which incorporates a mosaic pictorial panel; and the canopied Italianate tomb of George Edwards d.1874.

HEXHAM, Northumberland
St Andrew's Cemetery

Established 1858-9 overlooking the North Tyne valley, a Burial Board cemetery that is well looked after and remains notably complete. The buildings are by Archibald M.Dunn, who also won the competition for St Nicholas' Cemetery in Newcastle in 1855. Symmetrical lodge and office buildings in domestic Gothic either side of the gateway, with prominent traceried barge boards to the gables, patterned slate roofs and a weather vane. The chapels are placed on platforms some distance apart either side of the drive: fourteenth-century in detail, they both have pinnacled buttresses and varied Decorated tracery to the windows; their porches face each other across the drive and both are equipped with square turrets strongly battered up into open octagons with spirelets above. The layout is symmetrical about the central carriage drive, but includes delightfully serpentine subsidiary paths; the lime trees planted around the perimeter of the original cemetery still remain. Immediately inside the entrance, at the principal *rond-point*, is a tall cross erected in 1896 to the memory of Isaac Baty and carved by Robert Ball in imitation of Acca's Cross in Hexham Abbey – a late Victorian favourite. The cemetery has a good representative collection of monuments, among them: obelisks to William Pattinson d.1861, ironfounder of Hexham, and John Grey d.1858; a large square-based Gothic pinnacle to John King d.1859, and the pyramidal Wills memorial of 1864. A rarity is the monument to Joseph Fairless d.1873, which incorporates a photograph behind glass - most unusual at this date, though increasingly found from the 1930s, as in some nearby memorials here.

HEYWOOD, Lancashire
Heywood Cemetery

An extensive Burial Board cemetery laid out 1856-7 with buildings by T.D.Barry of Liverpool, who picked up a significant number of commissions for cemeteries for the heavily populated industrial belt of south Lancashire in the 1850s. The site is adjacent to Springfield Park, so the whole area has a rural character, emphasized by the picturesque layout of the cemetery, its chapels positioned on a knoll: twin Gothic chapels in rock-faced masonry, their porches facing each other, the Anglican chapel with a *flèche*. There are a number of good representative tombs, many to cotton magnates and manufacturers. Among others may be mentioned: the boldly simplified classical sarcophagus to Moses Cheetham, cotton spinner, who died in 1845 so the monument would seem to have been moved; an obelisk with portrait bust to Samuel Hill d.1857; the Gothic pinnacle to the local architect James Edward Mills d.1907, but erected in 1875 for his infant son and presumably designed by Mills himself.

HINDLEY, Lancashire
Hindley Cemetery

Laid out on a sloping site with meandering paths, and steps to manage the sharper changes of level, the cemetery was opened in 1879 with buildings in a muscular Decorated by George Heaton of Wigan, who won the competition for their design in 1877. The single, apsidally ended chapel is in rugged cream-coloured sandstone with red-sandstone dressings and polychromatic roof tiles: three bays in length with plate tracery cusped lancets below quatrefoils and a bellcote on the west gable. The large lodge is firmly managed, with bay windows and dormers; good cast iron gates and red sandstone gatepiers. The dominant monument is a marble angel on a tall grey granite pedestal, erected by public subscription to Dr John Brayton d.1892, 'The friend of the poor'.

KEIGHLEY, West Yorkshire
Utley Cemetery

A Burial Board cemetery founded in 1856 and laid out in terraces on a site sloping down to a railway cutting, crossed by a bridge in 1910 when the cemetery was extended to the other side of the line. Two entrances, both with lodges, that to the south Gothic, as also is the one chapel that remains, cruciform in plan with steep gables, now disused and threatened with demolition. The major feature of the cemetery is its sequence of ornate monuments to the manufacturing dynasties of Victorian Keighley: Hattersley, Smith, Craven, Midgley, Wilkinson and Prince-Smith. The outstanding memorial, however, is the Butterfield family chapel and vault of the 1870s, opposite the main gateway: chamfered plinth, corner buttresses with granite colonnettes and gablets, and a pyramided apex raised on colonnettes.

KETTERING, Northamptonshire
London Road Cemetery

Established in 1861, the cemetery occupies a flat site, originally of 5 acres, increased to 12 in 1894. The boundary wall to the road has cast-iron Gothic railings; at the main entrance a domestic Gothic lodge with a timber verandah; from the entrance the carriage drive curves to the chapels, which are on a raised terrace with steps up. The chapels are identical, Early English, the east end lancet triplets with stiff-leaf capitals; vestries link them to a *porte-cochère* above which a battered octagon carries a belfry stage and tall spire. All the buildings were designed by R.W.Johnson of Melton Mowbray, the ironstone of which they are constructed quarried on the site. East and west of the *porte-cochère* runs a fine avenue of limes; planting elsewhere is informal.

LEAMINGTON SPA, Warwickshire
Brunswick Street Cemetery

A large cemetery laid out in 1852-3: a lodge and single chapel were built at that date to the designs of

Brunswick Street Cemetery, Leamington Spa, Warwickshire; the Turnerell family memorial.

D.G.Squirhill. The chapel is Neo-Norman – still enjoying some popularity for cemetery chapels in the early 1850s – of brick, with a bellcote and rose window. A second chapel was added some distance to the north in 1868-9, this time Gothic with a much-pinnacled bell turret, but in overall design quite close to the earlier chapel: the architect was John Cundall who had been Squirhill's clerk-of-works in 1852-3 – hence, no doubt, the similarity between the two buildings. Paths are set out on a grid plan with a main promenade connecting the two chapels; there is much good planting of mixed conifers and broadleaves. Among the more notable monuments: a tall pedestal, triangular on plan, with corner columns and sculptured relief panels, to Adolphus Riley d.1867; a Greek pedestal with an aedicule containing a mourner and urn, to Mary Tewart d.1871; a solid block of roughly hewn stone with a rustic cross lying on top, in memory of Peter Turnerell d.1839, sculptor of the Burns memorial at Dumfries, erected by his son Tracy Turnerell, who also celebrated his wife Martha's eightieth birthday by inserting a commemorative plaque to her in the side of the block of stone – all very odd.

LEEDS

Beckett Street Cemetery

Also known as Burmantofts, Beckett Street was opened in 1845 by the Leeds Town Council Burial Grounds Committee, along with cemeteries at Woodhouse Hill, Holbeck and Armley, the total cost being £25,000: Leeds thus became the first of the great industrial towns to take civic responsibility for the provision of burial space. The cemetery forms a lopsided square, enclosed on three sides by walls, with railings on the fourth. It was equally divided into Anglican and nonconformist sections, each with its own entrance and lodge as well as chapel; the stone boundary posts between the two halves still survive. The present two lodges date from 1880, built of gritstone with steep gabled roofs and Tudor detailing; they are by W.S.Braithwaite, who later became architect to the Leeds School Board, and are probably his earliest work. Both chapels have been demolished. Most of the memorials are relatively humble, executed in local sandstone, but exhibiting a high level of craftsmanship. Gathered in phalanxes or small groups, and dating between the 1880s and 1930s, are a lot of 'guinea graves' – common graves so positioned as to share a headstone carrying memorial inscriptions on both sides: in death as in life, one might suppose, for back-to-back housing also persisted for a long time in Leeds. There are larger monuments as well; in particular, a polychromatic pinnacle of the 1860s to the Galli family, and, delightfully, a mill chimney 8 feet high to the memory of Thomas Kidney d.1914, 'the oldest steeplejack in England'. Threatened with clearance by Leeds Council in 1984, the cemetery was saved largely through the efforts of the Friends of Beckett Street Cemetery: a management scheme involving low-key maintenance and the encouragement of wildlife has been adopted.

Leeds General Cemetery

The first in the city, set up by the Leeds General Cemetery Company and opened in 1835; also known as Woodhouse Cemetery or St George's Fields. The architect was John Clark, whose buildings, somewhat surprisingly, still survive: an entrance arch, with offices on one side and sexton's lodge on the other, both in a weighty Graeco-Egyptian manner; the single chapel is Greek, with a portico towards the entrance, and square windows. Most of the cemetery's original planting has gone, and all but a few monuments have been cleared; some headstones have been used to make a footpath; among remaining memorials is that to Rev.R.W.Hamilton d.1851, by John Dobson of Newcastle.

LEICESTER

Leicester General Cemetery

Opened in 1849 by a joint stock company after much interdenominational bickering by Leicester Corporation, the cemetery occupies a sloping site south of the centre, near what was then the city lunatic asylum and is now part of the university. The architects, responsible for lay out as well as buildings, were the Gloucester firm of Hamilton and Medland, whose designs won a competition held in 1848. Interestingly, considering the location of the cemetery, the partnership made a success out of designing for the insane as well as the dead: they were the architects of lunatic asylums at Worcester in 1847 and Lincoln in 1848, as well as winning first prize in the competition for Plymouth Cemetery in 1848. With the exception of a decent but unremarkable domestic Gothic lodge, their

The General Cemetery, Leicester, 1848-9; view over the cemetery from the chapel terrace, the layout probably designed by William Gay.

The City of Liverpool Cemetery, Anfield, 1860-63; view from the catacomb range, the layout designed by Edward Kemp.

buildings at Leicester have been destroyed: they comprised two chapels and a long Decorated entrance screen with geometrical tracery. Fortunately, their layout survives. It combines formal and informal features: the chapels stood on a terrace cut from the hillside; by a flight of steps it leads down to another, broader terrace which has a fine promenade with views over the city. The cemetery's first superintendent was William Gay, who went on to plan Undercliffe in Bradford, which has an even more dramatic promenade as its main feature, so it seems likely he may have had a hand in landscaping Leicester as well. Away from the terraces, the paths curve picturesquely and the planting is informal. There are a number of good monuments: at the highest point, in the south east corner, with the best vistas over the city, a matching pair of tombs with urns under Greek canopies to Richard Harris d.1854, and his son, also Richard Harris d.1874, both of whom were mayors of Leicester. On the main promenade: a Gothic tomb chest with relief panels and angels, to Jane Broadbent d.1856, signed by a local mason, J.Firm; the Jessop memorial of 1869 by another local man, J.Barratt, a tall plinth with medallion heads; the Wakerley memorial of 1911 with spooky Art Nouveau angels. By the main drive from the lodge to the chapel terrace, the Evans memorial of 1886, a fine Jacobethan table tomb designed by the talented Leicester architect J.G.Goddard.

LIVERPOOL
City of Liverpool Cemetery, Walton Road

A grand municipal cemetery at Anfield, north of the centre of the city; 130 acres in extent, it was opened in 1863. The public competition for its buildings was held in 1860 and won by Liverpool's own cemetery specialist T.D.Barry, who had been architect for Toxteth Park Cemetery on the other side of the city a few years earlier. The irregular lozenge-shaped site was laid out by Edward Kemp, a protégé of Sir Joseph Paxton. The design is extraordinarily inventive: principal drives run straight from corner to corner of the lozenge – west to east and north to south – dividing the cemetery into irregular quarters, the path-plan in each one of which is different, though all are variations on formal rectilinear and circular layouts. The intriguing complex that results is further varied by changes in level and Kemp's use of both raised and sunken terraces. See p.53.

The principal entrance is off Walton Road at the western end of the west-east axial drive, its buildings, like all those of the cemetery, in the red local sandstone: a symmetrical pair of L-plan Gothic lodges stand to either side of the drive within the gates, which have big, square piers with massive tapering capstones; the wrought ironwork of the gates themselves is outstanding, and the pedestrian entrances that flank the carriageway have elaborate wrought-iron overthrows. In the centre of the whole group is a tall, free-standing clock tower, its plinth carved with the city arms; from the square base, the shaft is chamfered into an octagon, then back to a square again for the clock stage, the four faces set beneath tall gables that climb up the sides of a short spirelet. Originally there were three chapels, one on the west–east drive, two on the north-south. Only the Anglican one remains: early Decorated in style, its polygonally-apsed east end with slender lancets, a big west window with good geometrical tracery, and an elegant steeple asymmetrically placed on the north, its ground stage containing the entrance. The cemetery's two catacomb ranges also survive, though now semi-derelict: each range, long and low, has two chapels set end-to-end and linked by a *porte-cochère*; the interiors are arcaded to either side, with robust Early French piers and transverse arches for the roof; at the end of each chapel is a stone catafalque which contained a hydraulic lift – all the mechanism now gone – to lower the coffins into the vault below. Although parts of the cemetery have been cleared, and parts are covered with little modern headstones in uniform rows, many monuments of major quality and interest remain, along the axial drives, at intersections of the subsidiary paths, and grouped around the catacomb ranges. Their stylistic variety seems particularly wide, and the collection around the northern catacomb is representative: a mourning woman with urn on a Greek plinth decorated with inverted torches, to Margaret Chadwick d.1864; a polychromatic Gothic pinnacle, to James Smith d.1872; one of the oddest, an indecipherable headstone of 1884 crowned by a jagged row of spikes, all in white marble; tall Celtic crosses to John Highmett d.1890 and Samuel Waring d.1907, the latter with a small portrait medallion; set on a tall plinth, a polished granite sarcophagus with lion's claw feet, in memory of Mary Ann Barker d.1892; a baldacchino in grey granite to Robert Daglish d.1904, the urn or the bust it sheltered now gone; a compound monument to

Toxteth Park Cemetery, Liverpool, 1855-6; view from the principal drive, the chapel designed by T. D. Barry, the layout by William Gay.

members of the Noblett family, comprising a coped tomb chest carrying a free-standing Calvary with figures of the Virgin and St John, dating from 1911, set in front of a gabled Gothic headstone with a memorial date of 1856 – presumably moved from one of the city's churchyards.

St James's Cemetery, St James Road

Opened by Liverpool's Anglican community in 1829 as an alternative to the nonconformist Low Hill, now destroyed; its design by John Foster, the city's leading architect in the first half of the nineteenth century, makes spectacular use of the disused stone quarry in which the cemetery is sited; the original landscaping was by John Shepherd. For description see pp.9-10. The towering presence of Giles Gilbert Scott's Anglican cathedral immediately to the west makes of the whole an unforgettable *tour de force*. It is much to be regretted that most of the cemetery's monuments have been cleared away and its planting over-tidied. Still remaining, but visually isolated and looking rather like a funereal bandstand, is the fine memorial to William Huskisson, M.P. for Liverpool and Secretary of the Board of Trade, run down by a train at the opening of the Liverpool to Manchester railway in 1830. Based on the Choragic Monument of Lysicrates and designed by Foster, it is a raised drum of Corinthian columns with a glazed dome; it contained a statue to the accident-prone statesman by John Gibson, but, following vandalism, this has been removed for safe-keeping.

Toxteth Park Cemetery, Smithdown Road

Liverpool's first publicly funded cemetery, opened in 1856: the competitions for its design were held in the previous year, that for the buildings won by T.D.Barry, that for the grounds by William Gay, who had laid out Undercliffe in Bradford in 1853-4. The broad main entrance, on the north of the cemetery, is flanked by red-brick lodges, eclectically Gothic, with lots of gables and hipped roofs, and tall picturesque chimney shafts – not at all funereal in fact. Three drives run from the entrance: the central one straight to the south perimeter, those on either side curving away to the chapels which Gay set on terraces a third of the way into the cemetery. Flights of steps from the terraces go down to a straight promenade linking the chapels and crossing the central drive which runs between them. Only the Anglican chapel, the eastern of the two, survives: it is Decorated Gothic, quirkily handled, with rock-faced sandstone masonry and a very big roof decorated with bands of geometrically shaped tiles; at one end, polygonal porches are set in a kind of transept below hipped roofs; at the other end an octagonal corner bell tower, heavily buttressed, groups with another porch – this time more conventionally gabled – which faces the flight of steps down to the promenade. Eccentric as Barry's design certainly is, it is also strong and visually effective, particularly when seen from the promenade and drive against the backdrop provided by the buildings of Sefton General Hospital, adjoining the cemetery to the east. Except for a few individual trees – including a weeping willow – planting is restricted to the perimeter.

Toxteth Park has retained the great bulk of its Victorian and Edwardian memorials, and they form an impressive collection; many of the relatively modest headstones, for example, have fine flower and foliage carving. The grandest monuments are along the central drive and the promenade – which has much of the character of the main terrace Gay designed at Leicester, and, on a smaller scale, of the great promenade at Undercliffe. The promenade is lined with pedestal tombs, Greek tablets, obelisks, draped urns on plinths, and pinnacles. At the junction with the central drive is the monument to John Eills d.1886 and family – a tightly managed Ionic canopy, square in plan, set on a tall plinth with each face of the canopy pedimented and crested with a large acroterion, the whole thing executed in polished pink granite, sharply detailed. Opposite, where the promenade starts towards the nonconformist chapel, is a fine group of granite obelisks. On the main drive is the intricate Gothic memorial of the Simpson family, apparently dating from 1872: it has a tall, heavily buttressed base, integral to which is a ogival canopied niche containing a relief of a woman holding to the cross; pinnacles crown the buttresses and canopy, and from their midst rises a clustered shaft which supports the base of a finial cross. Adjacent to it is the cemetery's most extravagent monument, to Thomas Pennington: an angel, holding an open scroll which carries the memorial inscription, stands at a half open door, on the lintel of which is written 'O Death where is thy sting...'; above the door is a foliage swag and portrait medallion under a pediment which carries the date 1886; above this again is a frieze and pediment with foliage trails, ribbons and masks at the corners.

LONDON

All London's cemeteries are described in Hugh Meller's *London Cemeteries. An Illustrated Guide and Gazetteer*, which is the essential starting point for anybody interested in the cemeteries of the metropolis: the descriptions that follow, along with material in the main text, supplement his accounts. No attempt has been made to reproduce the lists of the famous – and not so famous – dead that Meller gives with each one of his entries.

Abney Park Cemetery, Stoke Newington High Street

London's most important nineteenth-century nonconformist cemetery, established in 1840 on a 32 acre site in Stoke Newington by the Abney Park Cemetery Company; for its history see pp.26-8. The main entrance is in Stoke Newington High Street: the single-storey Egyptian lodges with tapered clasping buttresses bracket the gates, which have severely rectilinear ironwork with minimal Egyptian detailing, and piers in the form of Egyptian pylons; the design was by the cemetery's architect, William Hosking, aided by the scholarship of Joseph Bonomi junior. With a bookish eye for detail, Bonomi also provided the hieroglyphic inscription in the cornices of the lodges: translated, it apparently means 'The Gates of the Abode of the Mortal Part of Man'. From the entrance drive, in the original layout, one main carriage-way curved to the right

Abney Park Cemetery, London; monument to Frank Bostock, d.1912, made by Millward and Company.

and led due east to the chapel, while another swung south at the beginning of its long circuit round the perimeter. An additional drive, New Road, was inserted between them in 1870. The chapel stands in the centre of the grounds, near the middle of an axial path, only part of it dating from the original layout but now running from the Church Street entrance on the south perimeter to the northern boundary, taking in Baily's imposing Isaac Watts statue and the small catacombs – now with the First World War memorial on top of them – on the way: both are south of the chapel. The chapel makes excellent landscape: brick-built and lanky in proportions, it has a cruciform plan with an octagonal tower and spire over the crossing and a *porte-cochère* in the south arm, its arches to the sides functionally severe, that to the south graced with an ogee and forming part of the principal elevation, which includes flanking towers and a wheel window. Stylistically, it is a medieval *mélange*: Hosking was the architect, evidently working without the blessings of scholarship. The chapel was badly damaged by fire but is being repaired by members of Save Abney Park Cemetery, who have also been trying to control the dense undergrowth and woodland that now fill much of the grounds, largely swamping the remains of the original planting by the great nurseryman George Loddiges.

There are no monuments on the grand scale of Kensal Green or Norwood, but there are many smaller memorials that are high in aesthetic quality, and particularly interesting because often the work of local funerary masons. The following is merely a selection. In the area between the chapel and the Watts chapel: to Frank Bostock d.1912, who owned a menagerie, a life-size sleeping lion on a high pedestal all in white marble, carved by Millward and Company, whose premises were opposite the cemetery gate and who carried out many good Edwardian monuments in Abney Park; a kneeling, heavily draped female mourner, her hands clasped in prayer, to the memory of Fanny Mechi d.1845; a robust High Victorian pedestal tomb in two stages below a pyramidal capstone, designed for John Spreat d.1865, and an early work of Alfred Waterhouse, architect of Manchester Town Hall and the South Kensington Natural History Museum; in memory of Elizabeth Tollady d. 1855, an angel in the Pre-Raphaelite manner carved by a mason called Dunkley. Along Dr Watts Walk, south of his statue: a baroque tomb chest topped by an urn, to John Beazley,

Abney Park Cemetery, London; memorial to Sarah Norwood, d.1851.

d.1851; a pair of identical capped obelisks , very chaste and still with their neo-classical railings, in memory of Andrew and John Hart, d.1868 and 1871; to John Jay d.1872, a stonemason in the City, a curvaceous tomb chest with excellent rococo foliage, apparently carved 1854-5 doubtless by Jay himself; in memory of Algernon Wells d.1850, a squatly powerful saddle-backed obelisk in granite, entirely unornamented. To the west of Watts statue, a baroque canopy over a policeman's helmet and cape commemorates Constable William Tyler, killed in the course of his duty in 1909. Near the Church Street entrance: the monuments to the founder of the Salvation Army, General William Booth d.1912, his wife and their son – aesthetically dull, but important additons to the cemetery's galaxy of dissent; to Alexander Fletcher d.1860, 'The Children's Friend', a tall red granite cross with pierced octagonal head, by W.H.Burke and Company of Marylebone; a tightly carved Celtic cross in memory of Andrew Reed d.1892, by O'Shea of Kilkenny, perhaps the same family that carried out the carvings for Oxford Museum in the 1850s; to Henry Richards, a gabled Early English tomb chest with portrait medallion erected in 1891. On the perimeter road between the two gates is one of the most distinguished memorials: by the leading sculptor James Forsyth in memory of his three-year-old daughter Agnes, d.1864, a coped Gothic tabernacle with a moving portrait medallion in high relief. There are oddities to be found as well, like the draped beehive of 1851 to Sarah Norwood, near the north boundary path. For further information, see Paul Joyce's excellent *Guide to Abney Park Cemetery.*

Brompton Cemetery, Old Brompton Road

Founded in 1840 by the ill-fated West of London and Westminster Cemetery Company; for history and description see pp.24-5. The cemetery's buildings, by Benjamin Baud, in conjunction with the layout, create an ensemble of high formality. Major monuments are along the principal drive and the parallel paths to either side, and huge numbers of late Victorian and Edwardian memorials fill the catacomb circle, spilling along the verges in front of the parallel catacomb ranges that lead to it. There are several good mausolea: a very elaborate Gothic construction, undated, to the MacDonald family with a pair of angels standing guard at the entrance; a severe little Egyptian mausoleum in polished granite, to Duncan Wilson, undated but signed by Barker and Son, whose showroom was near the main gate; near the catacombs, a plain marble box with a lancet entrance, the roof topped by a statue of Hope, in memory of Matilda France d.1871; at a *rond-point* on the parallel path east of the drive is one

Brompton Cemetery, London; the memorial figure of Blanche Roosevelt Macchetta, Marchesa d'Allegri, d.1898.

of the most imposing of the mausolea, tall and tapering, in the Egyptian manner and constructed of pink granite, its bronze door carrying an interlaced monogram framed by Egyptian symbols but no other indication of who it contains and no date; close by, the Tucker mausoleum of 1881 in well-managed Doric. Perhaps the finest monument in Brompton, however, is that to the patron of the aesthetic movement, Frederick Leyland d.1892, the man for whom Whistler created the Peacock Room: designed

Brompton Cemetery, London; tomb of Frederick Leyland, d.1892, designed by Edward Burne-Jones.

by Edward Burne-Jones, it stands east of the principal drive, and consists of a gabled marble tomb chest raised on short piers, its surfaces covered in prolifically curling foliation inlaid in copper, the whole enclosed by high railings; near it is the tomb of the painter Val Prinsep d.1904, an Italian medieval font, no less, in heavily veined and now badly-decayed marble, decorated with a continuous trefoliated arcade containing charming little figures of saints. An informative comparison to these arty products is the Faith, Hope and Charity group in memory of Maria Mutton d.1884, carved by Prowse of Hammersmith – and a very creditable job, particularly the mother and child that represent Charity. Among the monuments packed into the catacomb circle are the fine free-standing figure of Blanche Roosevelt Macchetta, Marchesa d'Allegri, d.1898, and the memorial to Sir Augustus Harris d.1896, the London theatrical manager, which has a female figure stretching up to crown his bust, set on a tall pedestal – a conception more common in the eighteenth than the nineteenth century, and as stagey as the grand productions for which he was famous. On the far side of the Anglican chapel, beyond the catacomb circle, the character of the cemetery is quite different: many of the earliest monuments are here, their modest style and informal distribution reminiscent of an English churchyard; among the more ambitious is the Greek pedestal in grey-brown granite to Louisa Salting d.1858, with an inset frieze of the empty tomb still in the Flaxman idiom, signed by G.C.Adems. As well as individual monuments, there is also the Chelsea Pensioners memorial, erected close to the main gate over ground where more than 2600 pensioners were buried between 1855 and 1893: an obelisk with bronze standards forming the finial and piles of cannon balls around the plinth.

City of London Cemetery, Aldersbrook Road

Situated at Little Ilford, on the edge of Epping Forest, this is the cemetery provided by the Burial Board of the City of London to replace the 88 burial grounds within the City. Instead of their paltry and polluted 8 acres, Little Ilford extends to nearly 200 acres; designed by William Haywood, with landscaping by Robert Davidson, it cost £45,450. Haywood's buildings, all based on the Gothic of the early fourteenth century, show considerable variety of design and an eye for picturesque outlines and effects: the triple-arched entrance screen, its stepped central gable inset with the arms of the City, is set forward of the superintendent's house and porter's lodge, both of which are emphatically asymmetrical, and both of which have towers with pyramidal roofs; the rather lanky Anglican chapel is spiky with pinnacles, has an octagonal bell tower and crocketted spire, and a densely traceried west window under a fancily decorated ogival arch; stockier and altogether more robust is the nonconformist chapel, the main part of which is octagonal. Little Ilford's layout, combining formal and picturesque elements, established much of the character of the mid-Victorian municipal cemetery. For description see pp.50-51. The two best

Hampstead Cemetery, London, opened in 1876; general view, the chapels designed by Charles Bell.

monuments were also designed by Haywood: one is the fine Gothic pinnacle, Veronese in some of its details, erected over reinterments from churchyards cleared during the building of the Holborn Viaduct in 1871; the other is the Decorated Gothic mausoleum – one of relatively few in Little Ilford – to Haywood himself, who died in 1894, and his wife. Substantial monuments, largely obelisks and draped urns on plinths, line the principal drives, many of them in polished grey and red granite, and there are good groups of tombs around both chapels. The cemetery's planting is carefully looked after, but substantial parts of the grounds have been selectively cleared of memorials. A Gothic crematorium was added to Little Ilford's complement of buildings in 1902, but this was much altered by conversion into offices in 1971, when a new and aggressively ugly crematorium was built.

Hampstead Cemetery, Fortune Green Road

A Burial Board cemetery of 37 acres opened in 1876 to serve the prosperous and fashionable population of Hampstead. Opposite the main gate are the business premises of John Cramb, monumental mason: dating from 1886, they are a three-storey advertisement, decorated in an eclectic style that combines Byzantine and Egyptian with an exuberant disregard for historical proprieties. The cemetery's buildings, designed by Charles Bell, are more conventional: a substantial domestic Gothic lodge, and paired Decorated chapels, apsidally ended and linked by a *porte-cochère*, over which rises a square tower, its traceried gables masking the base of the octagonal belfry stage and spire. Internally, each chapel has an arched brace roof on foliated corbels with a big arch on well-carved demi-angels into the apse, in one of which are three windows designed by J.Dudley Forsyth. The main carriage drive runs straight from the lodge to the chapels, and is crossed by a public footpath which cuts through the middle of the cemetery, tidily fenced between long lines of railings. Beyond the chapels the ground rises, giving views back over the extent of the cemetery: from formally managed *ronds-points* subsidiary paths wind through the memorials. The mixed planting is particularly attractive, dominantly evergreen, including a fine Cedar of Lebanon, but with flowering shrubs and poplars as well.

The outstanding feature of Hampstead, as one might expect from the wealth of its catchment area, is its monuments. The earliest, dating from the last years of the nineteenth century, are in the higher part of the grounds, where the best is a mourning female figure leaning against a draped pedestal which carries a portrait medallion of the deceased, Joseph Maas d.1888, 'a great singer and a good man'. But the most distinguished tombs date from the first thirty years of the twentieth century and are sited along the main drive, around the chapels, or bordering the principal path that loops through the area between the chapels and the main gate. Many are by north London firms of monumental masons, testimony to their quality and variety: Green and Edwards, Hussey of Kensington, Kelly and Company, Maile and Son, Macdonald and Company, E.H.Mills of Hampstead – and Cramb and Son from opposite the cemetery gates. Inside the entrance is the extraordinary tomb of the poet Arthur Frankau d.1904, all granite and bronze with a big vase on which, for some arcane symbolic purpose, a snake and eagle do battle; a little further down is a miniature Egyptian temple, by Macdonald, to James Wilson d.1906, an engineer in the service of the Egyptian government for over forty years; on a *rond-point* by the chapels, a tall baldacchino with seated female figures around the base, in memory of the architectural historian Banister Fletcher d.1899, designed by his son Banister Flight Fletcher; also near the chapels, the intensely expressed memorial to Jacob Arnhold d.1903, and Goscombe John's 1923 monument to his wife Marthe – see pp.72-4; in the main area of the cemetery, the tomb of Mordaunt Gwynne d.1910 has an upwardly mobile female figure helped heavenward by a pair of hovering angels, presumably an Italian import though the plinth is signed by E.H. Mills; more eccentric in its iconography is the 7 feet high church organ that commemorates Charles Barritt d.1929. Adjacent to it is Hampstead's most grandiose tomb, the Bianchi monument, undated though clearly of *c*.1930, and erected by an Italian restaurateur to his opera singer wife, Mattie, who died in childbirth: above a metal gate stands a streamlined futurist angel, wings spread, arms held aloft; in front of the gate a big ledger stone carries a poem, 'To Mattie in Heaven', as imperfect in rhyme and rythm as it is deeply felt; panels to either side carry shallow reliefs, the one showing an angelically assisted Mattie ascending to heaven, the other showing husband, wife and baby, sitting together on a park bench in paradise.

Highgate Cemetery, London; tomb of Tom Sayers, d.1865.

Highgate Cemetery, Swains Lane

Highgate comprises two distinct cemeteries, in the form of a lop-sided figure of eight divided by Swains Lane, climbing uphill to Highgate village. The west cemetery is the original, some 20 acres in extent, opened in 1839 by Stephen Geary's London Cemetery Company on the steep slope below the church of St Michael's. The layout, designed by David Ramsay is perhaps the most fully Romantic of any Victorian cemetery, and Highgate's architectural features are subordinate to the effect of the whole; see also p.22-4. The brick gatehouse on Swains Lane, probably designed by Stephen Geary himself, has a central gabled tower featuring a large oriel window stretched up above the gate, with short two-storey ranges to either side containing the chapels; the style is Gothic, but wholly indifferent to any historical precedent. Curving round one side of the courtyard inside the gate is an open arcade that buttresses the ground that rises beyond. From either side of the courtyard, principal drives begin their looping journeys round the lower half of the cemetery, and another path winds uphill from the centre of the arcade. The three paths come together again in the middle of the grounds, from where the main drive curves on up the slope. Half-way along is the Egyptian Avenue, a corridor of catacombs entered through an Egyptian arch with obelisks to either side, and open to the sky. At the end of the Avenue is the Catacomb Circle, the inner range

Highgate Cemetery, London; the outer catacomb circle, designed in the 1870s by Thomas Porter, and the mausoleum of Julius Beer, d.1880, designed by John Oldrid Scott.

Egyptian, probably designed by J.B.Bunning in 1839, the outer range classical, designed by Thomas Porter in the 1870s. In the centre of the Circle is a Cedar of Lebanon older than the cemetery itself. Higher again, and forming part of the northern boundary, is the Terrace, built above a range of Gothic catacombs. Finally, beyond the Terrace and outside the cemetery, is St Michael's church, its spire and tall east end forming the visual climax of the whole intricate journey up from the gatehouse.

Architecturally, the most important monument in the west cemetery is the mausoleum of the financier Julius Beer d.1880, centrally placed between the Catacomb Circle and the Terrace. It was designed by John Oldrid Scott, and is a putative reconstruction of the Mausoleum of Halicarnassus, one of the Seven Wonders of the Ancient World, a prototype which was nothing if not ambitious, and a model that thumbed the nose at the exclusiveness of English high society into which Beer could never gain entry. Internally, his Renaissance sarcophagus stands in front of a high relief of an angel raising a praying child, the whole framed by paired Corinthian pilasters with an enriched entablature. It cost £5000, with £800 for the plot, and Beer did not even get an obituary in *The Times*. None of Highgate's other monuments is on such a scale or of such extravagance. Most, indeed, are conventional, though certainly exhibiting much of the repertoire of Victorian funerary design. The most interesting are the most personalized: the famous sleeping lion in memory of George Wombwell d.1850, proprietor of the biggest travelling menagerie in England; a horse stands with bent head on the tomb of John Atcheler d.1853, in bizarre commemoration of the man who was horse slaughterer to Queen Victoria; easier for the animal lover is the Grecian tomb chest to the bare knuckle boxer Tom Sayers d.1865, with his loyal mastiff stretched full-length below his master's portrait. Away from the animal iconography – of which there is plenty more – the headstone of Charles Spencer d.1890, 'Aeronaut of Holloway', has an ascending balloon, and the gravestone of Alfred Prosser, a sports goods manufacturer who d.1923, shows a cricket ball clipping the bails off a wicket.

The east cemetery, 19 acres in extent and opened in 1855, is far less dramatic than the west. Its terrain slopes gently, and its paths meander informally through deciduous woodland. Inside the gate are a number of good classical mausolea, dating from the early twentieth century, two to men who made a fortune out of transport, Lord Strathcona d.1914, director of the Canadian Pacific Railway, and Lord Dalziel of Wooler d.1928, director of the Pullman Car Company. But the cemetery's most famous memorial – strange company for their lordships – is further down the main drive. It is, of course, the 1954 monument to Karl Marx, who d.1883 and was originally buried about a hundred yards away: a bronze bust, surely the biggest in any English cemetery, sternly purposeful in the manner of heroic Soviet realism, the whole effect ironically spoilt by the prissy little wrought iron railings that enclose the plot as if it were a bourgeois front garden. Almost opposite Marx is the monument of a home-grown radical, George Holyoake d.1906, who is commemorated by an excellent portrait bust. Immediately in front of him is the plain obelisk of 1880 to the novelist George Eliot, a good liberal who, in death at least, fetched up closer to the revolutionaries than to the capitalists who command the cemetery gate. Highgate Cemetery is now run by the Friends of Highgate, who have been carrying out an ambitious management and conservation programme since the early 1970s, for an account of which see pp.99-102.

Kensal Green Cemetery, Harrow Road

The first of the metropolitan cemeteries, founded in 1832 by the General Cemetery Company and still under their management. For the history of its establishment and an account of its layout see pp.10-15. Still largely intact, Kensal Green is without equal as a totality, and rivalled only by Norwood among London cemeteries in the quality and interest of its monuments. As one would expect, many of the best are in front of the Anglican chapel and either side of Centre Avenue, which runs from it to the lodge. Even of these, only a selection can be mentioned here. First, in the chapel range itself, is the Sievier family monument, sculpted by Robert Sievier, who d.1868 and was one of the directors of the General Cemetery Company: a life-sized group in the domestic manner popularized by Chantrey, presumably representing Sievier's parents, John and Frances; she kneels by his side as he reclines on a Greek *chaise longue*, one hand stroking her head, the other holding open a bible. In the opposite ambulatory is the recumbent effigy of Georgina Clementson d.1868, the daughter of the sculptor J.G. Lough, who carved the tomb. In front of the chapel, pride of place for its historical significance goes to the massively severe polished slab to Augustus Frederick, Duke of Sussex, sixth son of George III, whose burial at Kensal Green in 1843 set the seal on the cemetery's prosperity. On the other side of the drive is his sister, Kensal Green's second royal burial, Princess Sophia d.1848. Her tomb was an international production: a Renaissance sarcophagus designed by Ludwig Grüner – later to be architect of the royal mausoleum at Frogmore – and carved by the Signori Bardi, mounted on a tall classical podium carved by Edward Pearce, whose workshop was in the Euston Road. Accompanying the royalty in front of the chapel are a number of major memorials, including: a sarcophagus on podium *à la* Princess Sophia, to Harriet Browne, Viscountess D'Alte d.1862; the finely detailed Gothic mausoleum of Eustace Meredyth Martin, all in granite, right down to the doors, and facing one end of the chapel range; facing the other end, and clearly by the same

Kensal Green Cemetery, London; the sarcophagus over the family vault of William Holland, d.1856.

designer, the Bayly mausoleum of 1876; most eccentric is the memorial over the family vault of William Holland d.1856, a sarcophagus densely sculpted with angels, swags and inverted torches, held on the wings of eight wyverns.

At the intersection of Centre Avenue and Kensal Green's circular drive stand the monument to John St John Long and the Ducrow mausoleum, for which see pp.11-13. On Centre Avenue itself: an Early French tomb chest with gabled canopy to Frederick Tillson d.1870, presenting an instructive stylistic contrast to the adjacent tomb chest of Amelia Cowell d.1847, which is full-blown rococo; the mausoleum of Edmund Molyneux d.1864 and family, a polychromatic Italian Gothic octagon with clustered shafts surmounted by angels and pinnacles at each corner, each face with an elaborately decorated gable – designed by John Gibson, it is the largest monument in the cemetery, and as it once had an octagonal stone spirelet was originally even bigger; a few yards away, set back slightly from the drive, is Gibson's own tomb, a square Italianate Gothic canopy with a pyramidal roof, the central stage strongly striped, the whole design robustly High Victorian though Gibson did not die until 1892; opposite the Molyneux mausoleum is the delicately managed monument of Mary Gibson who d.1872 aged 18, a plain coped tomb chest below a baldacchino left open to the sky, with clustered Corinthian columns at each corner and, above the cornice, four heavenward pointing angels; it was made by the local firm of J.S. Farley; next to it, the undecorated granite mausoleum of the utilitarian politician, Sir William Molesworth d.1855, looks almost brutal by comparison; beyond the mausoleum is Godfrey Sykes' excellent memorial to William Mulready, who d.1863 and who lies in effigy below a six-poster Renaissance canopy, the base of the tomb decorated with little cartoons of his best-known paintings; on the other side of the drive is the monument to General Sir William Casement d.1844, a canopy supported by Indian caryatids in reference to his colonial service, over a plain sarcophagus on which are the General's cloak and plumed hat, the whole thing made by the local monumental mason, F.M.Lander, who carried out a number of tombs in the immediate vicinity.

There are a number of good monuments at the point where the North and South Avenues – the two perimeter drives – diverge from Centre Avenue. The finest is the French Gothic tomb to Commander Charles Ricketts d.1867, designed by William Burges: a canopy of gabled

Kensal Green Cemetery, London; the memorial to Mary Gibson, d.1872, made by J. S. Farley, and, beyond it, the Molesworth mausoleum of 1855 and the Mulready monument of 1863.

trefoliated arches, the gables sprouting with crockets and finials, tightly encloses a tomb chest which stands on its own stubby piers, its surface covered with decoration in shallow relief. Nearby is a massive gravestone with a bold sexafoil forming the head and an angel, now almost lost in undergrowth, on one side: it is in memory of the architect H.E.Kendall, who d.1853 and whose Gothic designs for Kensal Green won first place in the competition for the cemetery, only to be thrown out in favour of the present Greek buildings. One hopes that getting into Kensal Green at last was some small compensation.

Norwood Cemetery, Norwood High Street

Opened by the South Metropolitan Cemetery Company in 1837 with buildings and layout designed by William Tite, for many years Norwood was the most fashionable London cemetery south of the river; for an account of its original design see pp.20-22. Of Tite's buildings, only the entrance arch remains, along with the massive iron railings to Robson Road, which forms the northern boundary of the cemetery. Much of the original planting has also gone, and many memorials have been swept away; for an account of Norwood's recent sorry history see pp.92-5. Nevertheless, Norwood retains some of the most oustanding monuments to be found in any cemetery.

Kensal Green Cemetery, London; an angel from the monument of H. E. Kendall, d.1853.

Immediately inside the gate are some very large early-

Norwood Cemetery, London, 1836-7; the Greek Orthodox section, with the Ralli mortuary chapel of 1872, probably designed by John Oldrid Scott, John Ralli's Gothic mausoleum of 1863 designed by G. E. Street and the domed Renaissance mausoleum of Eustratio Ralli, d.1875, by Edward Barry.

twentieth-century mausolea; the biggest of them, topped by an extraordinary scooped-profile pyramidal roof, has neither name nor date. A little further on, occupying the prime site where the main drive divides, is William Tite's monument to the founding father of Joint Stock Banking, James Gilbart d.1863: a large-scale Decorated Gothic pinnacle, with an octagonal spire above paired traceried lights under tall gables, with lots of well-studied detail. Over the way – and the contrast could hardly be more dramatic – is the monolithic, roughly-hewn block of millstone grit that George Godwin, the editor of the *Builder* designed to commemorate the antiquarian John Britton d.1857. How odd that one of the leading proponents of medieval scholarship should get an elemental lump of rock, and the banker should get the best Gothic.

The most important group of tombs is in the Greek Orthodox section of the cemetery, separately fenced off, with its own Doric entrance and classicizing statues of the Virtues on the piers of the railings. Closely packed with large tombs, the section is dominated by the 1872 Ralli mortuary chapel in the south-west corner, from where the ground falls gently across the site. The chapel is Doric, aligned north–south, with tetrastyle porticos at both ends; the pediment over the north portico, which gives onto the Orthodox ground, carries a figural group and there are scenes from the life of Christ between the triglyphs on the entablature. With these exceptions everything is severely unornamented, the proportions beautifully judged. The architect may have been John Oldrid Scott; if so, his design here makes an interesting pendant to his Beer mausoleum of a few years later at Highgate. Within the section classical and Renaissance styles predominate, as one might expect. The Renaissance mausoleum of 1875 to Eustratio Ralli, designed by Edward Barry, is particularly ornate: all in white marble, its portico with putti stretched out in the pediment, its dome surmounted by a thickly scrolled iron cross. Renaissance again is the elegant octagonal mausoleum on the other edge of the ground, again with a portico but this time with a shallow pitched stone roof: there is no date or family name. Among the Greek-inspired monuments are a number of sarcophagi with shallow relief friezes on the sides, including one to the Sheridan family dating from 1862, and another, adjacent to it, which also has a dramatically intense female mourner draped across the top; several monuments work variations on the canopy motif, quite elaborately in the case of the Schilizzi memorial of 1872 which has a free-standing figure below a multi-cusped baldacchino; against the north perimeter are more mausolea, Greek with a delicately sharp foliage frieze for the Theologo family, Egyptian for P.A.Argenti. And there is Gothic as well, powerfully present in the shape of the 1863 mausoleum of John Ralli, designed by George Edmund Street: rectangular on plan, the tall plinth banded in grey and pink granite, a plate tracery wheel window above the segmentally headed door at the east end, stepped triple lancets at the west end, and a stone roof itself profiled like a lancet, massively ribbed externally and crested with a line of gargantuan trefoils – all very tough in its classical surroundings. Further variety is added to the Orthodox section by the early twentieth-century monuments, including eroticism – frequently an element in Italian cemeteries, but rarer in English: the memorial to John Schilizzi d.1908 and Virginia Schilizzi d.1929 has a lushly veined marble plinth topped by a half-naked woman languidly abandoning herself to grief.

Other major monuments at Norwood are concentrated around the site of the Anglican chapel, now occupied by a crematorium that manages to be simultaneously mean and sprawling, and a bleakly exposed Garden of Rest. To the south–west, just below the crest of the hill, is the outstanding monument to Alexander Berens d.1858, who made a fortune as a linen draper in the 'fancy trade'; the architect was Edward Barry. The coped tomb chest stands on a pink granite plinth above a frieze of encaustic tiles which carry the letter B for Berens and a bear, in punning reference to his name – a heraldic conceit lifted from aristocratic practice. Panels carved in deep relief showing scenes from the life of Christ adorn the ends and sides of the chest; from the densely foliated cornice, pointed canopies at the corners curve out to shelter figures of the four evangelists, and the cornice itself steps out to rest on paired barley sugar columns, free-standing to either side of the relief panels. Above each pair of columns a kneeling angel carries a shield. The whole tomb is not merely lavish, but authentically rich in plasticity and in the concentration of its details and textures. By contrast, next to the Berens tomb, is a polygonal Gothic chest of the 1860s to the Grissell family, made of cast iron. Down the hill is the tomb to John Wimble d.1851, 'thirty four years of whose eventful life was passed on the seas': a classical podium with the hull of a ship on top and a storm at sea in relief on the plinth.

Among the tombs closer to the crematorium are: a

Norwood Cemetery, London; commemorative angel by the Monteverde firm of Genoa, from the King family monument of 1923.

mausoleum in the northern Italian Gothic recommended by Ruskin, designed by Thomas Allom for George Dodd d.1865 and family; a small, steeply coped tomb chest in polished granite with notched decoration and geometrical patterns, to Sir Joseph Causton d.1871; the mausoleum of Sir Henry Doulton d.1897, but probably built for his wife who d.1888 – Perpendicular in style with a hipped roof gabled above the entrance, sharp detailing, mosaic decoration to the interior, and entirely made out of red terracotta, as is fitting for one of the great manufacturers of Victorian ceramics; nearby, on a corner of the crematorium, the mausoleum of the philanthropic sugar baron Sir Henry Tate d.1899, again in terracotta, eclectically Gothic with Renaissance detailing, designed by George and Peto, whose skill with terracotta can be seen all along Pont Street; next to Tate, the Johnston memorial of 1900, a refined design in Portland stone, with double stairs up to a small Ionic portico; next to it, by contrast, is the heavyweight tomb of the preacher C.H.Spurgeon d.1892, a massive sarcophagus in polished grey granite with free-standing corner shafts and a portrait medallion above a bible open at the aggressively assertive text 'I have fought the good fight'. Finally, on the other side of the crematorium – and a long way indeed from Spurgeon – another touch of eroticism to go with the Schilizzi tomb in the Orthodox section: the King family monument of 1923, with a sultry adolescent angel contemplating the cemetery from under her fringe; an identical figure by Monteverde of Genoa can be found on a tomb of the 1880s in the Staglieno Cemetery there.

Nunhead Cemetery, Linden Grove

Opened in 1840, Nunhead was established by the London Cemetery Company who intended it as the south London equivalent of their cemetery at Highgate in the north. The company's architect, James Bunstone Bunning, subsequently architect to the City of London, designed the entrance and lodges, and the layout. As at Highgate, the result was calculatedly Romantic, with long curving drives through hilly terrain, extensive planting, and broad views over the metropolis to the north. All this now survives only in a fragmentary state, the consequence of persistent financial difficulties, neglect and clearance; for the recent history of the cemetery see pp.95-7. On Bunning's plan, the main drive ran straight uphill from the principal entrance on Linden Grove to the Anglican chapel, while subsidiary drives looped through the consecrated area to the left of the entrance and the unconsecrated section to the right; beyond the chapel the main carriage-drive took a long circular route round the perimeter of the rest of the ground, while secondary paths meandered across the interior. What remains is the area between the Anglican chapel and Linden Grove, with the consecrated section to one side now overgrown and managed as a nature reserve, and almost all the most interesting monuments in the unconsecrated section. Bunning's entrance, one of the most dignified of any cemetery, testifies to the impressiveness

Nunhead Cemetery, London 1840; the main entrance, designed by J. B. Bunning.

of the original conception: four monolithic Portland stone piers with inverted torches in cast iron to the main faces, and iron wreaths on the square terminals above the capstones. His lodges also survive, that to the left only just – semi-ruinous, overgrown and fenced off. But the other has been restored, though much too heavily, and is occupied: it is Greek, of yellow stock brick with stone dressings, sash windows, and a number of Soanic elements. By contrast, the Anglican chapel that picturesquely closes the vista at the top of the principal drive is Gothic. Designed by Thomas Little, it is an octagon attached to an enormous *porte-cochère*; ogee arches open on three sides between polygonal clasping buttresses that soar upwards into tall pinnacles panelled with tracery; the octagon has two-light Decorated windows, set high, and was originally provided with an imitation vault; it is now a burnt-out ruin.

Around the chapel are a number of substantial monuments, largely classical: draped urns and mourning figures on plinths, obelisks, Greek sarcophagi. On the main drive is a tall polished granite column surmounted by a heavily draped woman, hands clasped in prayer, in memory of Maria Proom d.1872, signed by E.Burridge and Sons of Peckham, who must also have done the very similar monument, its inscription now gone, that is close to it. Most of the surviving major monuments are on the main path that curves through the unconsecrated ground, now heavily wooded: set well above the path with steps up to one side is the granite mausoleum of John Allan d.1865,

Nunhead Cemetery, London, 1840; monuments in the undergrowth.

with a pointed arch roof on cushion-capitalled shafts, panels of relief carving inset at either end, and a moulded tomb slab manneristically placed half in and half out of the bulk of the monument; just beyond is the Stearne mausoleum, undated, all in red terracotta with delightful Romanesque detailing; further on, in sharp contrast to the elaborateness of both mausolea, are the adjacent memorials to William Chadwick d.1852 and Thomas Wing d.1889, the one an unornamented obelisk, the other an unornamented rectangular block of stone – both instances of the synthesis of the High Victorian geometrical style with the traditions of Greek severity; standing in a clearing back from the path is the family vault of John Oppenheim d.1864, a substantial Grecian pedestal with figural reliefs; near the lodges is the sheer granite obelisk erected in 1851 from funds collected by the radical M.P. Joseph Hume to commemorate five 'Scottish Political Martyrs' transported in 1793. Away from Nunhead's main paths are thousands of headstones, crosses and memorials, most of them submerged in undergrowth, many of them of considerable interest and quality.

Putney Vale Cemetery, Kingston Road

Established by the London Borough of Wandsworth in 1891 and extended in 1909 and 1912 to a total of 45 acres, the flat site is bounded to the south and east by Wimbledon Common, to the north by the A3, separating the cemetery from the expanses of Richmond Park. The buildings and layout are conventional enough: a domestic

Putney Vale Cemetery, London; memorial to Annie Hull, d.1920, and her son, killed in the Great War.

Gothic lodge to one side of the short straight drive to the two chapels, in standard Decorated linked by a *porte-cochère* below a stumpy broach spire with large gabled lucarnes; between the chapels and extending beyond them, is the crematorium, opened in 1938, rebuilt in 1956, and decently maintaining the Gothic vocabulary. Putney Vale prospered from the beginning; on the edge of the suburban equivalent of countryside and – as the twentieth century advanced – easily accessible to the motor car, it attracted the wealthy middle classes and a sizeable slice of the London nobility as well. Their monuments fill the south-eastern acres of the cemetery, a great stretch of white marble from the chapels to the edge of the common. A sample may indicate the variety that Putney Vale offers: near the chapels, an Egyptian mausoleum in grey granite, complete with lotus columns and mystic symbols on the door, its date and even the name of the deceased unknown; opposite is the Lyons family vault of 1924, with a low flight of steps leading to a long Italianate canopy, at the entrance of which stand two life-sized angels, one strewing flowers, while, inside, another angel offers entry through a half-open door labelled 'The Gates of Life'; further along the perimeter path, a large, and now vandalized, figure group of Faith, Hope and Charity in memory of Elizabeth Stimpson d.1898; against the southern perimeter is the elegant mausoleum of Edwin Tate d.1928, with cleanly detailed Ionic columns in antis and armorials on the bronze door; close by, a large tablet to John Appleyard d.1924, with a sinuous female mourner embracing the inscription – a model that has literally dozens of variations on other tombs in the cemetery; against one of the cross paths, an attenuated mourning figure stands at the head of the grave of Annie Hull d.1920, looking sadly down towards the foot of the grave where a helmet and knapsack commemorate her only son, Arthur, killed on the Western Front in 1916.

St Marylebone Cemetery, East End Road

Founded in 1854 by the St Marylebone Burial Board, the cemetery was designed by the London firm of Barnett and Birch and cost £15,000. It is set back from the road behind a fine set of Gothic railings, with a substantial Gothic lodge at one end of the street frontage. At the other end, just inside the cemetery, is the Anglican chapel, Decorated in style and cruciform on plan, its lanky bellcote equipped with flying buttresses and a crocketted spirelet. The two principal drives run from the Anglican chapel, one taking a route down the eastern perimeter and returning back up through the cemetery, the other curving to the west where the ground slopes gently away. The nonconformist chapel – a modest, single cell building – is tucked into the south-west corner of the cemetery. Planting is mixed, with cedars near the entrance, some fine mature broadleaves, and avenues of yew bushes. The middle-class development of Marylebone in the second half of the nineteenth century is reflected in the significant number of major late Victorian and Edwardian monuments in the cemetery. Baroque first, in the pink granite monument to the engineer Sir Peter Russell d.1905, prominently sited by the Anglican chapel: a life-sized bronze figure of a young engineer leans on his hammer while an angel hovers at his shoulder pointing upwards to the laurelled bust of Sir Peter triumphantly set on top of the memorial; the memorial was designed by Sir Edgar MacKennal, later responsible for the figures on the tomb of Edward VII and Queen Alexandra at Windsor. Nearby is the Abraham family enclosure of 1912, graced by a decidedly pretty angel daintily dropping roses on the steps of the tomb. For the bronzes to Thomas Tate d.1909 and Harry Dillon-Ripley d.1914, south-west of the Anglican chapel, see p.72. Near the nonconformist chapel, on an island site enclosed within its own hedge, is the tomb of Thomas Skarratt Hall d.1903, a massive but finely detailed Greek sarcophagus in polished red granite on a high grey granite plinth; seemingly based on Napoleon's tomb – what fantasies of grandeur does that imply? – it originally had bronze angels at each corner, now, alas, no more. More conventional in its aspirations is the monument of Gaynor Rowlands d.1906, showing the deceased shepherded skyward by a pair of attendant angels: it is very similar to the Gwynne memorial of 1910 in Hampstead Cemetery.

Outdoing all the monuments in St Marylebone's, however, is the Glenesk mortuary chapel, probably larger than the nonconformist chapel and certainly far finer than any of the cemetery's buildings. It is a late work of Sir Arthur Blomfield. The chapel is built of ashlar masonry, its steeply pitched roof slated in diminishing courses, its style a freely handled version of Early English/Decorated. Rectangular on plan, it is of three bays with the central bay slightly stepped out; gabled angle buttresses with two

St Marylebone Cemetery, London; interior of the Glenesk mortuary chapel, designed c.1897 by Sir Arthur Blomfield with mosaics and stained glass by Powell's of Whitefriars. English Heritage.

set-offs, lancets to the sides, a cinquefoil window to the east end, a triplet above the door at the west end. In the west gable is a relief of the Resurrection, and, above the buttresses at the four corners of the chapel, seated figures of the evangelists on octagonal shafts. The interior is vaulted, with a complete set of stained glass windows, an altar decorated with mosaic, and a mosaic reredos, all by Powell's of Whitefriars. There are three alabaster sarcophagi, one in the centre of the chapel, the other two occupying the recessed central bays to either side: they contain Algernon Borthwick, 1st Baron Glenesk d.1908, friend of Napoleon III, editor and proprietor of the *Morning Post*, Conservative M.P. for South Kensington 1885-95; his wife Alice-Beatrice d.1898, one of the most celebrated of late Victorian hostesses; and their only son, Oliver, who d.1905 – so the title, which had only been created in 1895, became extinct when its first possessor was laid in the chapel that was meant to accommodate a dynasty.

St Pancras and Islington Cemetery, High Road, East Finchley

Opened in 1854, St Pancras cemetery was the first to be established by a Burial Board under the provisions of the 1852 Metropolitan Burial Act. In 1877 it became the St Pancras and Islington Cemetery when its 88 acres of former farmland on Finchley Common were extended by a further 94 acres, making it the largest cemetery in London. The architects of the original cemetery were Barnett and Birch, the London firm also responsible for nearby St Marylebone. The two lodges on the main road – actually a stretch of the Great North Road – bordering the site to the west, were linked by a large semi-circular drive with the Anglican chapel set in a carriage turn on the outermost edge of the curve; from the drive another branched off north to the nonconformist chapel. The northern of the two lodges – two-storey domestic Gothic with square-headed mullioned windows – survives, as does the Anglican chapel: of Kentish Rag, cruciform, Decorated in style, with angular geometrical tracery and an octagonal crossing tower and spire, the two-light windows of the belfry stage ornamented with ball-flower and set below steep gables. From the Anglican chapel and from the site of the nonconformist chapel, roads spread out into the further reaches of the cemetery in a complex web that combines straight, formal drives with meandering paths. The Islington cemetery occupies the eastern parts of the grounds, but its layout is continuous with the rest. It has its own Anglican chapel, however, designed in the spirit of Arts and Crafts by W.Forsyth and H.Maude of London in 1896: red brick with white stone dressings and bandings, a polygonal bell turret with a tented roof on the main ridge, free Perpendicular tracery to the windows, those to the side below large gables and breaking the eaves line, the roof of the polygonal apse brought down through the cornice on to jutting eaves. Throughout the cemetery the terrain is undulating and the planting extensive, arranged in every manner: avenues, single trees planted in isolation, clumps and belts of woodland. Equally varied are the species: lime, horse chestnut, maple, London plane among the broadleaves; yew, monkey puzzle, different firs, varieties of cypress and cedar among the conifers; evergreen bushes of laurel and rhododendron. St Pancras and Islington contains a great range of memorial types, but one of outstanding aesthetic quality: the Mond family mausoleum designed by Darcy Braddell for the millionaire chemicals industrialist Ludwig Mond d.1909. It is an Ionic temple, predominantly in grey granite, its distylar portico in antis, with the ends of the flanking walls treated as pilasters. Set against wooded rising ground and above a main junction of the cemetery's roads, with a broad path climbing through clear ground to the entrance steps, the mausoleum is consciously isolated as a grand architectural feature in the landscape. In this it is quite different from the Ralli chapel at Norwood, which mediates between the cemetery as a whole and the enclosed Orthodox ground, and is integral to both.

Tower Hamlets Cemetery, Southern Grove

Established by the City of London and Tower Hamlets Cemetery Company on a roughly rectangular site just south of the Mile End Road, and opened in 1841, Tower Hamlets Cemetery was shrewdly positioned to exploit the market that was constituted by the densely packed population of London's East End. Burial in a common grave cost 25s., which compared well with charges in the city churchyards and burial-grounds. As an investment, the cemetery prospered from the beginning, and business was sufficiently brisk to merit the building of two chapels, designed by Wyatt and Brandon, in 1848. In the 1850s more than 80% of the interments were in common graves. The ever-growing population of the East End, the brutally high mortality rate, and the difficulties of providing convenient public cemeteries in the area – partly the consequence of interdenominational squabbles – all meant that the cemetery continued to be heavily used. By the 1890s more than 250,000 bodies had been crammed into Tower Hamlets' 33 acres, and burials continued up to the 1960s, when the cemetery was finally closed; long before this, maintenance had been virtually abandoned. The cemetery is now surrounded by post-war housing estates and ringed round by high-rise blocks; all its buildings have been demolished, and a part of its grounds cleared; for its recent history see pp.97-9. Near the entrance, at the north west corner, is a small group of early tombs; they include the Greek sarcophagi of George Morris d.1843, raised on a large plinth and retaining its original railings, and of James Walker d.1846, its terminal oddly shaped like a mushroom; flanking the perimeter path to the south are some Edwardian angels and hefty Celtic crosses. But these statements of middle-class substance – relatively speaking, for they would be unremarkable in Kensal Green or Highgate – are not what matter at Tower Hamlets. What matter are the thousands of headstones, set at times without a space between them, all but submerged in the woodland and undergrowth that fill the cemetery. Along the eastern side, gravestones are raggedly ranked in the thick light below the trees, half buried in dead leaves or covered with ivy; subsidiary paths crossing the site are in places reduced to narrow grass tracks between walls of brambles and saplings; in the central parts of the cemetery, the undergrowth is largely impenetrable, and massed headstones can only be glimpsed through a tangle of stems and foliage. Tower Hamlets is unforgettable, and not a little uncanny: it is also moving, for nowhere in London now conveys the human density of the Victorian East End more clearly.

LOUGHBOROUGH, Leicestershire
Loughborough Cemetery

A Burial Board cemetery laid out in 1857 at a cost of some £8000 on a flat, rectangular site originally of 7 acres. The architects were Pearson Bellamy and J.Spence Hardy of Lincoln. An intact set of fleur-de-lys railings encloses the cemetery, more elaborate in design to the entrance front

Loughborough Cemetery, Leicestershire, 1857; memorial bronze to William Paltridge, d.1924, and the chapels by Bellamy and Hardy.

on Leicester Road, where a compact and picturesque Tudor lodge in red brick with diaper patterns in black and a prettily bargeboarded porch stands to one side of the gate, with a sympathetically designed early twentieth-century lodge opposite. The path layout is strongly axial, the main drive running straight from the lodge to the chapel group, then beyond to a carriage turn at the centre of a circular drive, continuing beyond that to the western perimeter. Decorated in style, with three-light west windows and distinct chancels, the chapels are linked by a triple *porte-cochère* above the central arch of which rises a tall steeple which has a needle spire on a slim two-stage tower; the whole chapel group is in limestone. The formality of the cemetery's layout is varied by carefully disposed coppices and single trees: broadleaves predominate – copper beech, oak, sycamore and horse chestnut – but interspersed with Cedar of Lebanon, deodar and cypress. Large tracts of the cemetery have been cleared of monuments, but several of substance remain in the vicinity of the chapels, among them: a free-standing figure of a woman and cross, to Richard Hale d.1868; an eclectic Gothic pinnacle with an upward pointing finger as finial, to George Wragg d.1868; the life-sized bronze figure of William Paltridge d.1924, a Doctor of Music and represented in full academic dress. The cemetery is now closed for burials and the chapels in an advanced state of delapidation.

MANCHESTER AND SALFORD

Agecroft Cemetery, Langley Road

Also known as The Northern Cemetery and actually within Salford, its eastern boundary formed by the River Irwell. With an extent of 45 acres, opened in 1903, it served the north west of the conurbation, effectively the fourth of the public cemeteries at the cardinal points around Manchester/Salford, following Phillips Park to the east, Weaste to the west and Manchester Southern in the south. The same conception underlay the provision of cemeteries for Napoleonic Paris and the early plans of the joint stock companies in London. Agecroft occupies a long rectangular site with buildings by W.R.Sharp and F.Foster of Manchester, whose designs were selected after a competition held in 1898. The main entrance on Langley Road has a Gothic lodge and offices in sandstone, the masonry both smooth-dressed and rock-faced, either side of a carriage arch which gives directly on to the circle in front of the Anglican chapel. This is the architectural focus, with a big, robust tower. From here an axial drive runs north to the nonconformist chapel and south to the Roman Catholic.

Cheetham Hill Cemetery, Thomas Street

Established as a Wesleyan burial-ground around 1815, but seems to have become a general nonconformist cemetery by the middle of the nineteenth century; closed for burials in 1955. A small rectangular plot, it is perhaps the most atmospheric cemetery in Manchester: it is also the most overgrown and, despite being completely walled in, one of the most vandalized; its single chapel has also been demolished. Yet it still contains an impressive concentration of monuments amidst the undergrowth: classical plinths and pedestals in freestone and granite, draped urns, a number of odd obelisks half way to becoming Gothic pinnacles, Celtic crosses.

Manchester Southern Cemetery, Barlow Moor Lane

At 187 acres the city's largest cemetery, laid out in the Didsbury suburbs in 1879 by Manchester Corporation with H.J.Paull as architect. Impressive main entrance to Barlow Moor Road, with offices and registrar's house to one side and sexton's lodge to the other; all Gothic. The main carriage road leads straight to an elliptical drive, which forms the central feature of the layout, having the Anglican chapel in the middle of its far side and the nonconformist and Roman Catholic chapels at its points, all three in their own carriage-turns; paths run in from the elliptical drive to a circle at its centre. The rest of the cemetery's paths form a grid of squares. See p.60. The kerbs and edgings of the cemetery's graves, more than 100,000 of them, have been removed and the mounds levelled; substantial parts of the Victorian shrubbery planting have been cleared. But the comprehensiveness with which Manchester Southern represents the late Victorian and Edwardian memorial repertoire is largely unimpaired. From the outset the cemetery authorities stipulated that no soft stones (how northern that sounds!) were to be used for memorials, no Bath or Caen: so marbles, black and white, and granites, red and grey, gleam everywhere among the earlier burials: whole columns and broken columns, obelisks and pinnacles, Celtic crosses and draped urns, all feature largely among the more modest headstones and crosses, as well as Italianate angels and other figure sculpture. Some monuments, like the granite and marble Rylands memorial stand out, but the cemetery's aesthetic impact and historical importance derives from its cumulative effect.

Manchester, Philips Park Cemetery, 1863-6; the Anglican chapel, designed by Paull and Ayliffe.

Philips Park Cemetery, Briscoe Lane

Sited north-east of the centre of the city, the cemetery's southern boundary is formed by the River Medlock, with Philips Park itself on the opposite bank. Opened in 1866, its buildings were designed by the talented Manchester firm of Paull and Ayliffe, placed first in an open competition of 1863. Originally there were three chapels, set well apart along the higher ground near the northern perimeter: the Roman Catholic chapel, in what is virtually a cemetery extension to the east, was demolished in 1971, the dissenters' chapel in 1972. The buildings that remain are of very high quality, which makes the loss of the two chapels even more deplorable. The entrance group around the main gate on the corner of Briscoe Lane and Hulme Hall Lane is immediately imposing: large offices and registry on an L-plan, part single- and part two-storeyed, mullioned and transomed windows flush to the wall plane, and a strong clock tower, square and tall with a pyramidal roof; the smaller lodge is forcefully massed, its gabled wings tightly packed around a short square tower which has a pyramidal roof and a half-round staircase bay. The Anglican chapel is big, Early French in its detailing, and apsidally ended, each face of the apse separately gabled; over the south transept is a tower with long, louvred openings to the belfry stage, each one gabled and breaking through the cornice of the tall pyramidal spire; the spire cornice itself is supported on slender free-standing marble columns – a finely judged piece of delicacy to counter the power of the overall design. All the buildings are in buff-coloured sandstone, rock-faced apart from the occasional band of dressed stone, and have grey slate roofs. The layout of the grounds is informal and the monuments disappointing, mostly dating from after the First World War. Much of the original work on the cemetery was done by unemployed cotton operatives during the Cotton Famine, set to it by the Manchester Poor Law Guardians amidst many arguments as to how much heavy labour could be expected from men who were weak through lack of food. One wonders what they thought about building a cemetery?

Weaste Cemetery, Cemetery Road

In Salford, of 21 acres when it was opened in 1857, extended by a further 18 acres in 1888. Weaste had no less than four chapels, each with little spires, designed by the cemetery specialists Pritchett and Sons of York; it also had an octagonal glazed summer-house – evidence for the cemetery as rural oasis amidst the industrial desert. Disgracefully, all these have been demolished: the only building left is the unremarkable Gothic lodge. Despite its losses, however, Weaste still has major cultural and aesthetic interest, for many of the most successful families of Victorian Manchester lived nearby and were buried here. The most distinguished monument – and one of the finest in any English cemetery – is that to Salford's first M.P., Joseph Brotherton (1783-1857), who had inspected Weaste, then newly opened, only five days before he died and had picked the spot where he wished to be buried. His memorial cost £1000, raised by public subscription, was designed by Thomas Holmes and William Walker, and

Weaste Cemetery, Salford; the Brotherton memorial of 1857, designed by Thomas Holmes and William Walker, carved by Thomas Williams.

carved by Thomas Williams – all three of them, despite a national competition, Mancunians. They created a densely enriched pinnacle monument: from an arcaded and buttressed octagonal base rises an open arcaded octagon – the shafts replaced by standing angels – which carries a tall gabled and crocketted spirelet; within the open arcade, rather oddly, is a draped urn, a motif taken over from Greek, though its decoration here is Gothic.

MANSFIELD, Nottinghamshire
Mansfield Cemetery

Opened in 1857 by the Mansfield Burial Board, the cemetery was originally 20 acres in extent, to which 10 acres were added in 1898; the initial cost was £3500. A competition for the design of the buildings was won by the York firm of J.P.Pritchett & Sons, a practice which made a speciality of cemeteries; a competition for the layout, held at the same time, was won by the Mansfield architect, C.J.Neale. The principal entrance is through a gabled Gothic arch, free-standing, but set close to the more northerly of two lodges, one the gravedigger's house, the other the cemetery superintendent's. Both are modest buildings, two-storeyed, vernacular in idiom, their steep gables matching that of the entrance arch: both have been spoilt by the insertion of modern windows. The cemetery occupies an undulating hillside site, with serpentine paths often following the natural rise and fall of the ground; planting is informal and entirely coniferous, with the exception of some ancient oaks retained from the natural woodland that pre-dated the cemetery and that still remains beyond its western perimeter on the other side of the hill. The Decorated chapels, simply detailed and identical apart from variations in tracery design, are single vessels of three bays, one of which is taken by a large porch; the chapels are joined by a *porte-cochère*, its square tower surmounted by an octagonal belfry stage and spire, the elegantly long belfry openings continuously gabled and filled with openwork tracery. The major monuments in the cemetery are a surprise. There is a decidedly tough Greek mausoleum of the late 1850s, its plain pediment and corner pilasters set off against rock-faced masonry. But it seems light against the Walker mausoleum of 1858: a cyclopean blockhouse with a straight cornice and weathered chunks of stone that were once over-sized acroteria at the corners; apart from these, the only decoration is in the simple moulding of the door surround. There are few monuments in any British cemetery that achieve this level of atavism. Other tombs in the vicinity, like the Walkden monument of 1878 – a sarcophagus with clumping palmettes and acroteria –

continue the theme of Greek primitivism. Against all this, the Wildman memorial of 1859 strikes a note of Gothic refinement: a coped chest tomb, its steeply pitched, hipped canopy varied with gablets and raised on a trefoliated arcade that has slender pink granite colonettes.

NEWCASTLE UPON TYNE

All Saints Cemetery, Jesmond Road

Opened 1856, some 5 acres in extent, its grandiose gateway a Gothic riposte by the architect, Benjamin Green, to Dobson's Greek a few yards away along Jesmond Road. The carriage arch takes the form of a very tall thirteenth-century arch, with capitalled shafts and deeply cut mouldings, below a big traceried gable: more modest Tudor arches to either side give pedestrian access. The two chapels are distinguished by the detailing of their tracery, but both make much of their buttressing and both have quirky corner turrets with spirelets facing the main entrance – an appropriate touch of the picturesque. Among the monuments, a tall quatrefoil shaft with a foliated capital, on top of which are angels with a cross: it is to the memory of C.W.West, who drowned when his schooner foundered in 1869: on the base is a relief of the stricken ship.

General Cemetery, Jesmond Road

Founded in 1836 by the Newcastle General Cemetery Company with buildings, planting and layout by John Dobson. The architecture is Greek, severe and geometrically simplified. The main gateway on Jesmond Road is conceived as a single composition with the chapels: the deep carriage arch flanked between square towers which have corner pilasters to their upper stage; outside of these are the chapels, projecting somewhat into the street and further into the cemetery, with windows only to the cemetery side, plain pediments, and deeply overhanging eaves. The secondary entrance is on Sandyford Road, with pedestrian entrances through massive gatepiers topped by sarcophagi. See also pp.17-18. Architecturally, one of the grandest and most urban of early nineteenth-century cemetery designs, although the grounds are only some 10 acres in area. The ground undulates slightly, the main carriageway taking a gentle serpentine route between the two gates. Informal mixed planting, with plenty of mature trees including weeping willow, holly, lime and copper beech. According to Dobson's daughter, 'the cemetery is ornamentally laid out, and yet there is no mistaking it for a mere garden'. Amidst the headstones there is one substantial group of monuments – a double row of obelisks, pedestals and plinths – largely to leading commercial and industrial figures from the early Victorian city. One outstanding monument is that of 1843 to Archibald Reed: a great Gothic pinnacle, its heavy square base topped by a rather elegant octagonal spirelet. The designer was John Dobson, as willing to go Gothic as he was Greek, just like J.P.Pritchett at York.

NORWICH

Earlham Road Cemetery

Originally of 35 acres, now over 85 acres, the cemetery was established in 1855 by the Norwich Burial Board as the final remedy for the city's congested churchyards: though much mauled over the last thirty years, it offers an informative comparison with The Rosary. The original design was by E.Edward Benest, surveyor to the Corporation. The paired Anglican and nonconformist chapels, both of which had *porte-cochères* were ruthlessly altered to form a crematorium in 1964, when the present, brutally inappropriate concrete tower was erected between them. A small Gothic Roman Catholic chapel remains, as well as a chapel in the separate Jewish ground. The main lodge is of brick, with triple Gothic windows; it has a companion lodge, smaller, but similar in design. Planting comprises single trees and numerous shrubs, informally distributed. Extensive clearance has sanitized large tracts of the cemetery, but some worthwhile monuments remain, among others: a square-sectioned iron pillar to Mary Ann Lack d.1884; a table tomb with a horse on it, in memory of John Abel d.1883; and the large army memorial of 1878, in Portland stone and terracotta surmounted by a figure, 'The Spirit of the Army', carved by John Bell.

The Rosary Cemetery

The first interdenominational cemetery in England, established on a 6 acre site east of the city by Rev.Thomas Drummond in 1819. For history see pp.8-9. The site slopes up quite steeply; the cemetery is entered by a lane which runs from Rosary Road, where the lodge and office is, to the chapel, so the whole approach is essentially rural, a character enhanced by the informal planting – principally native broadleaves. Originally The Rosary had no chapel; the present one dates from 1872 and is quite an elaborate affair designed by the local architect Edward Boardman, whose output included a number of good nonconformist churches. Built in knapped flint with a tiled roof, it is early Decorated in style and apsidally ended, its pinnacled buttresses ornamented by small arches with detached shafts. On the south elevation is a large *porte-cochère*, open on three sides, with big, pinnacled buttresses to the corners and a tiled pyramidal roof finished off by an open timber belfry stage with a small broach spire. There are a number of interesting monuments, aesthetically as well as historically, among them: a large iron sarcophagus crested by an iron flame, in memory of Jeremiah Cozens d.1823; to the cemetery's founder, Thomas Drummond d.1852, a ledger stone with two outsized urns; the mausoleum to Emanuel Cooper d.1878, in a simplified Egyptian mode; the extraordinary cast-iron memorial to Charles Hines d.1896, a small fountain-like structure with filigree decoration that gives it a saracenic character; and a white marble bust under an open canopy in memory of John Barker d.1897, a steam circus proprietor who was crushed by one of his own waggons. In recent years The Rosary has been the subject of an excellent conservation management scheme by Norwich City Council: see pp.103-5.

NOTTINGHAM
Church Cemetery, Mansfield Road

The city's Anglican cemetery, founded in 1848 to provide an alternative to the General Cemetery. It had no chapel until 1878-9, when one was built to the designs of E.W.Godwin, beyond question one of the most talented and original later Victorian architects: a fine work, cruciform, with a strongly managed central tower and pyramidal spire, it has been demolished – a major loss. Without the chapel, the building to which the cemetery relates visually is St Andrew's church, opposite the main gate onto Mansfield Road, its strong steeple a dominant feature from the whole of the eastern half of the grounds. The cemetery occupies a steeply sloping north-facing hillside, laid out originally by Edwin Patchett of Nottingham: out of the site he created one of the finest of cemetery landscapes. It consists of four distinct parts: the

The Church Cemetery, Nottingham; late Victorian and Edwardian angels.

top terrace, where the chapel stood; the central and north-west section, terraced, with tooled ashlar retaining walls; an almost circular catacomb range, with exposed bedrock supporting a sequence of pointed arched recesses with buttresses between; the north-west corner, dramatically and romantically exploiting a natural declivity in the rock, with cliffs, caves, outcrops and natural arches, the weathered sandstone dotted with dwarf conifers. In this last section are the best Victorian monuments, for example: the tomb of William Hannay d.1862, a crocketted gable over a recess quarried into the sandstone; the Sylvester memorial of 1877, a trefoiled canopy

The General Cemetery, Nottingham, 1837-40.

supported by three stubby piers, all in granite; the canopy tomb of George Stokes d.1881, containing a badly smashed figure group 'Resignation' by the Nottingham sculptor W. Jackson; in stylistic contrast, the Renaissance baldacchino of 1882 to the Cutts family, in grey and pink granite surmounted by an angel. Quite different in character from the Victorian tombs in the quarry are the early twentieth-century monuments that fill one side of the top terrace between the Mansfield Road gate and the site of the chapel. Packed tightly together, they form a major – and visually extraordinary – collection of funerary sculpture, with angels predominating. Angels, in fact, in every attitude: hands clasped in prayer, pointing upwards, bearing babies heavenward, embracing crosses, carrying wreaths and sprays of lily. The origin of most must be Italian, but the signatures are of local firms of monumental masons – A. Hardy, S. Drake, Hoyles, among others.

General Cemetery, Canning Circus

Established in 1837 by the Nottingham General Cemetery Company, with buildings completed in 1840 to the designs of S.S.Rawlinson. The entrance is part of a complete architectural elevation in which the gatehouse forms the central feature of a terrace of almshouses. Impressive and heavily detailed, the gatehouse has projecting side wings of two storeys and a large round-headed carriage arch with giant 'keystones' cut in the stucco; above is a two-stage tower with pedimented belfry. The double gates are of 1839 by Falconer and Company of Derby. The two-storeyed ranges to either side of the entrance each contains three almshouses, with round headed arches to the doors and windows on the ground floor, and the central house brought forward under a pediment. The whole front proclaims civic improvement, but hardly announces its function as the entrance to a cemetery. See also pp.18-19. Nottingham General originally had a neo-

Greek chapel with a tetrastyle Ionic portico approached up a flight of steps: like Godwin's chapel in the Church Cemetery, it has been demolished. The site is an approximate rectangle, gently undulating and rising to the south west, where the chapel stood. Paths wind picturesquely through informal planting, relaxed and uncluttered; almost all the trees are native broadleaves, as one would expect at the time of the cemetery's foundation: lime, weeping beech, beech, ash, sycamore, horse chestnut. Among the monuments headstones predominate, many in Swithland slate and exhibiting the craftsmanship of the north east Midlands slate-cutting tradition. Some of the older memorials have been removed to the perimeter paths, but many remain *in situ*, crowded around the site of the chapel. Of particular interest are: the obelisk by Samuel Pratt of Nottingham to D.S. Churchill, who drowned in 1838 and must have been one of the first to be buried here; the lantern cross with foliated shaft and octagonal base to the Bright family, apparently of 1903 and all in white ceramic; the Greek pedestal with portrait medallion in memory of Charles Bell Taylor d.1909, 'an opponent of every form of cruelty and oppression'.

OAKHAM, Leicestershire
Oakham Cemetery

A small cemetery of 4 acres established by the Oakham Burial Board and opened in 1860 with buildings designed by Pearson Bellamy and J.Spence Hardy of Lincoln, a firm that made something of a speciality of cemeteries: their buildings are the distinctive features here. The main entrance is through a carriage arch with an oriel window over, on one side the two-storeyed lodge, on the other the cemetery office, banded green and grey slate roofs with fleur-de-lys cresting, the whole conceived as a group and markedly asymmetrical. The layout is largely formal, the principal drive leading straight to the chapels: these are linked by a *porte-cochère* which has a square tower and tall

Oakham Cemetery, Leicestershire, 1860; buildings designed by Pearson Bellamy and J. Spence Hardy.

spire, lantern-like openings to the belfry stage and angle buttresses with big pinnacles. The chapels have open traceried parapets to the gables and Decorated tracery to the windows.

OUNDLE, Northamptonshire
Oundle Cemetery

A very complete rural cemetery, only 3 acres in extent, south-west of the town, established by the Oundle Burial Board and opened in 1860 at a total cost of £2650. The architect was Edward Browning of Stamford. All the buildings are in rock-faced limestone: the attractive lodge is Gothic, two-storeyed, with flush tracery; the chapels, which have nicely varied window forms, are arranged on a T-plan with a common lobby entrance between them; the eastern chapel has a corner turret with tall cusped lancets to the octagonal belfry stage and a heavily crocketted spire. The cemetery is laid out on a grid plan with clipped yews scattered among the graves. Immediately to the east of the chapels is a pinnacle with similar detailing, its inscription now illegible; also, a good table tomb to Thomas Norby d.1862, its cusped arcade with polished granite shafts, now in need of repair.

OXFORD
St Sepulchre's Cemetery

On its small rectangular site, now all but enclosed by twentieth-century factories, St Sepulchre's is one of the most poignant of Victorian cemeteries. Between the houses on Walton Street, a path leads to the gatehouse, a strongly asymmetrical Gothic design of *c.*1850 by E.G.Bruton, with one of the rooms of the lodge over the entrance arch itself. From the gate an avenue of yews, short but dense, curves to the site of the chapel; now demolished, this was a little Romanesque building of 1848 designed by H.J.Underwood. The cemetery is crowded with monuments, none of them aesthetically assertive. Deliberately so, for St Sepulchre's is in Jericho, a slum area in nineteenth-century Oxford and a prime focus for missionary activity, particularly by the Tractarians and their followers, but also by the university's radicals. Among the better-known names are: Marian Rebecca Hughes d.1912, the first Anglican woman to profess the life of a religious since the Reformation, and founder of the Society of the Trinity in Oxford; surrounding her lie members of her sisterhood; Thomas Combe d.1872 of Oxford University Press, patron of the Pre-Raphaelites and founder of the great mission church of St Barnabas; the Tractarian publisher, J.H.Parker d.1882, commemorated by a low table tomb; the influential liberal philosopher, T.H.Green of Balliol d.1882; nearby, Green's friend Edward Caird d.1907, Master of Balliol, champion of the entrance of women into the university and supporter of working-class education. All in all, the cemetery is an extraordinary and moving document of Victorian seriousness. Neglected, overgrown, and vandalized as it now is, it is also a testimony to our corporate indifference.

St Sepulchre's Cemetery, Oxford, established 1848.

REDRUTH, Cornwall
St Day Road Cemetery

A small windswept cemetery opened in 1878 a mile east of Camborne, with views over the mining district around the town. The paths are bordered with low hedges of clipped yew and laid out on a simple grid. It has a single chapel building, rendered, with rudimentary lancets in granite and a gabled bellcote over the centrally placed porch. Almost all the graves between the gate and the chapel have high kerbs and are packed quite closely together. A representative selection of monuments, with a variety of types perhaps surprising in so small a cemetery. The best is a large Gothic headstone, with crocketted gable and cross finial, and a portrait medallion of the deceased, Samuel Trounson d.1904, by Hems and Sons of Exeter.

ST AUSTELL, Cornwall
Watering Hill Cemetery

A Burial Board cemetery established in 1878 just south of the town on a rectangular 7 acre site, extended to the east in 1903. The path layout is formal with a main drive running straight north to south; the entrance towards the town has rusticated granite piers and decent cast iron gates. The chapels, arranged on a T-plan, are immediately inside: squared rubble masonry with granite dressings, Gothic in style, with plate tracery and a full set of prettily patterned glass. The planting is excellent: mature yews, laurels and cypresses bordering the carriage turn in front of the chapels; an avenue of yews and laurels to the south gate; a line of beeches marking the original eastern boundary, and now demarcating the 1903 extension; privet and hydrangea bushes to the perimeters. Few monuments are assertive – Cornwall's Low Church tradition deprecated display – but the headstones constitute a fascinating and rather rustic collection of funerary symbolism: clasped hands, trumpeting cherubs, heavenward-pointing fingers, hearts and flowers in every conceivable combination: the most poignant is a little bird singing on a leafless branch in memory of Fanny Hudd d.1888; the most exuberant commemorates Clara Grose d.1903, and has clasped hands draped with a scroll, a heart, a dove with a sprig of what looks like laurel, passion flowers, roses and an ivy-covered cross for good measure.

SALE, Cheshire
Brooklands Cemetery

In two distinct halves, either side of the main road; the earlier half, of 6 acres containing the cemetery's buildings, was established by the local Burial Board in 1862. This was extended by a further 12 acres on the other side of the road in 1895. Early English chapels with linking *porte-cochère*, designed by William Wilson of Manchester. The spire over the *porte-cochère* was added by a local stonemason called Spence in 1903, and very appropriate it looks; unfortunately, the archway itself has been blocked in more recently. Also of Wilson's design is the single storey lodge and registrar's house, around which the planting is concentrated – deciduous trees with some evergreen shrubs. Around the perimeter are beds of flowering shrubs, and there are further beds, including azaleas, in the newer part of the cemetery: all the planting is maintained to a very high standard. A good variety of middle-class monuments around the chapels, including: a portrait bust to George Benton d.1887, under a Gothic canopy; an elaborately crocketted Gothic headstone framing a representation of Christ in stained glass, the monument's inscription unfortunately indecipherable; a large and refined Greek tablet to Max Essayan d.1923, with a seated female figure at its base staring wistfully at a funerary wreath of coloured ceramic flowers.

SHEFFIELD
General Cemetery

Opened in 1836 by the Sheffield General Cemetery Company, and originally only 6 acres in extent, but on a fine site in Sharrow Vale, sloping down to the River Porter. Buildings and layout were designed by the Sheffield architect, Samuel Worth between 1834 and 1836. The gateway is Doric, with a pair of columns *in antis* framing a round-headed entrance arch; uphill from the entrance and approached by a curving drive is the chapel, Doric again, with a tetrastyle portico, triglyph frieze, acroteria along the eaves, and simply framed Egyptian windows to the sides; higher again is the minister's house, domestically Greek with a pediment and Doric pilasters to the corners. Below the chapel are two curving tiers of catacombs – more than 250 in all – terraced into the hillside, the Egyptian balustrade to the upper range forming the barrier to one side of the main drive to the chapel. The buildings are set with studied informality amidst extensive broadleaf planting, much of which originally incorporated trees that were already growing on the site: the whole effect is a highly successful blend of the artificial and the natural. The cemetery was used exclusively by nonconformists until an 8 acre extension was opened for Anglicans in 1848, with a Gothic chapel, complete with spire, designed by William Flockton and Son. The grounds were laid out under the direction of Robert Marnock, who had designed the Botanic Gardens in Regent's Park in 1840 and who, for a number of years, edited the *Floricultural Magazine*. His first major work had been the Sheffield Botanic Gardens of 1834, also in Sharrow Vale, and his advocacy of natural effects must have had a direct influence on Worth's planning of the original cemetery. Sheffield General was purchased by the City Council in 1979: all the buildings are listed and the whole cemetery is a Conservation Area.

Rivelin Glen Cemetery

A Roman Catholic cemetery opened in 1862 on a steeply sloping 4 acre site to the east of the Rivelin Valley Road. The outstanding feature of the cemetery is its chapel, built in 1877-8 at a cost of £2000 to the designs of M.E.Hadfield and Son of Sheffield; the chapel was given by a Quaker couple, George Harvey Foster and his wife, as a mark of respect for the work of Father Fitzgerald among the city's working class – who lived in some of the worst housing in England. Externally, the small chapel is entirely simple: Early English, of Greenmoor stone with a western bell turret and south porch. The interior is richly decorated, with work by major nineteenth-century craftsmen and designers: beneath the marble and alabaster altar is a white alabaster figure of The Dead Christ by Richard Lockwood Boulton of Cheltenham, responsible – among much else – for the sculpture on the west front and in the chancel of Gloucester Cathedral, and on the front of Godwin's Northampton Town Hall; the stained glass in the three chancel lancets was made by the leading London firm of Lavers, Barraud and Westlake, and designed by John Francis Bentley, the architect of Westminster Cathedral. In 1884 the chapel was decorated by N.H.J.Westlake and Charles Hadfield, son of M.E.Hadfield: in the chancel, an all-over pattern in red, green and gold, with four paintings of resurrection scenes; the west window is also designed by Westlake. Around the walls of the nave are the Stations of the Cross in terracotta – by whom?

SOUTH SHIELDS, Tyne and Wear
Harton Cemetery

A late-Victorian cemetery of 33 acres founded by the Joint Burial Board for the parishes of South Shields and Westoe, with distinctive and elaborate buildings of 1888-91 designed by Henry Grieves. A tripartite entrance with a large gabled carriage arch and gabled pedestrian entrances to either side; a substantial and consciously pretty

The General Cemetery, Sheffield, 1834-6; general view soon after opening, buildings designed by Samuel Worth; from a print by T. C. Hofland. Sheffield Library Bibliographical Services.

lodge that nods in the direction of the Vernacular Revival with its mullioned bay windows and timber framed porch. The twin chapels with *porte-cochère* form a complex ensemble with much free Perpendicular detailing: over the *porte-cochère* an elegant lantern with distinctive ogee-capped buttresses, the whole topped by a spire. The layout is on the grid plan with avenues mainly of lime. The whole cemetery cost £22,000.

STROUD, Gloucestershire
Bisley Road Cemetery

Established by the Stroud Burial Board in 1856 on a large, long site splendidly situated on a hillside well above the town. The chapel group, just below the crest of the hill, is Decorated Gothic, managed with considerable assurance and historical accuracy, the detailing excellent and the Cotswold stone masonry of high quality. The identical chapels, bulky though quite short, with big roofs, diagonal buttresses and curvilinear tracery to the east and west windows, are set parallel to one another and linked by a *porte-cochère* in a three-stage tower with a broach spire. The chapels are currently disused and boarded up. The architect is unknown, but the distinction of the group has led to its being attributed to Benjamin Bucknall, a local man, architect of the remarkable Woodchester Park just outside Stroud, and, though his output was small, one of the most accomplished exponents of mid Victorian Gothic. East of the chapels a curving avenue of mixed trees and bushes runs to the *porte-cochère*; west of the chapels the ground falls steeply and is informally planted.

Harton Cemetery, South Shields, Tyne and Wear, 1889-91; the chapels, designed by Henry Grieves.

TORQUAY, Devon
Barton Road Cemetery

Established in 1852 on a triangular 17 acre site by the Torquay Extra-Mural Cemetery Company in response to the rapid growth of the resort in the first half of the nineteenth century. From the single-storey lodge, set back from the carriage sweep on the road, paths curve right and left to the chapels, the areas of the cemetery that they serve still divided by a wall. The Anglican chapel, to the north, has segmental headed windows and a slender corner tower with an octagonal belfry and spirelet; the nonconformist chapel is a plain Perpendicular box: all the buildings are in pale grey Torquay limestone. The outstanding feature of the cemetery is its monuments, their quality reflecting the considerable – but most genteel – prosperity the resort enjoyed in the later nineteenth and early twentieth centuries. Apart from the Greek pedestal in polished granite to the Congregationalist minister Robert Vaughan d.1868, founder of the *British Quarterly Review*, all the major memorials are in the Anglican section. Dominant is the sumptuous Renaissance sarcophagus to the founder of the Singer sewing machine company, Isaac Merritt Singer d.1875, entirely in marble, made by the Monumental Company of Kensal Green, and reported to have cost 'several thousand pounds'. To one side of it is a Greek tablet to Rosamond Hofmann d.1860 with a touching relief of the young mother ascending to heaven with her baby in her arms, still in the Flaxman manner. To the other side of the Singer tomb, the monument to Robert Marillier d.1903 has an intensely human female mourner seated at the foot of a tall Greek tablet, all in white marble and undoubtedly Italian – could the figure of the mourner be a portrait? Italian as well is the exquisite Quattrocento-style relief of the Madonna and Child to Kitty, Baroness de Reede de Ter Aa d.1896. In contrast to all the white marble is the Gothic tabernacle and canopy in coloured terracotta in memory of the sculptor Frederick Thrupp d.1895, and, near the main gate, a pile of rocks incorporating a headstone with inset enamel painted panel showing poppies, lilies, a butterfly and an overturned vase: a real oddity, it commemorates Alice Knight d.1878.

TRING, Hertfordshire
Tring Cemetery

Established at the west end of the town on a 9 acre site in 1892, the buildings and landscape all the work of a local architect, William Huckvale, who lived near the cemetery and is buried there: he died in 1936. He provided an inventive layout, nostalgic for the picturesque prettiness that the late nineteenth century had learnt to associate with the Georgians: the raised main carriage drive curves gently through an avenue of trees, across the saucer-shaped site, to finish at a knoll on which the chapel stands – Gothic, flint, with brick and stone dressings. The entrance lodge is of the same materials, but Queen Anne in style, as befits the character of the whole cemetery: gates and boundary wall are kept plain. The perimeter beds are planted with clipped and shaped bushes, very much as in a Kate Greenaway illustration. Entirely complete, the cemetery, just as Huckvale designed it, is kept immaculately.

Barton Road Cemetery, Torquay, Devon; memorial of Robert Marillier, d.1903, the mourning figure probably a portrait.

TROWBRIDGE, Wiltshire
Trowbridge General Cemetery

A Burial Board cemetery opened in 1855, all its buildings designed by C.E.Davis of Bath, who was also the architect for Weston super Mare Cemetery in the same year, and Lyncombe Cemetery in Bath itself in 1859. For a small town, Trowbridge Cemetery is of remarkable interest and quality, both in its buildings and its monuments. The main entrance has gabled gate piers with octagonal shafts above, with a separate pedestrian entrance through a heavily moulded arch to one side. The large Gothic lodge, in ashlar masonry, has a two-storeyed porch open on three sides at ground level, flush windows and tall chimney shafts. From the lodge the main drive, with a fine gloomy avenue of yew bushes, runs axially straight through the cemetery; the chapels are set to either side and staggered slightly. The Anglican is first, on the north side; the chapel itself in a conventional lancet style, cruciform, with broad transepts, but south-west of it and virtually free-standing, a steeple of eccentric but highly effective design: of three stages, the stretched central stage open on three sides through long paired lancets, the stumpy octagonal spire rising from a gabled lantern, a big weathercock topping off the whole thing. The nonconformist chapel, further down the drive and south of it, is also in the lancet style, but this time with a polygonal apse and a steeple, again virtually free-standing, with triple lancets open on all four sides and an Italianate upper stage capped by a pyramidal roof. Two large mausolea against the southern perimeter path appear integral to the cemetery's buildings. The easternmost has a triple-arched Early French entrance front, the central doors with outstanding ironwork decoration, the interior rib-vaulted: it is now in poor condition, partly overgrown and, for much of the year, flooded. The westernmost mausoleum has a segmental-headed front wall – giving the whole thing a bunker-like profile – with a Romanesque central entrance and inscription panels to either side in Romanesque recesses: it contains members of the Hastings and Kingston families. Against the western perimeter is the Brown mausoleum, of pink granite with an octagonal dome and bronze gates: it dates *c.*1900 and was possibly designed by A.S.Goodridge. Many lesser monuments are of considerable quality, including many to members of the main local clothier families, the Clarks, Salters and Browns, mostly designed by the local architect William Smith.

Trowbridge General Cemetery, Wiltshire, 1855; buildings by C. E. Davis.

UPTON UPON SEVERN, Worcestershire
Rectory Road Cemetery

A very small rural cemetery opened in 1867, entirely complete, with a good set of buildings designed in 1865-6 by George Row Clarke. The main gates are simple, well-detailed cast iron; the lodge picturesque, with an outsize bargeboarded porch. The two Gothic chapels, grey masonry with Bath stone dressings, arranged on a T-plan, the chapel office between them topped by a stocky tower with pyramidal roof; the Anglican chapel – the cross-stroke of the T – is apsidally ended with a hammerbeam roof and three stained glass windows by Heaton, Butler and Bayne; the nonconformist chapel is plainer. The short main drive runs straight from the gate to the chapels and is lined with yews, so that the tower is framed by them when seen from the entrance. Though G.R.Clarke had an office in London, he had many connections in south Gloucestershire and was the architect of a number of local schools and church restorations: he must have been pleased with his little cemetery, for he is buried south east of the Anglican chapel; he died in 1908.

WELLINGBOROUGH, Northamptonshire
London Road Cemetery

A Burial Board cemetery of 6 acres, opened in 1858. Its lodge has a dwarf tower topped by a pyramidal roof, mullioned windows, a tall chimney, and emphatically cusped bargeboards to the main gable – all very jolly and picturesque. The identical paired chapels are early Decorated in style and quite ambitious: tall, with a west doorway above which is a three-light window with Geometrical tracery; both chapels have corner steeples, placed to balance one another, with nice grotesques clinging on below the spires. The architect for the cemetery was E.F.Law of Northampton. The main carriage drive is bordered with flower beds and there are some fine mature trees informally planted in the rest of the cemetery: yew, monkey puzzle, silver birch, sycamore, holly, laurel and laburnum.

WESTBURY, Wiltshire
Bratton Road Cemetery

Opened in 1857, with the entrance lodge and pair of Gothic chapels by E.G.Bruton of Oxford. The cemetery is significant for its three mausolea. Most impressive is that to J.L.Phipps of Leighton House, Westbury, who died in 1871: Gothic, octagonal, with a tall spire, the lofty interior vaulted, with fine armorial floor tiles and a Gothic tomb chest. Nearby is another octagonal mausoleum, smaller, with rock-faced masonry and an ogee roof; no memorial date, but it must be late nineteenth century. On the main avenue, an apsidal mausoleum in the Romanesque style for the family of Lopes, Baron Ludlow: the peerage was created in 1897 and extinct by 1922. Elsewhere in the cemetery some good representative memorials, most notably the solid Gothic cross to A.Laverton d.1886, the reviver of the cloth trade in the town; in front of it, a good granite and bronze slab dating from 1906.

WOKING, Surrey
Brookwood Cemetery

The largest cemetery in England, founded in 1852 by the London Necropolis and National Mausoleum Company, who purchased an astonishing 2000 acres of heathland for the site. Similar in conception to Chadwick's National Cemeteries, Brookwood drew for its custom upon the whole of south and central London, and was connected to the metropolis by train. Of the original site, about a quarter was laid out first, to the designs of William Tite. Enormous numbers of trees were planted, including many redwoods and monkey puzzles; these still remain, many now of great size, along with a wide variety of conifers and other evergreens. Inevitably, it is the sheer scale of the cemetery which creates its dominant character, and it is a tribute to the original planning that the tree-planting is in keeping with this. The general feeling of openness is enhanced by the ground cover, which remains a heathland mix, with heather, coarse grass and bracken predominating, as well as areas of birchwood. The main road that runs through the site divides the cemetery into consecrated and unconsecrated areas. Various chapels are dotted around the landscape of the unconsecrated section: none, perhaps rather surprisingly, is of any great size, and all are suffering from neglect. The best individual memorials in this part are a series of mausolea to members of the Parsee community, many of which are quite recent in date though stylistically there is little indication of this – they are all approximately Classical. A substantial part of the unconsecrated ground is taken up by military cemeteries dating from both world wars and belonging to a number of different countries. Many parts of the consecrated half of Brookwood have reverted to woodland, with dense bracken and brambles overwhelming the memorials. Areas bordering the main drives are generally clear, however, and, though they are scattered, there are many monuments of quality and interest. Three, quite close together, will have to suffice to indicate the range: a cross and kneeling angel on a tapering base decorated and lettered in mosaic, to the memory of Giulio Salviati d.1898, a member of the nineteenth century's leading family of

Brookwood Cemetery, Woking, Surrey; anonymous bronze figure group in the consecrated section, c.1910.

mosaic craftsmen; a bronze angel on an Ionic plinth with a bronze portrait bust, to Lieut.Rex Moir d.1915 – the sculptor was Lilian Wade; beneath a bunch of pines, a bronze group that is surely one of the most dramatic of any English cemetery group: a grief-striken man crouches over the corpse of a young woman, his hand cupped behind her head; above him, her angelic form soars aloft, wings spread, her face turned in sympathy towards him – the monument is unsigned, and the date and inscription have gone.

YORK
Fulford Cemetery

Established south east of the city in 1836-7, the layout and architecture to the designs of the major local practitioner James Piggott Pritchett, whose firm went on to make a speciality of Burial Board cemeteries. Here, however, he is in the mainstream of 1830s cemetery design, that is, Greek – and of a high quality. An oblong chapel in Roche Abbey stone, with an Ionic portico and pediment in the centre of one of the long sides and Ionic demi-columns in antis to the ends. The lodge had an Ionic portico as well, but this went in the 1920s; the corner piers of the boundary wall have a sarcophagus on top of one of them and a sphinx on the other; the cast iron gates were made by John Walker of York, who made those of the British Museum a few years later. Pritchett's layout of the original 8 acres has, as its major features, circulating paths – an intriguing synthesis between formality and the picturesque – and a grand double avenue of lime trees. Planting elsewhere includes copper beech, chestnut, plane, tulip ash and mountain ash. The monuments are rewarding both aesthetically and historically: they include memorials to the antiquarians William Hargrove and Harvey Brook, the sculptors John Atkinson and William Plows, and the engraver Henry Cave, as well as tombs of major York families. The Gothick Gray monument of 1837 is striking, and particularly interesting as it was designed by Pritchett himself – willing to medievalize in the midst of his own Neo-Greek. Also striking, indeed rather alarming, is the monument to Charles Ellis Hessey d.1874 – a recumbent effigy covered in a sheet. Until recently the whole cemetery was neglected and the chapel dilapidated, but in 1988, thanks to the York Cemetery Trust, a programme of repair and restoration began on the grounds and buildings.

SELECTIVE BIBLIOGRAPHY

1. GENERAL

Primary Sources

Anonymous — *Extramural Burial. The Three Schemes* (London, 1850).

Chadwick, Edwin — *Report on the Sanitary Condition of the Labouring Population of Great Britain. A Supplementary Report on the Results of a Special Inquiry into the Practice of Interment in Towns* (London, 1843).

Geary, Stephen — *Cemetery Designs for Tombs and Cenotaphs* (London, 1840).

Hakewill, Arthur — *Modern Tombs, gleaned from the Public Cemeteries of London* (London, 1851).

Holmes, Mrs Basil — *The London Burial Grounds. Notes on their History from the earliest times to the Present Day* (London, 1896).

(Lewis, Thomas) — *Seasonable Considerations on the Indecent and Dangerous Custom of Burying in Churches and Church-yards* (London, 1721).

Loudon, John Claudius — *On the Laying out, planting and managing of Cemeteries; and on the improvement of Churchyards* (London, 1843).

Robinson, William — *God's Acre Beautiful, or the Cemeteries of the Future* (London, 1880).

Strang, John — *Necropolis Glasguensis with Observations on Ancient and Modern Tombs and Sepulture* (Glasgow, 1831).

Trendall, E. W. — *Monuments, Cenotaphs, Tombs, Tablets, etc. etc. with their details drawn to a large scale* (London, 1850).

Walker, George Alfred — *Gatherings from Graveyards; particularly those of London; with a concise history of the modes of interment among different nations, from the earliest periods* (London, 1839).
Interment and Disinterment; or a further exposition of the practices pursued in the metropolitan places of burial, and the results as affecting the health of the living (London, 1843).
Burial-Ground Incendiarism: the last fire at the bone-house in the Spa-Fields Golgotha, or, the minute anatomy of grave-digging in London (London, 1846).

Wren, Christopher — 'Note to page 128, on Sir Christopher Wren's plan for extra mural interments, and for excluding graveyards on the rebuilding of the City of London'; reprinted in Chadwick (1843), pp. 234-5.

Secondary Sources

Ariès, Philippe — *The Hour of our Death*, trans. Helen Weaver (Harmondsworth, 1981).

Bailey, Brian — *Churchyards of England and Wales* (London, 1987).

Briggs, Asa — *Victorian Cities* (Harmondsworth, 1968).

Burgess, Frederick — *English Churchyard Memorials* (London, 1979).

Curl, James Stevens — *The Victorian Celebration of Death* (Newton Abbot, 1972).
The Cemeteries and Burial Grounds of Glasgow (Glasgow, 1974).
A Celebration of Death (London, 1980).

de Brunhoff, Anne — *Souls in Stone. European Graveyard Sculpture* (New York, 1979).

Dyos, H. J. and Wolff, Michael (eds.) — *The Victorian City. Images and Realities*, 2 vols. (London, 1973).

Elliott, Brent — *Victorian Gardens* (London, 1986).

Etlin, R. A. — *The Architecture of Death: the Transformation of the Cemetery in eighteenth-century Paris* (London, 1984).

Gillon, Edmund V. — *Victorian Cemetery Art* (New York, 1972).

Meller, Hugh — *London Cemeteries. An Illustrated Guide and Gazetteer*, 2nd edn. (London, 1985).

Morley, John — *Death, Heaven and the Victorians* (London, 1971).

Read, Benedict — *Victorian Sculpture* (New Haven & London, 1982).

Stamp, Gavin — *Silent Cities* (London, 1977).

2. INDIVIDUAL CEMETERIES

Barker, Felix — *Highgate Cemetery. Victorian Valhalla* (London, 1984).

Barker, Thomas — *Abney Park Cemetery: A complete Descriptive Guide* (London, 1869).

Blair, George — *Biographic and Descriptive Sketches of Glasgow Necropolis* (Glasgow, 1857).

Brown, Frederick — *Père Lachaise. Elysium as Real Estate* (New York, 1973).

Chapple, Christine E. — *Undercliffe Cemetery* (Bradford, 1988).

Clark, B. — *Hand-book for Visitors to the Kensal Green Cemetery* (London, 1843).

Coones, Paul — 'Kensal Green Cemetery: London's First Great Extramural Necropolis', *Transactions of the Ancient Monuments Society*, New Series vol. 31 (1987).

Curl, James Stevens — 'Nunhead Cemetery', *Transactions of the Ancient Monuments Society*, New Series vol. 23 (1977).

Haywood, William — *Plans and Views of the City of London Cemetery at Little Ilford* (London, 1856).

Joyce, Paul — *A Guide to Abney Park Cemetery* (London, 1984).

Justyne, William — *Illustrated Guide to Kensal Green Cemetery* (London, 1858).
Guide to Highgate Cemetery (London, 1865).

Keeling, Dennis — 'The City of London and Tower Hamlets Cemetery', *East London Papers*, vol. 12 (1969-70).

Smith, Eric — 'The South Metropolitan Cemetery, West Norwood and its Memorials', *London and Middlesex Archaeological Society Special Papers 2* (1978).

3. CONSERVATION

There is now an extensive literature dealing with the practical conservation and repair of historic structures and materials. For guidance to the whole field readers should consult John F. Smith's *A Critical Bibliography of Building Conservation* (London, 1978). The most comprehensive and up-to-date work on architectural conservation is John and Nicola Ashurst's *Practical Building Conservation. English Heritage Technical Handbooks*, 5 vols. (Gower Technical Press, 1988): Vol. 1 *Stone Masonry*, Vol. 2 *Brick, Terracotta and Earth*, Vol. 3 *Plasters, Mortars and Renders*, Vol. 4 *Metals*, Vol. 5 *Wood, Glass and Resins;* the last volume also contains a Technical Bibliography which includes more recent material than that in Smith (1979). Dealing with an area cognate to cemeteries and an excellent source of practical guidance is *The Churchyards Handbook. Advice on their Care and Maintenance* by Henry Stapleton and Peter Burman, published for The Council for Places of Worship, 2nd edn. (London, 1976). Invaluable also is the series of *Technical Pamphlets* published by The Society for the Protection of Ancient Buildings, from whom practical advice may also be had; the society's address is 37 Spital Square, London E1 6DY. For general historical and architectural information readers should contact the Victorian Society, 1 Priory Gardens, London W4 1TT.

4. NATURAL HISTORY

Rather than attempt to select a few works from the vast literature that covers natural history and nature conservation, it seems more valuable to direct readers to organizations which can give specific help and advice; a useful guide to such organizations is the Department of Education and Science handbook *Environmental Education: Sources of Information*, published by HMSO. The Nature Conservancy Council, 19-20 Belgrave Square, London SW1X 8PY, produces a wide range of publications including a bibliography of urban natural history, *Wildlife in the City*. Practical advice on management can be sought from The Council for Environmental Conservation at the Zoological Gardens, Regent's Park, London NW1 4RY. London natural history generally is covered by the activities of The London Natural History Society which, among much else, publishes the journals *London Naturalist* and *London Bird Report;* the society's address is The Natural History Museum, Cromwell Road, London SW7 5BD. Specialist organizations cover those topics discussed specifically in this book: for geology, The Institute of Geological Sciences, The Geological Museum, Exhibition Road, London SW7 2DE or, for advice on a broad range of geological matters, The Geologists' Association, The Department of Geology, University College, London; for molluscs, The Conchological Society of Great Britain and Ireland, through the Secretary at 51 Wychwood Avenue, Luton, Bedfordshire LU2 7HH; for insects, The Royal Entomological Society, 41 Queens Gate, London SW7 5HU; for birds, The Royal Society for the Protection of Birds, The Lodge, Sandy, Bedfordshire SG19 2DC.

INDEX

Illustrations are denoted by italicized page numbers.

1. INDIVIDUAL CEMETERIES

2. ARCHITECTS, DESIGNERS AND CRAFTSMEN

3. GENERAL